P9-CNB-245

DISCARD

PART 6 • PRESENTATION AIDS   155

20. Speaking with Presentation Aids   156
21. Designing Presentation Aids   161
22. A Brief Guide to Microsoft PowerPoint   164

PART 7 • TYPES OF SPEECHES   175

23. Informative Speaking   176
24. Persuasive Speaking   189
25. Speaking on Special Occasions   219

PART 8 • ONLINE, GROUP, AND BUSINESS
CONTEXTS   231

26. Preparing Online Presentations   232
27. Communicating in Groups   238
28. Presenting in Teams   243
29. Business and Professional Presentations   247

PART 9 • SPEAKING ACROSS THE CURRICULUM   254

30. Presentations Assigned across the Curriculum   255
31. Science and Mathematics Courses   261
32. Technical Courses   265
33. Social Science Courses   267
34. Arts and Humanities Courses   270
35. Education Courses   272
36. Nursing and Allied Health Courses   274

APPENDICES

A. Citation Guidelines   278
B. Question-and-Answer Sessions   292
C. Preparing for Mediated Communication   294
D. Tips for Non-Native Speakers of English   296

Glossary   300
Index   337

A Pocket Guide to Public Speaking

FOURTH EDITION

Getting Started ■ Development ■ Organization ■ Starting, Finishing, and Styling ■ Delivery ■ Presentation Aids ■ Types of Speeches ■ Online, Group, and Business Contexts ■ Speaking across the Curriculum ■ Citation Guidelines

Dan O'Hair
University of Kentucky

Hannah Rubenstein

Rob Stewart
Texas Tech University

Bedford / St. Martin's   Boston ◆ New York

For Bedford/St. Martin's

Publisher for Communication: Erika Gutierrez
Developmental Editor: Mae Klinger
Senior Production Editor: Harold Chester
Senior Production Supervisor: Jennifer Peterson
Marketing Manager: Stacey Propps
Copy Editor: Denise P. Quirk
Indexer: Leoni Z. McVey
Photo Researcher: Connie Gardner
Permissions Manager: Kalina K. Ingham
Art Director: Lucy Krikorian
Text Design: Claire Seng-Niemoeller
Cover Design: Marine Miller
Composition: S4Carlisle Publishing Services
Printing and Binding: Quad/Graphics

President, Bedford/St. Martin's: Denise B. Wydra
Presidents, Macmillan Higher Education: Joan E. Feinberg and Tom Scotty
Director of Development: Erica T. Appel
Director of Marketing: Karen R. Soeltz
Production Director: Susan W. Brown
Associate Production Director: Elise S. Kaiser
Managing Editor: Shuli Traub

Library of Congress Control Number: 2012942634

Acknowledgments
Acknowledgments and copyrights are continued at the back of the book on page 335, which constitutes an extension of the copyright page. It is a violation of the law to reproduce these selections by any means whatsoever without the written permis-

How to Use This Book

A Pocket Guide to Public Speaking, Fourth Edition, is designed to provide quick, clear answers to your questions about public speaking—whether you're in a public speaking class, in a course in your major, on the job, or in your community. Here, you will find the tools you need to prepare and deliver a wide range of speeches and presentations.

In Parts 1 through 6, you will find chapters covering all the steps necessary to create a speech—from planning, research, and development to organization, practice, and delivery. Chapters in Part 7 contain guidelines for creating three of the most commonly assigned speeches in public speaking classes: *informative, persuasive,* and *special occasion.* For specific guidelines on preparing online presentations, communicating and speaking in small groups, and speaking on the job, see Part 8. Part 9 contains advice on speaking in other college courses, from science and math to engineering, education, and nursing and allied health.

Finding What You Need

TABLES OF CONTENTS. Browsing through the brief table of contents inside the front cover will usually guide you to the information you need. If not, consult the more detailed table of contents included inside the back cover.

INDEX. If you can't locate what you need in either set of contents, consult the index at the back of the book, beginning on page 337. This can be especially useful if you're looking for something specific and you know the term for it. For example, if you need to prepare a sales presentation for a business course, you could simply look under "sales presentations" in the index and then go to the designated pages.

LISTS OF FEATURES. On pages 352–55 (just before the end of the book), you'll find a quick guide to some of the most often consulted parts of this book: the Checklists, Quick Tips, Visual Guides (illustrated explanations of key points), and full-length model speeches.

SPEAKING BEYOND THE SPEECH CLASSROOM. In Part 8, "Online, Group, and Business Contexts," you'll find useful information on preparing online presentations, communicating and speaking in teams, and speaking in the workplace. In Part 9, "Speaking across the Curriculum," you'll find detailed directions for speaking in a range of college classes, including courses in the social sciences, arts and humanities, education, science and mathematics, engineering and architecture, and nursing and allied health.

GLOSSARY. For definitions of key terms highlighted in the book, see pages 300–320.

Quick Speech Preparation

If you have to prepare a speech quickly (for example, giving a first speech early in the semester), consult Chapters 1–3 in *A Pocket Guide:*

- Chapter 1, "Becoming a Public Speaker," provides a brief discussion of public speaking basics.
- Chapter 2, "From A to Z: Overview of a Speech," offers quick guidance on each step in the speechmaking process, from selecting a topic to delivery.
- Chapter 3, "Managing Speech Anxiety," provides techniques that will help you overcome any fears you may have.

For more on specific types of speeches, consult Chapters 23–25 in Part 7 on informative, persuasive, and special occasion speeches, or the appropriate chapter in Part 8 or Part 9.

Other Useful Tools

CITATION GUIDELINES. Appendix A (pp. 278–92) contains guidelines for documenting sources in the following styles: *Chicago,* American Psychological Association (APA), Modern Language Association (MLA), Council of Science Editors (CSE), and Institute of Electrical and Electronics Engineers (IEEE).

TIPS FOR NON-NATIVE SPEAKERS OF ENGLISH. Appendix D (pp. 296–99) addresses the most common ESL challenges, including difficulty pronouncing words and problems in being understood.

Preface

A *Pocket Guide to Public Speaking,* Fourth Edition, represents our belief in offering a truly effective speech resource that is comprehensive yet brief, affordable, and student friendly, with solid scholarship and an emphasis on the rhetorical tradition. This guide is designed to be useful in the widest possible range of situations, from the traditional speech classroom and courses across the curriculum to applications on the job and in the community.

In developing *A Pocket Guide,* our goal has always been to meet the needs of speech instructors who find mainstream, full-size introductory speech texts either too overwhelming or too constraining for their classes. In addition, we hope to satisfy instructors in other disciplines who want an easy and affordable tool for teaching basic presentation skills that is also manageable enough to allow them to focus on their own course material. And with this new edition, we also aim to adapt to the changing realities of technology in the discipline, both in terms of content—by providing helpful guidance on online research and online presentations—and in terms of content delivery—by offering *A Pocket Guide* in multiple digital formats that students can access easily on a number of devices.

Happily, *A Pocket Guide to Public Speaking* seems to have struck a chord. Since the first edition was published in 2003, more than 200,000 instructors and students across the academic spectrum—from courses in speech and the humanities to education, engineering, and business—have embraced the book, making it the most successful pocket-size speech text available. We have used their generous feedback to create this fourth edition.

Features

A Pocket Guide to Public Speaking addresses all of the topics and skills typically covered in an introductory speech text. And because the book is meant to be used throughout students' academic careers and in a wide variety of classroom settings, examples are drawn from a broad range of speech situations and disciplines. In addition to diverse examples, speech excerpts, sample outlines, and full-length annotated sample speeches provide useful models that help students see how speech fundamentals can be applied effectively.

Throughout the text, users will find many tools to help them focus on key public speaking concepts: charts and tables that summarize salient points; Checklists that reinforce critical content; insightful Quick Tips that offer succinct and practical advice; Visual Guides that illustrate the steps for accomplishing challenging speech tasks; and Appendices offering citation guidelines, help with question-and-answer sessions and mediated communication, and support for non-native speakers of English.

New to This Edition

Based on feedback from hundreds of instructors about the challenges of teaching public and presentational speaking, this fourth edition is designed to help students master basic skills while also addressing the new challenges that digital technology brings to public speaking:

- **Digital choices for every course need**. Because students learn in new ways and on different platforms, *A Pocket Guide to Public Speaking* is available in a variety of e-book formats, for use on computers, tablets, and other devices. New *SpeechClass for A Pocket Guide to Public Speaking* puts all our online resources for public speaking in one customizable space, including the e-book; hundreds of student and professional speech clips and full sample speeches from *VideoCentral: Public Speaking*; an outlining tool; video uploading, embedding, and annotating tools; rubrics; and more. For more information, see the "Supplements" section that follows.

- **Even better coverage of public speaking fundamentals.** Students will benefit from updates such as new advice on overcoming anxiety, expanded coverage of locating supporting material, and more on understanding subordination and coordination. All chapters have been thoroughly updated for the most recent scholarship on all facets of speechmaking.

- **Up-to-the minute coverage of speaking online**. Speakers are increasingly expected to prepare and deliver digital presentations, and a new Chapter 26 delivers practical guidance on the techniques and tools that will help students excel in mediated speaking, whether for online classes, virtual meetings, recorded presentations, or other contexts.

- **More help navigating the tricky terrain of Internet research.** An updated Chapter 10 provides useful guidance that helps students find credible sources online and evaluate the sources they discover. It includes new tips and strategies on fact checking, using online journals and library portals, and searching accurately by keyword and subject heading.

- **New coverage of service learning and health presentations.** Updated guidelines help students give service learning presentations across disciplines, and a fully updated chapter on nursing and allied health presentations provides even better support for speaking in health courses and careers.

- **A new organization emphasizes the skills students need to succeed beyond the classroom.** Part 8 prepares students for the demands of group communication and team, workplace, and online presentations, while Part 9 provides advice on speaking in other college courses.

- **New Visual Guides.** Eight Visual Guides, including two new guides on narrowing a speech topic to suit an audience and delivering a speech using presentation software, walk students through course challenges visually.

- **Updated sample speeches.** A new sample speech by J. K. Rowling brings us to a total of four full-length annotated sample speeches, all exemplifying core tenets of speechmaking.

Supplements

For more information on student resources or to learn about package options, please visit the online catalog at **bedfordstmartins.com/pocketspeak/catalog.**

Media Options for Students

- **E-books.** *A Pocket Guide to Public Speaking* is available in a variety of e-book formats, for use on computers, tablets, and e-readers. See **bedfordstmartins.com/aboutebooks** to learn more.

- *SpeechClass for A Pocket Guide to Public Speaking.* SpeechClass is an online course space designed to support students in all aspects of the public speaking course. It's fully loaded with an e-book, hundreds of speech video clips and full sample speeches from *VideoCentral: Public Speaking*, outlining and relaxation tools, and opportunities for students to assess their learning. Even better, video uploading, evaluating, and annotating tools make working with speech video easy—from assignments to peer review and collaboration. Upload video from students or embed clips from sites like YouTube and then use the SpeechClass annotation tool and preloaded, fully customizable rubrics for evaluation. Once in SpeechClass, get all our premium content and tools in one fully customizable course space, then assign, rearrange, and mix our resources with yours.

- **Free and open book companion site at bedfordstmartins .com/pocketspeak.** Here students will find an abundance of free study tools to help them excel in class, including help with speech topics, tutorials for evaluating sources and avoiding plagiarism, exercises for speaking in other college courses, and more. In addition, the book companion site is the gateway to *VideoCentral: Public Speaking* and other premium products (described below).

- ***VideoCentral: Public Speaking* at bedfordstmartins.com /pocketspeak.** The most extensive video offering available for the public speaking course, VideoCentral provides more than 200 student and professional speech clips and 28 full student speeches that model key speech concepts. Searchable by chapter or term, these model videos help students *see* speech concepts in action and learn how to *apply* them to their own speeches. Access to VideoCentral also connects students with additional premium resources, including the *Bedford Speech Outliner 2.0,* Video Quizzes, and the *Relaxation Audio Download.*

Print Resources for Students

- ***The Essential Guides.*** These brief yet comprehensive and affordable print booklets focus on a range of topics and are designed to supplement a main text in a public speaking course. These guides are available to be packaged with *A Pocket Guide to Public Speaking* for a very low price. Versions include *The Essential Guide to Rhetoric* by William M. Keith and Christian O. Lundberg; *The Essential Guide to Presentation Software* by Allison Ainsworth and Rob Patterson; *The Essential Guide to Intercultural Communication* by Jennifer Willis-Rivera; *The Essential Guide to Interpersonal Communication* by Dan O'Hair and Mary O. Wiemann; and *The Essential*

Guide to Group Communication by Dan O'Hair and
Mary O. Wiemann.

Instructor Resources

For more information or to order or download the instructor
resources, please visit the online catalog at **bedfordstmartins
.com/pocketspeak/catalog**.

- *Instructor's Resource Manual* **(print and electronic versions).** Karin Becker, University of North Dakota; Paula
  Baldwin, George Mason University; Elaine Wittenberg-
  Lyles, University of North Texas; and Melinda M. Villagran,
  George Mason University. This comprehensive manual
  offers useful guidance for new and experienced instructors, and outlines and activities for every chapter in the
  main text. The Instructor's Resource Manual for this
  fourth edition offers new guidance on online instruction and using video from *VideoCentral: Public Speaking*
  in the speech course, new advice about civility in the
  classroom, suggestions for preparing mediated presentations, and updated guidelines on presentations across the
  curriculum.

- *Test Bank* **(print and electronic versions).** Diana Rehling,
  St. Cloud State University; Paula Baldwin, George
  Mason University; Elaine Wittenberg-Lyles, University
  of North Texas; and Merry Buchanan, University of
  Central Oklahoma. The Test Bank contains more than
  1,500 true/false, multiple-choice, fill-in-the-blank, and
  essay/short answer questions that have been carefully
  crafted to test students' specific knowledge of the text.

- *ESL Students in the Public Speaking Classroom: A Guide
  for Teachers.* Robbin Crabtree and Robert Weissberg,
  New Mexico State University. This guide specifically
  addresses the needs of ESL students in the public speaking
  course and offers instructors valuable advice for helping
  students deal successfully with the challenges they face.

- **Professional Speeches.** In DVD and VHS formats, multiple volumes of the Great Speeches series are available to
  adopters, along with more videos from the Bedford/St.
  Martin's Video Library.

- **Student Speeches.** Three volumes of student speeches
  are available in DVD and VHS formats. For more
  on receiving copies of our professional and student
  speech collections, please contact your local publisher's
  representative.

- *A Pocket Guide to Public Speaking,* **Fourth Edition, Coursepacks.** A variety of student and instructor resources for this textbook are ready for use in systems such as Blackboard, WebCT, Angel, Desire2Learn, Moodle, and Sakai. To access CMS content, go to **bedfordsmartins.com/coursepacks.**

Acknowledgments

We would like to thank all our colleagues at Bedford/St. Martin's: President Denise Wydra, Publisher Erika Gutierrez, Marketing Manager Stacey Propps, Managing Editor Shuli Traub, Senior Project Editor Harold Chester, Senior Production Supervisor Jennifer Peterson, and Senior New Media Editor Tom Kane—we are truly grateful for your knowledge, creativity, expertise, and hard work throughout this process. We are especially grateful for the many contributions of our editor, Mae Klinger, who expertly guided us through every step of this revision.

Thanks to all the instructors who participated in reviews for the fourth edition: Sharee Broussard, *Spring Hill College*; Glen F. Byne, *Boston University*; Michael S. Carr, *Cleveland State Community College*; Carolyn Clark, *Salt Lake Community College*; Elaine Vander Clute, *Wor-Wic Community College*; Sarah Lynn Mohundro Contreras, *Del Mar College*; Kristopher Copeland, *Northeastern State University*; Donna Craine, *Front Range Community College*; Gabrielle Cuan, *Valencia Community College–Osceola Campus*; Oscar Cuan, *Valencia Community College–Osceola Campus*; Patricia Gowland, *University of Illinois at Chicago*; Lynette Jachowicz, *Metropolitan Community College–Maple Woods*; Nancy Jennings, *Cuyamaca College*; Debra S. Jones, *Chattanooga State Community College*; A'Isha Malone, *Tarrant County College–Northwest Campus*; Jodie D. Mandel, *College of Southern Nevada*; William Maze, *Northwest Mississippi Community College*; Brad Mello, *George Washington University*; Thomas A. Nelson, *Elon University*; Heidi Ochoa, *Saddleback College*; Mary Haslerud Opp, *University of North Dakota*; Diana Rehling, *St. Cloud State University*; Clifford J. Ruth, *Riverside City College*; Sudeshna Roy, *Stephen F. Austin State University*; Brian Simmons, *University of Portland*; Amy M. Smith, *Salem State University*; Jason Stone, *Oklahoma State University–Oklahoma City*; Barbara Tarter, *Marshall University*; Gretchen Aggertt Weber, *Horry-Georgetown Technical College*; Dennis Wemm, *Glenville State College*; Arnold Wood Jr., *Florida State College at Jacksonville*; Thomas S. Wright, *Temple University*.

Part 1
Getting Started

1. Becoming a Public Speaker 2
2. From A to Z: Overview of a Speech 9
3. Managing Speech Anxiety 14
4. Ethical Public Speaking 22
5. Listeners and Speakers 30

1   Becoming a Public Speaker

Whether in the classroom, workplace, or community, the ability to speak confidently and convincingly before an audience is empowering. This pocket guide offers the tools you need to create and deliver effective speeches, from presentations made to fellow students, co-workers, or fellow citizens, to major addresses to larger audiences. Here you will find concise explanations of the building blocks of any good speech and acquire the skills to deliver presentations in a variety of specialized contexts—from the college classroom to civic, business, and professional situations. You'll also find proven techniques to build your confidence by overcoming the anxiety associated with public speaking.

Gain a Vital Life Skill

Skill in public speaking will give you an unmistakable edge in life, leading to greater confidence and satisfaction. Now, more than ever, public speaking has become both a vital life skill and a potent weapon in career development.[1] Recruiters of top graduate school students report that what distinguishes the most sought-after candidates is not their "hard" knowledge of their areas of expertise, which employers take for granted, but the "soft skills" of communication, which fewer candidates display.[2] Similarly, dozens of surveys of managers and executives reveal that ability in oral and written communication is among the most important skills they look for in hiring new college graduates. In an annual survey of employers, for example, oral communication skills consistently rank in the top three among such critical areas as leadership, strong work ethic, teamwork, and problem-solving skills.

SKILLS EMPLOYERS SEEK
1. Ability to work in a team
2. Leadership
3. Communication skills
4. Problem-solving skills
5. Strong work ethic

Source: National Association of Colleges and Employers, "Attributes Employers Seek on Candidate's Resume," *Job Outlook 2012,* November 2011, www.naceweb.org.

Enhance Your Career as a Student

Preparing speeches calls upon numerous skills that you can apply in other college courses. As in the speech class, many courses also require that you research and write about topics, analyze audiences, outline and organize ideas, and support claims. These and other skill sets covered in this pocket guide, such as working with visual aids and controlling voice and body during delivery, are valuable in any course that includes an oral-presentation component, from English composition to nursing or engineering.

Find New Opportunities for Civic Engagement

While skill in public speaking contributes to both career and academic advancement, it also offers you ways to enter the public conversation about social concerns and become a more engaged citizen. Public speaking gives you a voice that can be heard and can be counted.

Climate change, energy, government debt, immigration reform—such large civic issues require our considered judgment and action. Yet today too many of us leave it up to politicians, journalists, and other "experts" to make decisions about critical issues such as these. Not including presidential elections, only about 37 percent of people in the United States regularly vote. Of these, only 24 percent are 18 to 29 years old.[3] When we as citizens speak up in sufficient numbers, change occurs. Leaving pressing social issues to others, on the other hand, is an invitation to special interest groups who may or may not act with our best interests in mind.

As you study public speaking, you will have the opportunity to research topics that are meaningful to you, consider alternate viewpoints, and choose a course of action.[4] You will learn to distinguish between argument that advances constructive goals and uncivil speech that serves merely to inflame and demean others. You will learn, in short, the "rules of engagement" for effective public discourse.[5] As you do, you will gain confidence in your ability to join your voice with others in pursuit of issues you care about.

The Classical Roots of Public Speaking

Originally, the practice of giving speeches was known as **rhetoric** (also called **oratory**). Rhetoric flourished in the Greek city-state of Athens in the fifth century B.C.E. and referred to making effective speeches, particularly those of a persuasive nature.

Athens was the site of the world's first direct democracy, and its citizens used their considerable skill in public speaking to enact it. Meeting in a public square called the **agora**, the Athenians routinely spoke with great skill on the issues of public policy, and to this day their belief that citizenship demands active participation in public affairs endures. As Greece fell and Rome rose (ca. 200 B.C.E.), citizens in the Roman republic (the Western world's first known representative democracy) plied their public speaking skills in a public space called a **forum**.

From the beginning, public speakers, notably the great classical rhetorician Aristotle (384–322 B.C.E.), and later, the Roman statesman and orator Cicero (106–43 B.C.E.), divided the process of preparing a speech into five parts—*invention, arrangement, style, memory,* and *delivery*—called the **canons of rhetoric**. *Invention* refers to adapting speech information to the audience in order to make your case. *Arrangement* is organizing the speech in ways best suited to the topic and audience. *Style* is the way the speaker uses language to express the speech ideas. *Memory* is the practice of the speech until it can be artfully delivered, and *delivery* is the vocal and nonverbal behavior you use when speaking.

Although the founding scholars surely didn't anticipate the omnipresent PowerPoint slide show that accompanies contemporary speeches, the speechmaking structure they bequeathed to us as the canons of rhetoric remains remarkably intact. Often identified by terms other than the original, these canons nonetheless continue to be taught in current books on public speaking, including this pocket guide.

QUICK TIP

Voice Your Ideas in a Public Forum

The Greeks called it the agora; *the Romans the* forum. *Today, the term* **public forum** *denotes a variety of venues for the discussion of issues of public interest, including traditional physical spaces such as town halls as well as virtual forums streamed to listeners online. Participation in forums offers an excellent opportunity to pose questions and deliver brief comments, thereby providing exposure to an audience and building confidence. To find a forum in your area, check with your school or local town government, or check online at sites such as the National Issues Forum (www.nifi.org/index.aspx).*

Learning to Speak in Public

None of us is born knowing how to speak in public. As with anything else, public speaking is an acquired skill that improves with practice. It is also a skill that shares much in common with other familiar activities, such as conversing and writing, and it can be much less daunting when you realize that you can draw on related skills that you already have.

Draw on Conversational Skills

In several respects, planning and delivering a speech resemble engaging in a particularly important conversation. When speaking with a friend, you automatically check to make certain you are understood and adjust your meaning accordingly. You also tend to discuss issues that are appropriate to the circumstances. When a relative stranger is involved, however, you try to get to know his or her interests and attitudes before revealing any strong opinions. These instinctive adjustments to your audience, topic, and occasion represent critical steps in creating a speech. Although public speaking requires more planning, both the conversationalist and the public speaker try to uncover the audience's interests and needs before speaking.

Draw on Skills in Composition

Preparing a speech also has much in common with writing. Both depend on having a focused sense of who the audience is.[6] Both speaking and writing often require that you research a topic, offer credible evidence, employ effective transitions to signal the logical flow of ideas, and devise persuasive appeals. The principles of organizing a speech parallel those of organizing an essay, including offering a compelling introduction, a clear thesis statement, supporting ideas, and a thoughtful conclusion.

Develop an Effective Oral Style

Although public speaking has much in common with everyday conversation and with writing, it is, obviously, "its own thing." More so than writers, successful speakers generally use familiar words, easy-to-follow sentences, and transitional words and phrases. Speakers also routinely repeat key words and phrases to emphasize ideas and help listeners follow along, and even the briefest speeches make frequent use of repetition.

Spoken language is often more interactive and inclusive of the audience than written language. Audience members want to know what the speaker thinks and feels and that he or she recognizes them and relates the message to them. Speakers accomplish this by making specific references to themselves and to the audience. Yet, because public speaking usually occurs in more formal settings than everyday conversation, listeners generally expect a more formal style of communication from the speaker. When you give a speech, listeners expect you to speak in a clear, recognizable, and organized fashion. Thus, in contrast to conversation, in order to develop an effective oral style you must practice the words you will say and the way you will say them.

Good conversationalists, captivating writers, and engaging public speakers share an important quality: They keep their focus on offering something of value for the audience.

Become an Inclusive Speaker

Every audience member wants to feel that the speaker has his or her particular needs and interests at heart, and to feel recognized and included in the message. To create this sense of inclusion, a public speaker must be able to address diverse audiences with sensitivity. As David C. Thomas and Kerr Inkson explain, more than ever, public speakers must cultivate their *cultural intelligence*,[7] which they define as:

> being skilled and flexible about understanding a culture, learning more about it from your ongoing interactions with it, and gradually reshaping your thinking to be more sympathetic to the culture and developing your behavior to be more skilled and appropriate when interacting with others from the culture.[8]

Striving for inclusion and adopting an audience-centered perspective will bring you closer to the goal of every public speaker—establishing a genuine connection with the audience.

Public Speaking as a Form of Communication

Public speaking is one of four categories of human communication: dyadic, small group, mass, and public speaking. **Dyadic communication** happens between two people, as in a conversation. **Small group communication** involves a small number of people who can see and speak directly with one another. **Mass communication** occurs between a speaker and a large audience of unknown people who usually are not present with the speaker, or who are part of such an immense crowd that there can be little or no interaction between speaker and listener.

In **public speaking**, a speaker delivers a message with a specific purpose to an audience of people who are present during the delivery of the speech. Public speaking always includes a speaker who has a reason for speaking, an audience that gives the speaker its attention, and a message that is meant to accomplish a specific purpose.[9] Public speakers address audiences largely without interruption and take responsibility for the words and ideas being expressed.

Public Speaking as an Interactive Communication Process

In any communication event, including public speaking, several elements are present. These include the source, the receiver, the message, the channel, and shared meaning (see Figure 1.1).

The **source**, or sender, is the person who creates a message. Creating, organizing, and producing the message is called **encoding**—the process of converting thoughts into words.

The recipient of the source's message is the **receiver**, or audience. The process of interpreting the message is called **decoding**. Audience members decode the meaning of the message selectively, based on their own experiences and attitudes. **Feedback**, the audience's response to a message, can be conveyed both verbally and nonverbally.

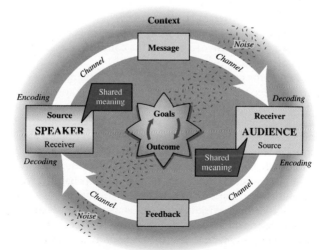

FIGURE 1.1 The Communication Process

The **message** is the content of the communication process: thoughts and ideas put into meaningful expressions, expressed verbally and nonverbally. The medium through which the speaker sends a message is the **channel**. If a speaker delivers a message in front of a live audience, the channel is the air through which sound waves travel. Other channels include the telephone, television, computers, and written correspondence.

Noise is any interference with the message. Noise can disrupt the communication process through physical sounds such as cell phones ringing and people talking, through psychological distractions such as heated emotions, or through environmental interference such as a frigid room or the presence of unexpected people.

Shared meaning is the mutual understanding of a message between speaker and audience. The lowest level of shared meaning exists when the speaker has merely caught the audience's attention. As the message develops, a higher degree of shared meaning is possible. Thus listener and speaker together truly make a speech a speech—they "co-create" its meaning.

Two other factors are critical to consider when preparing and delivering a speech—context and goals. **Context** includes anything that influences the speaker, the audience, the occasion—and thus, ultimately, the speech. In classroom speeches, the context would include (among other things) recent events on campus or in the outside world, the physical setting, the order and timing of speeches, and the cultural orientations of audience members. Successful communication can never be divorced from the concerns and expectations of others.

Part of the context of any speech is the situation that created the need for it in the first place. All speeches are delivered in response to a specific **rhetorical situation**, or a circumstance calling for a public response.[10] Bearing the context and rhetorical situation in mind ensures that you remain **audience centered**—that is, that you keep the needs, values, attitudes, and wants of your listeners firmly in focus.

A clearly defined *speech purpose* or goal—what you want the audience to learn or do as a result of the speech—is a final prerequisite for an effective speech. Establishing a speech purpose early on will help you proceed through speech preparation and delivery with a clear focus in mind.

2 From A to Z: Overview of a Speech

Persons with little experience in public speaking—and that includes most of us—will benefit from preparing and delivering a first short speech. An audience of as few as two people will be enough to test the waters and help you gain confidence in your ability to "stand up and deliver."

This chapter presents a brief overview of the process of preparing a first speech or presentation (see Figure 2.1). Subsequent chapters expand on these steps.

Analyze the Audience

Every audience is unique, with members who have personalities, interests, and opinions all their own, and these factors will influence their responses toward a given topic, speaker, and occasion. Thus, the first task in preparing any speech is to consider the audience. *Audience analysis* is a systematic process of getting to know audience members' attributes and motivations through techniques such as interviews and

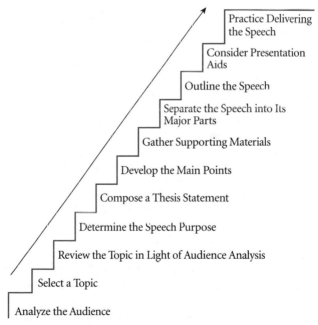

Practice Delivering the Speech

Consider Presentation Aids

Outline the Speech

Separate the Speech into Its Major Parts

Gather Supporting Materials

Develop the Main Points

Compose a Thesis Statement

Determine the Speech Purpose

Review the Topic in Light of Audience Analysis

Select a Topic

Analyze the Audience

FIGURE 2.1 Steps in the Speechmaking Process

questionnaires (see Chapter 6). For a brief first speech, however, gather what information you can about the audience in the time allotted. Consider some *demographic characteristics*: ratio of males to females, age ranges, cultural background, and socioeconomic status. As you mull over topics and the different ways you might present them, think about the potential impact of these variables on audience receptivity.

Select a Topic

Unless the topic is assigned, use your interests and those of the audience to guide you in selecting something to speak about. What are your areas of interest and expertise? Is there an important current event or outstanding issue affecting the audience that could serve as a topic? Whatever you settle on, you should feel confident that the topic is suitable for both the audience and the speech occasion.

Determine the Speech Purpose

Decide what you want to accomplish with your speech. For any given topic, you should direct your speech toward one of three *general speech purposes*—to *inform*, to *persuade*, or to *mark a special occasion*. Thus you need to decide whether your goal is to inform your audience about an issue or event, to persuade them to accept one position to the exclusion of other positions, or to mark a special occasion such as a wedding, a funeral, or a dinner event.

Your speech should also have a *specific purpose*. This is a single phrase stating precisely what you want the audience to learn or do as a result of your speech. For example, if your general purpose is to inform, your specific purpose might be "to inform my audience about three key qualities of distance courses." If your general purpose is to persuade, the specific purpose might be "to convince my audience that they should support funds for the development of distance courses."

QUICK TIP

Speak with Purpose
To ensure that the audience learns or does what you want them to as a result of your speech, keep your speech goals in sight. Write your specific purpose on a Post-it note and place it on the edge of your computer monitor. It will be an important guide in developing your speech.

Compose a Thesis Statement

Next, compose a thesis statement that clearly expresses the central idea of your speech. While the specific purpose focuses your attention on what *you* want to achieve with the speech, the *thesis statement* concisely communicates to your audience, in a single sentence, what the speech is about:

GENERAL PURPOSE: To inform

SPECIFIC PURPOSE: To inform my audience about the crucial role played by the nitrogen cycle in preserving biodiversity and maintaining healthy ecosystems.

THESIS STATEMENT: Excessive nitrogen additions to the nitrogen cycle from human activities such as crop fertilization and burning of fossil fuels pose serious threats to plant and animal life.

Wherever you are in the planning stage, always refer to the thesis statement to make sure that you are on track to illustrate or prove the central idea of your speech.

Develop the Main Points

Organize your speech around two or three *main points.* These are the primary pieces of knowledge (in an informative speech) or the key claims (in a persuasive speech). If you create a clear thesis statement for your speech, the main points will be easily identifiable, if not explicit:

THESIS: The Post-9/11 GI Bill offers eligible members of the U.S. military enhanced opportunities to fund their education and pay for housing and ancillary expenses.

   I.   The Post 9/11 Bill provides financial support for education and housing to individuals with at least three months' service on or after September 11, 2001.

   II.   The bill will pay full tuition for public institutions of higher learning for up to thirty-six months.

   III.   The bill will pay partial tuition for private institutions of higher learning.

Gather Supporting Materials

Supporting materials illustrate speech points by clarifying, elaborating, and verifying your ideas. They include the entire world of information available to you—from personal experiences to every conceivable kind of external source. Plan to research your topic to provide evidence for your assertions and lend credibility to your message (see Chapters 9–11).

Separate the Speech into Its Major Parts

Every speech will have an *introduction,* a *body*, and a *conclusion.* Develop each part separately, then bring them together using transition statements (see Chapter 12). The *introduction* serves to introduce the topic and the speaker, to alert the audience to your thesis, and to catch the audience's attention and interest (see Chapter 15). Just like the body of a written essay, the speech *body* contains the speech's main points and subpoints, all of which support the speech's thesis. The *conclusion* restates the speech thesis and reiterates how the main points confirm it (see Chapter 15).

MAJOR SPEECH PARTS
INTRODUCTION
• Pique the audience's curiosity with a quotation, a short story, an example, or other kind of attention-getting device.
• Introduce the speech topic and demonstrate its relevance to the audience.
• Preview the thesis and main points.
• Establish your credibility as a speaker to address the topic.
(Use a transition to signal the start of the speech body.)
BODY
• Develop the main points using an organizational pattern that suits the topic, audience, and occasion.
(Use a transition to signal the conclusion.)
CONCLUSION
• Restate the thesis and reiterate how the main points confirm it.
• Leave the audience with something to think about, or challenge them to act.
(Be prepared to answer questions.)

Outline the Speech

An outline is the framework upon which to arrange the elements of your speech in support of your thesis. Outlines are based on the principle of *coordination and subordination*—the logical placement of ideas relative to their importance to one another. *Coordinate points* are of equal importance and are indicated by their parallel alignment. *Subordinate points* are given less weight than the main points they support and are placed to the right of the points they support. (For a full discussion of outlining, see Chapters 12 and 14.)

COORDINATE POINTS

I.   Main Point 1

II. Main Point 2

    A. Subpoint 1

    B. Subpoint 2

SUBORDINATE POINTS

1. Main Point 1

    A. First level of subordination

        1. Second level of subordination

        2. Second level of subordination

            a. Third level of subordination

            b. Third level of subordination

As your speeches become more detailed, you will need to select an appropriate *organizational pattern* (see Chapters 13 and 24). You will also need to familiarize yourself with developing both working and speaking outlines (see Chapter 14). To allow for the full development of your ideas, *working outlines* generally contain points stated in complete sentences. *Speaking outlines* are far briefer and use either short phrases or key words. Speaking outlines are printed out on separate sheets or written on 4″ × 6″ index cards for use during the speech.

Consider Presentation Aids

As you prepare your speech, consider whether using visual, audio, or a combination of different *presentation aids* will help the audience understand points. A presentation aid can be as simple as writing the definition of a word on a blackboard or as involved as a multimedia slide show. (See Chapters 20–22.)

Practice Delivering the Speech

Preparation and practice are necessary for the success of even your first speech in class. You will want to feel and appear "natural" to your listeners, an effect achieved by rehearsing both the verbal and nonverbal delivery of your speech (see Chapters 18 and 19). So practice your speech often. It has been suggested that a good speech is practiced at least six times. For a four- to six-minute speech, that's only thirty to forty minutes (figuring in restarts and pauses) of actual practice time.

Practice Your Vocal Delivery

Vocal delivery includes speech volume, pitch, rate, variety, pronunciation, and articulation. As you rehearse, do the following:

- Pay attention to how loudly or softly you are speaking.
- Pay attention to the rate at which you speak. Aim to speak neither too fast nor too slowly.
- Avoid speaking in a monotone.
- Decide how you want to phrase your statements, and then practice saying them.
- Pronounce words correctly and clearly.

Be Aware of Your Nonverbal Delivery

Audiences are highly attuned to a speaker's facial expression, gestures, general body movement, and overall physical appearance. As you rehearse, do the following:

- Practice smiling and otherwise animating your face in ways that feel natural to you. Audiences want to feel that you care about what you are saying, so avoid a deadpan, or blank, expression.
- Practice making eye contact with your listeners. Doing so will make audience members feel that you recognize and respect them.
- Practice gestures that feel natural to you, steering clear of exaggerated movements.

3   Managing Speech Anxiety

All speakers, even the most experienced, often feel jittery before they give a speech. According to one study, at least 75 percent of students in public-speaking courses approach the course with anxiety.[1] It turns out that feeling nervous is not only normal but desirable! Channeled properly, nervousness may actually boost performance.

The difference between seasoned public speakers and the rest of us is that the seasoned speakers know how to make their nervousness work *for* rather than *against* them. They use specific techniques, described in this chapter, to help them cope with and minimize their tension.

> I focus on the information. I try not to think about being graded. I also practice my speech a ton to really make sure I do not speak too quickly. I time myself so that I can develop an average time. This makes me more confident [in dealing] with time requirements. And, because I know that I am well prepared, I really try to just relax.
>
> —*Kristen Obracay, student*

Identify What Makes You Anxious

Lacking positive public-speaking experience, feeling different from members of the audience, or feeling uneasy about being the center of attention—each of these factors can lead to the onset of **public-speaking anxiety**, that is, fear or anxiety associated with either actual or anticipated communication to an audience as a speaker.[2] Identifying what makes you anxious can help you lessen your fear.

Lack of Positive Experience

If you have had no exposure to public speaking or have had unpleasant experiences, anxiety about what to expect is only natural. And with no positive experience to fall back on, it's hard to put these anxieties in perspective. It's a bit of a vicious circle. Some people react by deciding to avoid making speeches altogether. Gaining more experience, however, is key to overcoming speech anxiety.

Feeling Different

Novice speakers often feel alone—as if they were the only person ever to experience the dread of public speaking. The prospect of getting up in front of an audience makes them extra-sensitive to their personal idiosyncrasies, such as having a less-than-perfect haircut or an accent. They may believe that no one could possibly be interested in anything they have to say.

As inexperienced speakers, we become anxious because we assume that being different somehow means being inferior.

Actually, everyone is different from everyone else in many ways. Just as true, nearly everyone experiences nervousness about giving a speech.

> I control my anxiety by mentally viewing myself as being 100 percent equal to my classmates.
>
> —*Lee Morris, student*

Being the Center of Attention

Certain audience behaviors—such as lack of making eye contact with the speaker, or conversing with a neighbor—can be disconcerting. Our tendency in these situations is to think we must be doing something wrong; we wonder what it is and whether the entire audience has noticed it.

Left unchecked, this kind of thinking can distract us from the speech itself, with all our attention now focused on "me." Our self-consciousness makes us feel even more conspicuous and sensitive to what we might be doing wrong, which increases our anxiety! In fact, an audience generally notices very little about us that we don't want to reveal.

> It's always scary to speak in front of others, but you just have to remember that everyone's human.... Nobody wants you to fail; they're not waiting on you to mess up.
>
> —*Mary Parrish, student*

Pinpoint the Onset of Nervousness

Different people become anxious at different times during the speechmaking process. Depending on when it strikes, the consequences of public-speaking anxiety can include everything from procrastination to poor speech performance. But by pinpointing the onset of speech anxiety, you can address it promptly with specific anxiety-reducing techniques.

Pre-preparation Anxiety

Some people feel anxious the minute they know they will be giving a speech. **Pre-preparation anxiety** at this early stage can have several negative consequences for speakers, from feeling reluctant to begin planning for the speech to becoming so preoccupied with anxiety that they miss vital information necessary to fulfill the speech assignment. If this form of anxiety affects you, start very early using the stress-reducing techniques described in this chapter.

Preparation Anxiety

For a minority of people, anxiety arises only when they actually begin to prepare for the speech. They might feel overwhelmed at the amount of time and planning required or hit a roadblock that puts them behind schedule. Preparation pressures produce a cycle of stress, procrastination, and outright avoidance, all of which contribute to **preparation anxiety**. If you find yourself feeling anxious during this stage, defuse the anxiety by taking short, relaxing breaks to regain your confidence and focus.

Pre-performance Anxiety

Some people experience anxiety as they rehearse their speech. This is when the reality of the situation sets in: Soon they will face an audience that will be watching and listening only to them. They may feel that their ideas don't sound as focused or as interesting as they should, or sense that the time left to polish the speech is short. If this **pre-performance anxiety** is strong enough, and is interpreted negatively, they may even decide to stop rehearsing. If you experience pre-performance heightened anxiety, consider using the **anxiety stop-time technique**: Allow your anxiety to present itself for up to a few minutes until you declare time for confidence to step in so you can proceed to complete your practice.[3]

> I experience anxiety before, during, and after the speech. My "before speech" anxiety begins the night before my speech, but then I begin to look over my notecards, and I start to realize that I am ready for this speech. I practice one more time and I tell myself I am going to be fine.
>
> — *Paige Mease, student*

Performance Anxiety

For most people, anxiety levels tend to be highest just before they begin speaking.[4] This is true even of actors, who report that their worst stage fright occurs just as they walk onstage. **Performance anxiety** in speechmaking is probably most pronounced when we utter the first words of the speech and are most aware of the audience's attention. Audiences we perceive as negative usually cause us to feel more anxious than those we sense are positive or neutral.[5] However, experienced speakers agree that if they control their nervousness during the introduction, the rest of the speech will come relatively easily.

Regardless of when anxiety about a speech strikes, try to manage your anxiety and not let it manage you—by harming your motivation, or by causing you to avoid investing the time and energy required to deliver a successful speech.

Use Proven Strategies to Boost Your Confidence

A number of proven strategies exist to help you rein in your fears about public speaking, from *meditation* and *visualization* to other forms of relaxation techniques. The first step in taming speech anxiety is to have a thorough plan for each presentation.

Prepare and Practice

If you are confident that you know your material and have adequately rehearsed your delivery, you'll feel far more confident in front of an audience than otherwise. Preparation should begin as soon as possible after a speech is assigned. Once you have prepared the speech, be sure to rehearse it several times.

Modify Thoughts and Attitudes

Negative thoughts about speechmaking increase speech anxiety.[6] A positive attitude, on the other hand, actually results in lowered heart rate and reduced anxiety during the delivery of the speech.[7] As you prepare for and deliver your speech, envision it as a valuable, worthwhile, and challenging activity. Remind yourself of all the reasons that public speaking is helpful personally, socially, and professionally. Think positively about public speaking, and focus on it as an opportunity toward, not a threat to, personal growth.

> Just before a speech those feelings of anxiety undoubtedly try to sneak in. The way I keep them from taking over is to not let my mind become negative. As long as I keep positive thoughts of confidence in my head, anxiety doesn't stand a chance!
> —*Morgan Verdery, student*

QUICK TIP

Envision Your Speech as a Conversation
Rather than thinking of your speech as a formal performance where you will be judged and critiqued, try thinking of it as a kind of ordinary conversation. By doing so, you will feel less threatened and more relaxed about the process.[8]

Visualize Success

Visualization is a highly effective way to reduce nervousness.[9] The following is a script for visualizing success on a public-speaking occasion. This exercise requires you, the speaker, to close your eyes and visualize a series of positive feelings and reactions that will occur on the day of the speech.

Close your eyes and allow your body to get comfortable in the chair in which you are sitting. Take a deep, comfortable breath and hold it ... now slowly release it through your nose. Now take another deep breath and make certain that you are breathing from the diaphragm ... hold it ... now slowly release it and note how you feel while doing this. Now one more deep breath ... hold it ... and release it slowly ... and begin your normal breathing pattern.

Now begin to visualize the beginning of a day in which you are going to give an informative speech. See yourself getting up in the morning, full of energy, full of confidence, looking forward to the day's challenges. You are putting on just the right clothes for the task at hand that day. Dressing well makes you look and feel good about yourself, so you have on just what you want to wear, which clearly expresses your sense of inner well-being. As you are driving, riding, or walking to the speech setting, note how clear and confident you feel, and how others around you, as you arrive, comment positively regarding your fine appearance and general demeanor. You feel thoroughly prepared for the target issue you will be presenting today.

Now you see yourself standing or sitting in the room where you will present your speech, talking very comfortably and confidently with others in the room. The people to whom you will be presenting your speech appear to be quite friendly and are very cordial in their greetings and conversations prior to the presentation. You feel absolutely sure of your material and of your ability to present the information in a forceful, convincing, positive manner.

Now you see yourself approaching the area from which you will present. You are feeling very good about this presentation and see yourself move eagerly forward. All of your audiovisual materials are well organized, well planned, and clearly aid your presentation.[10]

Activate the Relaxation Response

Before, during, and sometimes after a speech you may experience rapid heart rate and breathing, dry mouth, faintness, freezing-up, or other uncomfortable sensations. These are automatic physiological reactions that result from the "fight-or-flight" response. Research shows that you can counteract these sensations by activating the relaxation response[11] using techniques such as meditation and controlled breathing.

Briefly Meditate

You can calm yourself considerably with this brief meditation exercise:

1. Sit comfortably in a quiet space.
2. Relax your muscles, moving from neck to shoulders to arms to back to legs.
3. Choose a word, phrase, or prayer that is connected to your belief system (e.g., "Namaste," "Om," "Hail Mary, Full of Grace"). Breathe slowly and say it until you become calm (about ten to twenty minutes).

Use Stress-Control Breathing

When you feel stressed, the center of your breathing tends to move from the abdomen to the upper chest, leaving you with a reduced supply of air. The chest and shoulders rise, and you feel out of breath. With *stress-control breathing,*[12] you will feel more movement in the stomach than in the chest. Try stress-control breathing in two stages.

STAGE ONE   Inhale air and let your abdomen go out. Exhale air and let your abdomen go in. Do this for a while until you get into the rhythm of it.

STAGE TWO   As you inhale, use a soothing word such as "calm" or "relax," or use a personal mantra, such as the following: "Inhale calm, abdomen out, exhale calm, abdomen in." Go slowly. Each inhalation and exhalation of stress-control breathing takes about three to five seconds.

Begin stress-control breathing *several days* before you're scheduled to speak. Then, once the speaking event arrives, use it while awaiting your turn at the podium and just before you start your speech.

> I have two ways to cope with my nervousness before I'm about to speak. I draw a couple of deep breaths from my stomach; I breathe in through my nose and out through my mouth. This allows more oxygen to the brain so you can think clearly. I also calm myself down by saying, "Everything will be okay, and the world is not going to crumble before me if I mess up."
> —*Jenna Sanford, student*

> **QUICK TIP**
>
> **Stretch Away Stress**
> You can significantly lessen pre-speech jitters by stretching.
> A half-hour to one-hour session of whole body stretches and
> yoga poses, combined with deep breathing, will help dis-
> charge nervous energy.

Use Movement to Minimize Anxiety

During delivery, you can use controlled movements with your
hands and body to release nervousness.

Practice Natural Gestures

Practice some controlled, natural gestures that might be useful
in enhancing your speech, such as holding up your index finger
when stating your first main point. Think about what you want
to say as you do this, instead of thinking about how you look
or feel. (See Chapter 19 for tips on practicing natural gestures.)

Move as You Speak

You don't have to stand perfectly still behind the podium
when you deliver a speech. Walk around as you make some
of your points. Movement relieves tension and helps hold the
audience's attention.

> **QUICK TIP**
>
> **Seek Pleasure in the Occasion**
> Most people ultimately find that giving speeches can indeed be
> fun. It's satisfying and empowering to influence people, and a
> good speech is a sure way to do this. Think of giving a speech
> in this way, and chances are you will find pleasure in it.

Learn from Feedback

When you've finished your speech, welcome feedback as an
opportunity to do even better next time. Although you can
learn a great deal from your own evaluation, research suggests you can learn even more from the objective evaluations
of others.[13] Feedback is given in the spirit of helping you to
present your speech to the best of your ability.

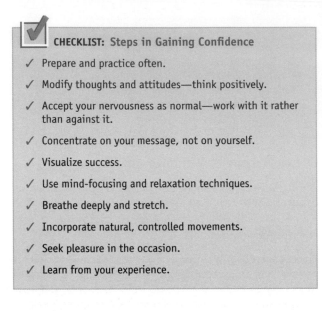

CHECKLIST: Steps in Gaining Confidence

✓ Prepare and practice often.

✓ Modify thoughts and attitudes—think positively.

✓ Accept your nervousness as normal—work with it rather than against it.

✓ Concentrate on your message, not on yourself.

✓ Visualize success.

✓ Use mind-focusing and relaxation techniques.

✓ Breathe deeply and stretch.

✓ Incorporate natural, controlled movements.

✓ Seek pleasure in the occasion.

✓ Learn from your experience.

4   Ethical Public Speaking

When we have an audience's attention, we are in a unique position to influence or persuade listeners and, at times, to move them to act—for better *or* worse. With this power to affect the minds and hearts of others comes *responsibility*—"a charge, trust, or duty for which one is accountable."[1] Taking responsibility for your message lies at the heart of being an ethical speaker.

Earn Your Listeners' Trust

Ethics is derived from the Greek word **ethos**, meaning "character." As Aristotle first noted so long ago, audiences listen to and trust speakers if they demonstrate *positive ethos*, or good character. Speakers in ancient Greece were regarded positively if they were well prepared, honest, and respectful toward their audience. Today, surprisingly little has changed. Modern research on **speaker credibility** reveals that people place their greatest trust in speakers who:

- Have a solid grasp of the subject.
- Display sound reasoning skills.
- Are honest and unmanipulative.
- Are genuinely interested in the welfare of their listeners.[2]

Respect Audience Values

Our ethical conduct is a reflection of our *values*—our most enduring judgments or standards of what's good and bad in life, of what's important to us. Like the individuals who hold them, values can conflict and clash. The more diverse the society, the greater these conflicts tend to be. One only has to think of the so-called values divide in the United States between "red states" (representing conservative values) and "blue states" (representing liberal values).

Conflicting values make it difficult to speak about certain topics without challenging cherished beliefs. The United States is a country of immigrants, for example, but half of the population with only a high school education believe that immigrants threaten traditional U.S. values, while only a quarter of college-educated Americans agree.[3] As you prepare speeches on controversial topics, anticipate that audience members will hold a range of values that will differ not only from your own, but from each other's. Demonstrate respect for your audience's values, even when you do not share them. (See Chapter 6 on identifying audience members' values.)

Use Your Rights of Free Speech Responsibly

Codes of ethical speech are built on moral rather than legal principles. Thus the **First Amendment**, which guarantees freedom of speech, assures protection both to speakers who treat the truth with respect and to those whose words are inflammatory and offensive.

Though often legally protected, racist, sexist, homophobic, pornographic, and other forms of negative speech clearly are unethical and should be avoided at all costs. *Be aware that certain types of speech are actually illegal:*

- Speech that provokes people to violence ("incitement" or "fighting words")
- Speech that can be proved to be **defamatory**, or that potentially harms an individual's reputation at work or in the community
- Speech that invades a person's privacy, such as disclosing information about an individual that is not in the public record

How can you tell if your speech contains defamatory language? If you are talking about public figures or matters of public concern, you will not be legally liable unless it can be shown that you spoke with a **reckless disregard for the truth**—that is, if you knew that what you were saying was false but said it anyway. If your comments refer to private persons, it will be easier for them to assert a claim for defamation. You will have the burden of proving that what you said was true.[4]

Contribute to Positive Public Discourse

An important measure of ethical speaking is whether it contributes something positive to **public discourse**—speech involving issues of importance to the larger community, such as the need to increase safety on campus or take action to slow climate change.

Perhaps the most important contribution you can make to public debates of this nature is the *advancement of constructive goals.* An ethical speech appeals to the greater good rather than narrow self-interest. It steers clear of **invective**, or verbal attacks designed to unfairly discredit, demean, and belittle those with whom you disagree. Ethical speakers avoid arguments that target a person instead of the issue at hand (*ad hominem* attack) or that are built upon other fallacies of reasoning (see Chapter 24).

QUICK TIP

Follow the Rules of Engagement
*Verbal attacks, heckling, and other forms of **conversation stoppers** breach the acceptable "rules of engagement" for public conversations. Originally used as a military term to describe how soldiers may use their weapons, the concept can also be applied to the ways we relate to one another in the public arena. Here, the **rules of engagement** oblige us to "speak the truth, to disclose one's purposes, to respond to others, to listen, and to understand."[5]*

Observe Ethical Ground Rules

Whether your speech focuses on a sensitive social issue or a dispassionate factual matter, the qualities of *dignity* and *integrity* should infuse every aspect of a speech. **Dignity** refers to ensuring that listeners feel worthy, honored, or respected as individuals.[6] **Integrity** signals the speaker's incorruptibility—that he or she will avoid compromising the truth for the sake of personal expediency.[7]

Speaking ethically also requires that we adhere to certain "pillars of character," or ethical ground rules.[8] These include being *trustworthy, respectful, responsible,* and *fair* in our presentations.

Trustworthiness is a combination of honesty and dependability. Trustworthy speakers support their points truthfully and don't offer misleading or false information.

We demonstrate **respect** by addressing audience members as unique human beings and refraining from any form of personal attack. The respectful speaker focuses on issues rather than on personalities and allows the audience the power of rational choice.

Responsibility means being accountable for what you say. For example, will learning about your topic in some way benefit listeners? Do you use sound evidence and reasoning? Do you offer emotional appeals because they are appropriate rather than to shore up otherwise weak arguments?

Fairness refers to making a genuine effort to see all sides of an issue and acknowledging the information listeners need in order to make informed decisions.[9] Few subjects are black and white; rarely is there only one right or wrong way to view a topic.

Avoid Offensive Speech

To be an ethical speaker, you must scrupulously avoid expressions of ethnocentrism, stereotypes, or outright prejudice. **Hate speech** is any offensive communication—verbal or nonverbal—that is directed against people's racial, ethnic, religious, gender, or other characteristics. This kind of speech is never acceptable.

✓ CHECKLIST: An Ethical Inventory

✓ Have you distorted any information to make your point?

✓ Have you acknowledged each of your sources?

✓ Does your speech focus on issues rather than on personalities?

✓ Have you tried to foster a sense of inclusion?

✓ Is your topic socially constructive?

✓ Do any of your arguments contain fallacies of reasoning? (see pp. 199–201)

✓ Is the content of your message as accurate as you can make it?

✓ Do you avoid speech that demeans those with whom you disagree?

Avoid Plagiarism

Crediting sources is a crucial aspect of any speech. **Plagiarism**—the passing off of another person's information as one's own—is as unethical in a speech as it is elsewhere. To plagiarize is to use other people's ideas or words without acknowledging the source. You are obviously plagiarizing when you simply "cut and paste" material from sources into your speech and represent it as your own. But it is also plagiarism to copy material into your speech draft from a source (such as a magazine article or Web site) and then change and rearrange words and sentence structure here and there to make it appear as if it were your own.[10] Whether it's done intentionally or not, plagiarism is stealing.

Orally Acknowledge Your Sources

The rule for avoiding plagiarism as a public speaker is straightforward: *Any source that requires credit in written form should be acknowledged in oral form.* These sources include direct quotations, as well as paraphrased and summarized information—any facts and statistics, ideas, opinions, or theories gathered and reported by others. For each source that requires citation, you need to include the *type of source* (magazine, book, personal interview, Web site, etc.), the *author or origin of the source*, the *title or a description of the source*, and the *date of the source*.

Oral presentations need not include the full bibliographic reference (that is, full names, dates, titles, volume, and page numbers). However, you should include a complete reference in a bibliography or at the end of the speech outline. (For more on creating a written bibliography for your speeches, see Appendix A.) Rules for avoiding plagiarism apply equally to print and online sources. It may be tempting to copy information from a Web site without attribution, but you must always accurately credit direct quotations, paraphrased information, facts, statistics, or other information posted online that was gathered and reported by someone other than yourself. For specific guidelines on how to record and cite sources found on Web sites, see "From Source to Speech" on pp. 80–81

One exception to sources needing citation is the use of **common knowledge**—information that is likely to be known by many people (though such information must *truly* be widely disseminated). For example, it is common knowledge that in March 2011 a massive earthquake in Japan triggered a tsunami. It is not common knowledge that it has been 1,200 years since an earthquake of this magnitude has hit the plate boundary of Japan. This fact requires acknowledgment of a source—in this case, a compilation of facts published by Francie Diep in *Scientific American*.[11]

Citing Quotations, Paraphrases, and Summaries

When citing other people's ideas, you can present them in one of three ways:

- **Direct quotations** are verbatim—or word for word—presentations of statements made by someone else. Direct quotes should always be acknowledged in a speech.
- A **paraphrase** is a restatement of someone else's ideas, opinions, or theories in the speaker's own words.[12] Because paraphrases alter the *form* but not the *substance* of another person's ideas, you must acknowledge the original source.
- A **summary** is a brief overview of someone else's ideas, opinions, or theories. While a paraphrase contains approximately the same number of words as the original source material stated in the speaker's own words, a summary condenses the same material, distilling only its essence.

Note how a speaker could paraphrase and summarize, *with credit*, the following excerpt from an article published in the *New Yorker* titled "Strange Fruit: The Rise and Fall of Açai," by John Calapinto.

ORIGINAL VERSION:
Açai was virtually unknown outside Brazil until 10 years ago, when Ryan and Jeremy Black, two brothers from Southern California, and their friend Edmund Nichols began exporting it to the United States. Since then, the fruit has followed a cycle of popularity befitting a teenage pop singer: a Miley Cyrus-like trajectory from obscurity to hype, critical backlash, and eventual ubiquity. Embraced as a "superfruit"—a potent combination of cholesterol-reducing fats and anti-aging antioxidants—açai became one of the fastest-growing foods in history. . . ."

Compare the original version of the excerpt to how it could be properly quoted, paraphrased, or summarized in a speech. Oral citation language is bolded for easy identification.

DIRECT QUOTATION:

As John Calapinto states in an article titled "Strange Fruit: The Rise and Fall of Açai," published in the May 30, 2011, issue of the *New Yorker,* "The fruit has followed a cycle of popularity befitting a teenage pop singer: a Miley Cyrus-like trajectory from obscurity to hype, critical backlash, and eventual ubiquity."

ORAL PARAPHRASE:

In an article titled "Strange Fruit: The Rise and Fall of Açai," published in the May 30, 2011, issue of the *New Yorker,* **John Calapinto explains that** until two brothers from Southern California named Ryan and Jeremy Black, along with their friend Edmund Nichols, began exporting açai to the United States ten years ago, it was unknown here. Now, says Calapinto, açai is seen as a "superfruit" that can help with everything from lowering cholesterol to fighting aging through its antioxidant properties.

ORAL SUMMARY:

In an article titled "Strange Fruit: The Rise and Fall of Açai," published in the May 30, 2011, issue of the *New Yorker,* **John Calapinto says that** açai, a fruit grown in Brazil that was unknown in this country until ten years ago, is now marketed as a "superfruit" that has powerful health benefits.

For detailed directions on crediting sources in your speech, see Chapter 11, "Citing Sources in Your Speech."

✓ **CHECKLIST: Correctly Quote, Paraphrase, and Summarize Information**

✓ If *directly quoting* a source, repeat the source word for word and acknowledge whose words you are using.

✓ If *paraphrasing* someone else's ideas, restate the ideas in your own words and acknowledge the source.

✓ If *summarizing* someone else's ideas, briefly describe their essence and acknowledge the source.

Fair Use, Copyright, and Ethical Speaking

Copyright is a legal protection afforded the creators of original literary and artistic works.[13] When including copyrighted materials in your speeches—such as reproductions of charts or photographs, a downloaded video clip, and so forth—you must determine when and if you need permission to use such works. For information on integrating media (such as downloaded videos and sound recordings) into your speech while respecting the laws of copyright, see Chapter 22, "A Brief Guide to Microsoft PowerPoint."

When a work is copyrighted, you may not reproduce, distribute, or display it without the permission of the copyright holder.[14] For any work created from 1978 to the present, a copyright is good during the author's lifetime, plus fifty years. After that, unless the copyright is extended, the work falls into the **public domain**, which means anyone may reproduce it. Not subject to copyright are federal (but *not* state or local) government publications, common knowledge, and select other categories.

An exception to the prohibitions of copyright is the doctrine of **fair use**, which permits the limited use of copyrighted works without permission for the purposes of scholarship, criticism, comment, news reporting, teaching, or research.[15] This means that when preparing speeches for the classroom, you have much more latitude to use other people's creative work without seeking permission, but *with* credit in all cases, including display of the copyright symbol (©) on any copyrighted handouts or visual aids you include in your speech. Different rules apply to the professional speaker, whose use of copyrighted materials is considered part of a for-profit "performance." (For more information, see www.copyright.gov.)

Creative Commons is an organization that allows creators of works to decide how they want other people to use their copyrighted works. It offers creators six types of licenses, three of which are perhaps most relevant to students in the classroom: *attribution* (lets you use the work if you give credit the way the author requests); *noncommercial* (lets you use the work for *noncommercial purposes* only); and *no derivative works* (lets you use only verbatim—exact—versions of the work).

The rules of fair use apply equally to works licensed under Creative Commons and the laws of copyright. Student speakers may search the Creative Commons Web site for suitable materials for their speech at creativecommons.org. Note that the rules for copyright, Creative Commons, and fair use also apply equally to print and online sources.

Most of us understand that giving a speech involves preparation and practice, but few recognize the hard work that listening to a speech requires. Rather than being a passive activity that simply "happens" to us, **listening** is the conscious act of *receiving, comprehending, interpreting, evaluating,* and *responding* to messages.[1]

Recognize That We Listen Selectively

In any given situation, no two audience members will process the information in exactly the same way. The reason lies in **selective perception**—people pay attention selectively to certain messages while ignoring others. Several factors influence what we listen to and what we ignore:

- We pay attention to what we hold to be important.
- We pay attention to information that touches our experiences and backgrounds.
- We sort and filter new information on the basis of what we already know (i.e., one way we learn is by analogy).[2]

With these principles in mind, try to:

- Identify what's important to your listeners, including their interests, needs, attitudes, and values.
- Show them early on what they stand to gain from listening to you.
- Touch upon their experiences and backgrounds.
- Build repetition of key ideas into the speech.
- Use analogies to help listeners learn new ideas.
- When appropriate, use presentation aids to visually reinforce your message.

QUICK TIP

Beat the Odds by Listening
Each of us devotes between 20 and 40 percent of our daily lives to listening.[3] For executives, the figure rises to 45 percent.[4] Yet most people retain only half of what they hear immediately and only 35 percent of what they heard after twenty-four hours.[5] Employers actively seek out new hires who can beat these averages, and those who do so tend to get hired and promoted first.[6]

Listen Responsibly

As a speaker, you have the power of the podium; but as a listener, you also have considerable power that you can wield constructively or destructively. As listeners, we are ethically bound to refrain from disruptive and intimidating tactics—such as heckling, name-calling, or interrupting—that are meant to silence those with whom we disagree. If we find the arguments of others morally offensive, we are equally bound to speak up appropriately in refutation.

Strive for the Open Exchange of Ideas

In contrast to *monologue*, in which we try merely to impose what we think on another person or group of people, **dialogic communication** is the open sharing of ideas in an atmosphere of respect.[7] For the speaker, this means approaching a speech not as an argument that must be "won," but as an opportunity to achieve understanding with audience members. For listeners, it means maintaining an open mind and listening with empathy.

Speakers and listeners are always responding to one another's signals—whether of interest or disinterest, agreement or disagreement, and so forth. This continual adjustment between speaker and listener is called the **feedback loop**.[8] As a listener, you can encourage dialogic communication and a positive feedback loop by approaching the speaker with an attitude of openness and giving him or her your full attention. This in turn will enable the speaker to deliver the message without impediment.

Anticipate the Common Obstacles to Listening

Active listening—listening that is focused and purposeful—isn't possible under conditions that distract us.[9] As you listen to speeches, try to identify and overcome some common obstacles.

Minimize External and Internal Distractions

A **listening distraction** is anything that competes for the attention we are trying to give to something else. Distractions can originate outside of us, in the environment (external distractions), or within us, in our thoughts and feelings (internal distractions).

To minimize *external listening distractions*, such as the din of jackhammers or competing conversations, try to anticipate and plan for them. If you struggle to see or hear at a distance, arrive early and sit in the front. To reduce *internal listening distractions*, avoid daydreaming, be well rested, monitor yourself for lapses in attention, and consciously focus on listening.

✓ **CHECKLIST: Dealing with Distractions While Delivering a Speech**

✓ *Problem*: *Passing distractions* (chatting, entry of latecomers)

✓ *Solution*: Pause until distraction recedes

✓ *Problem*: *Ongoing noise* (construction)

✓ *Solution*: Raise speaking volume

✓ *Problem: Sudden distraction* (collapsing chair, falling object)

✓ *Solution*: Minimize response and proceed

✓ *Problem: Audience interruption* (raised hand, monologue)

✓ *Solution*: Acknowledge audience reaction and either follow up or defer response to conclusion of speech[10]

Guard against Scriptwriting and Defensive Listening

When we engage in *scriptwriting*, we focus on what we, rather than the speaker, will say next.[11] Similarly, people who engage in **defensive listening** decide either that they won't like what the speaker is going to say or that they know better. When you find yourself scriptwriting or listening with a defensive posture, remind yourself that effective listening precedes effective rebuttal.[12] Try waiting for the speaker to finish before devising your own arguments.

Beware of Laziness and Overconfidence

Laziness and overconfidence can manifest themselves in several ways: We may expect too little from speakers, ignore important information, or display an arrogant attitude. Later, we discover we missed important information. Never assume that you already know exactly what a speaker will say; you'll seldom be right.

Work to Overcome Cultural Barriers

Differences in dialects or accents, nonverbal cues, word choice, and even physical appearance can serve as barriers to listening, but they need not if you keep your focus on the message rather than the messenger. Consciously refrain from judging a speaker on the basis of his or her accent, appearance, or demeanor; focus instead on what is actually being said. Whenever possible, reveal your needs to him or her by asking questions.

When speaking, the following will minimize confusion:

- Watch for **idioms**, or colloquial expressions such as "apple of his eye," that non-native speakers might not know. Either eliminate or define them.
- Speak at a rate that is neither too fast nor too slow. Pay particular attention to pronunciation and articulation.
- Be alert to nonverbal cues that suggest that listeners may not comprehend you, and clarify points when indicated.

Practice Active Listening

Taking the following practical steps can help you listen actively:

- Set listening goals and state them in a way that encourages action: "In my colleagues' presentation, I will learn why it took them six months to complete the last phase."
- Listen for the speaker's main ideas and take note of key points.
- Watch for the speaker's nonverbal cues.
- Try to detect the speaker's organizational pattern.

Evaluate Evidence and Reasoning

As you listen to speeches, use your critical faculties to do the following:

- *Evaluate the speaker's evidence.* Is it accurate? Are the sources credible?
- *Analyze the speaker's assumptions and biases.* What lies behind the speaker's assertions? Does the evidence support or contradict these assertions?

- *Assess the speaker's reasoning.* Does it betray faulty logic? Does it rely on fallacies in reasoning? (See Chapter 24.)
- *Consider multiple perspectives.* Is there another way to view the argument? How do other perspectives compare with the speaker's?
- *Summarize and assess the relevant facts and evidence.*

Offer Constructive and Compassionate Feedback

Follow these guidelines when evaluating the speeches of others:

- *Be honest and fair in your evaluation.*
- *Adjust to the speaker's style.* Don't judge the content of a speaker's message by his or her style.
- *Be compassionate in your criticism.* Always start by saying something positive, and focus on the speech, not the speaker.
- *Be selective in your criticism.* Make specific rather than global statements. Rather than statements such as, "I just couldn't get into your topic," give the speaker something he or she can learn from: "I wanted more on why the housing market is falling. . . ."

Part 2
Development

6. Analyzing the Audience 36

7. Selecting a Topic and Purpose 47

8. Developing Supporting Material 55

9. Locating Supporting Material 62

10. Finding Credible Sources on the
    Internet 72

11. Citing Sources in Your Speech 85

Advertisers are shrewd analysts of people's needs and wants, extensively researching our buying habits and lifestyle choices to identify what motivates us. To engage your listeners and encourage their involvement in your message, you too must investigate your audience. **Audience analysis** is the process of gathering and analyzing information about audience members' attributes and motivations with the *explicit aim of preparing your speech in ways that will be meaningful to them*. This is the single most critical aspect of preparing for any speech.

Maintaining an **audience-centered** approach throughout the entire speech preparation process—from selection and treatment of the speech topic to making decisions about how you will organize, word, and deliver it—will help you prepare a presentation that your audience will want to hear.

Adapt to Audience Psychology: Who Are Your Listeners?

As you prepare your speeches, seek to learn about the audience's attitudes, beliefs, and values—their *feelings and opinions*—toward the topic, toward you as the speaker, and toward the speech occasion. This "perspective taking" will help you learn more about your audience and see things from their point of view.

Taking the measure of the audience is critical because people tend to evaluate information in terms of their own—rather than the speaker's—point of view. You may want your school administrators to support a new online degree program, but unless you know their current perspective on such a program, you won't know how to appeal to them effectively.

Attitudes, beliefs, and values, while intertwined, reflect distinct mental states that reveal a great deal about us. **Attitudes** are our general evaluations of people, ideas, objects, or events.[1] To evaluate something is to judge it as relatively good or bad, useful or useless, and desirable or undesirable. People generally act in accordance with their attitudes (although the degree to which they do so depends on many factors).[2]

Attitudes are based on **beliefs**—the ways in which people perceive reality.[3] Beliefs are our feelings about what is true. The less faith listeners have in the existence of something—UFOs, for instance—the less open they are to hearing about it.

Both attitudes and beliefs are shaped by **values**—our most enduring judgments about what's good and bad in life, as shaped by our culture and our unique experiences within it.

Values run deeper than attitudes or beliefs and are more resistant to change. Values usually align with attitudes and beliefs.

As a rule, people are more interested in and pay greater attention to topics toward which they have positive attitudes and that are in keeping with their values and beliefs. The less we know about something, the more indifferent we tend to be. It is easier (though not simple) to spark interest in an indifferent audience than it is to turn negative attitudes around.

Appeal to Listeners' Attitudes, Beliefs, and Values

Evoking some combination of the audience's attitudes, beliefs, and values in the speeches you deliver will make them more personally relevant and motivating. For example, the Biodiversity Project, a group that helps speakers raise public awareness about the environment, counsels clients to appeal directly to the values their audience members hold about the environment (discovered in surveys), offering the following as an example:[4]

> You care about your family's health (value #1) and you feel a responsibility to protect your loved ones' quality of life (value #2). The local wetland provides a sanctuary to many plants and animals. It helps clean our air and water and provides a space of beauty and serenity (value #3). All of this is about to be destroyed by irresponsible development.[5]

Gauge Listeners' Feelings toward the Topic

Try to learn what your listeners know about the topic. What is their level of interest? Do they hold positive, negative, or neutral attitudes toward it? Once you have this information, adjust the speech accordingly:

If the topic is *new* to listeners,

- Start by showing why the topic is relevant to them.
- Relate the topic to familiar issues and ideas about which they already hold positive attitudes.

If listeners know *relatively little* about the topic,

- Stick to the basics and include background information.
- Steer clear of jargon, and define unclear terms.
- Repeat important points, summarizing information often.

If listeners are *negatively disposed* toward the topic,

- Focus on establishing rapport and credibility.
- Don't directly challenge listeners' attitudes; instead begin with areas of agreement.
- Discover why they have a negative bias in order to tactfully introduce the other side of the argument.
- Offer solid evidence from sources they are likely to accept.
- Give good reasons for developing a positive attitude toward the topic.[6]

If listeners hold *positive attitudes* toward the topic,

- Stimulate the audience to feel even more strongly by emphasizing the side of the argument with which they already agree.
- Tell stories with vivid language that reinforce listeners' attitudes.[7]

If listeners are a *captive audience*,

- Motivate listeners to pay attention by stressing what is most relevant to them.
- Pay close attention to the length of your speech.

QUICK TIP

Custom-Fit Your Message

Audience members like to feel that the speaker recognizes them as unique individuals. You can do this by making positive references to the place where you are speaking and the group to whom you are addressing your comments. Personalize the speech by applying relevant facts and statistics in your speech directly to the audience. If your topic is hurricanes, for example, you could note that "Right here in Carla, Texas, you endured and survived a Category 4 hurricane in 1961."

Gauge Listeners' Feelings toward You as the Speaker

How audience members feel about you will also have significant bearing on their responsiveness to the message. A speaker who is well liked can gain an initial hearing even when listeners are unsure what to expect from the message itself.

To create positive audience attitudes toward you, first display the characteristics of speaker credibility (ethos) described in Chapter 4. Listeners have a natural desire to identify with the speaker and to feel that he or she shares their perceptions,[8] so establish a feeling of commonality, or **identification**, with them. Use eye contact and body movements to include the audience in your message. Relate a relevant personal story, emphasize a shared role, focus on areas of agreement, or otherwise stress mutual bonds. Even your physical presentation can foster a common bond. Audiences are more apt to identify with speakers who dress in ways they find appropriate.

✓ **CHECKLIST: Respond to the Audience as You Speak**

Audience analysis continues as you deliver your speech. During your speech, monitor the audience for signs of how they are receiving your message. Look for bodily clues as signs of interest or disengagement:

✓ Large smiles and eye contact suggest a liking for and agreement with the speaker.

✓ Arms folded across the chest may signal disagreement.

✓ Averted glances, slumped posture, and squirming usually indicate disengagement.

Engage with the audience when it appears they aren't with you:

✓ Invite one or two listeners to relate briefly their own experiences about the topic.

✓ Share a story linked to the topic to increase identification.[9]

Gauge Listeners' Feelings toward the Occasion

Depending on the circumstances calling for the speech, people will bring different sets of expectations and emotions to it. For example, members of a **captive audience**, who are required to hear the speaker, may be less positively disposed to the occasion than members of a **voluntary audience** who attend of their own free will. Whether planning a wedding toast or a business presentation, failure to anticipate and adjust for the audience's expectations risks alienating them.

Adapt Your Message to Audience Demographics

Demographics are the statistical characteristics of a given population. At least six such characteristics are typically considered in the analysis of speech audiences: *age, ethnic or cultural background, socioeconomic status* (including *income, occupation,* and *education*), *religion, political affiliation,* and *gender.* Any number of other traits—for example, disability, group membership, sexual orientation, or place of residence—may be important to investigate as well.

Knowing where audience members fall in relation to audience demographics will help you identify your **target audience**—those individuals within the broader audience whom you are most likely to influence in the direction you seek. You may not be able to please everyone, but you should be able to establish a connection with your target audience.

Age

Each age group has its own concerns and, broadly speaking, psychological drives and motivations. In addition to sharing the concerns associated with a given life stage, people of the same generation often share a familiarity with significant individuals, local and world events, noteworthy popular culture, and so forth. Being aware of the audience's age range and generational identity, such as the Millennials (those born between 1977 and 1995), allows you to develop points that are relevant to the experience and interests of the widest possible cross section of your listeners.

Ethnic or Cultural Background

An understanding of and sensitivity to the ethnic and cultural composition of your listeners are key factors in delivering a successful (and ethical) speech. Some audience members may have a great deal in common with you. Others may be fluent in a language other than yours and must struggle to understand you. Some members of the audience may belong to a distinct **co-culture**, or social community whose perspectives and style of communicating differ significantly from yours. All will want to feel recognized by the speaker. (See "Adapt to Cultural Differences," p. 43.)

Socioeconomic Status

Socioeconomic status (SES) includes income, occupation, and education. Knowing roughly where an audience falls in terms of these key variables can be critical in effectively targeting your message.

INCOME *Income* determines people's experiences on many levels. It directly affects how they are housed, clothed, and fed, and determines what they can afford. Beyond this, income has a ripple effect, influencing many other aspects of life. For example, depending on income, home ownership is either a taken-for-granted budget item or an out-of-reach dream. The same is true for any activity dependent on income. Given how pervasively income affects people's life experiences, insight into this aspect of an audience's makeup can be quite important.

OCCUPATION In most speech situations, the *occupation* of audience members is an important and easily identifiable demographic characteristic. The nature of people's work has a lot to do with what interests them. Occupational interests are tied to several other areas of social concern, such as politics, the economy, education, and social reform. Personal attitudes, beliefs, and goals are also closely tied to occupational standing.

EDUCATION Level of *education* strongly influences people's ideas, perspectives, and range of abilities. Higher levels of education lead to increased lifetime earnings, decreased levels of crime, better health outcomes, and greater civic engagement;[10] such factors may be important to consider when preparing a speech. Depending upon audience members' level of education, you may choose to clarify your points with fewer or more examples and illustrations.

Religion

Beliefs and practices and social and political views vary by religious traditions, making *religion* another key demographic variable. At least a dozen major religious traditions coexist in the United States and these, in turn, are divided into hundreds of distinct religious groups.[11] Not all members of the same religious tradition will agree on all issues, however. For example, Catholics disagree on birth control and divorce, Jews disagree on whether to recognize same-sex unions, and so forth.

Political Affiliation

As with religion, beware of making unwarranted assumptions about an audience's *political values and beliefs*. Some people like nothing better than a lively debate about public-policy issues. Others avoid anything that smacks of politics. And many people are very touchy about their views on political issues. Unless you have prior information about the audience's political values and beliefs, you won't know where your listeners stand.

Gender

Gender is another important factor in audience analysis, if only as a reminder to avoid the minefield of **gender stereotyping**. Distinct from the fixed physical characteristics of biological sex, **gender** is our social and psychological sense of ourselves as males or females.[12] Making assumptions about the preferences, abilities, and behaviors of your audience members based on their presumed gender can seriously undermine their receptivity to your message. Beyond ensuring that you treat issues of gender evenly, try to anticipate the audience members' attitudes with respect to gender and plan accordingly.

QUICK TIP

Be Sensitive to Disability When Analyzing an Audience

One out of every five people in the United States has some sort of physical or mental disability;[13] 14 percent of those enrolled in college and graduate school are counted as disabled. Problems range from sight and hearing impairments to constraints on physical mobility and employment. Knowing this, make certain that your speech reflects language that accords dignity, respect, and fairness to persons with disabilities (PWD).

Adapt to Cultural Differences

In the United States, one-third of the population, or nearly 112 million people, belong to a racial or ethnic minority group, and 38.5 million people, or 12.5 percent, are foreign-born.[14] Nearly half of the population living in the western United States identify themselves as members of a minority group. Worldwide, there are 194 independent states, and many more distinct cultures within these countries.[15] What these figures suggest is that audience members will hold different cultural perspectives and employ different styles of communicating that may or may not mesh with your own.

How might you prepare to speak in front of an ethnically and culturally diverse audience, including that of your classroom? In any speaking situation, your foremost concern should be to treat your listeners with dignity and to act with integrity. Since values are central to who we are, identifying those of your listeners with respect to your topic can help you to avoid ethnocentrism and deliver your message in a culturally sensitive manner.

Consider Cross-Cultural Values

In the United States, researchers have identified a set of core values seen in the dominant culture, including *achievement and success, equal opportunity, material comfort, hard work, practicality and efficiency, change and progress, science, democracy,* and *freedom.*[16] A survey of Mexican society reveals such core values as *group loyalty, mañana* (cyclical time), *machismo, family closeness,* and *fatalism.*[17] People in every culture possess values related to their personal relationships, religion, occupation, and so forth. Understanding these values can help you deliver your message sensitively.

QUICK TIP

Consult Global Opinion Polls

Cross-cultural surveys can be extremely useful for learning about how values vary across cultures. The Pew Global Attitudes Project *(http://pewglobal.org/) is a series of worldwide opinion surveys conducted in 57 countries.* Gallup World View *(worldview.gallup.com) surveys 150 countries on attitudes related to issues ranging from well-being to the environment. The* World Values Survey *(www.worldvaluessurvey.org) offers a fascinating look at the values and beliefs of people in 97 countries.*

Focus on Universal Values

As much as possible, it is important to try to determine the attitudes, beliefs, and values of audience members. At the same time, you can focus on certain values that, if not universally shared, are probably universally aspired to in the human heart. These include love, truthfulness, fairness, freedom, unity, tolerance, responsibility, and respect for life.[18]

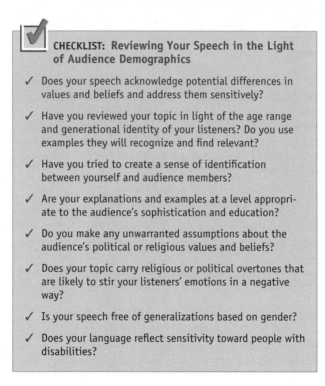

CHECKLIST: Reviewing Your Speech in the Light of Audience Demographics

✓ Does your speech acknowledge potential differences in values and beliefs and address them sensitively?

✓ Have you reviewed your topic in light of the age range and generational identity of your listeners? Do you use examples they will recognize and find relevant?

✓ Have you tried to create a sense of identification between yourself and audience members?

✓ Are your explanations and examples at a level appropriate to the audience's sophistication and education?

✓ Do you make any unwarranted assumptions about the audience's political or religious values and beliefs?

✓ Does your topic carry religious or political overtones that are likely to stir your listeners' emotions in a negative way?

✓ Is your speech free of generalizations based on gender?

✓ Does your language reflect sensitivity toward people with disabilities?

Interview and Survey Audience Members

Now that you know the kind of information to look for when analyzing an audience, how do you actually uncover it? Unlike a professional pollster, you cannot survey thousands of people and apply sophisticated statistical techniques to analyze your results. On a smaller scale, however, you can use the same techniques. These include interviewing, surveying, and consulting published sources. Often, it takes just a few questions to get some idea of where audience members stand on each of the demographic factors.

Conduct Interviews

Interviews, even brief ones, can reveal a lot about the audience's interests and needs. You can conduct interviews one-on-one or in a group, in person or by telephone or e-mail. Consider interviewing a sampling of the audience, or even just one knowledgeable representative of the group that you will address. As in questionnaires (see "Survey the Audience," which follows), interviews usually consist of a mix of open- and closed-ended questions. (See Chapter 9, pp. 70–71, for more on conducting interviews.)

Survey the Audience

Surveys can be as informal as a poll of several audience members or as formal as the pre-speech distribution of a written survey, or **questionnaire**—a series of open- and closed-ended questions.

Closed-ended questions elicit a small range of specific answers supplied by the interviewer:

> "Do you or did you ever smoke cigarettes?"

Answers will be either "Yes," "No," or "I smoked for X number of years." Closed-ended questions may be either fixed-alternative or scale questions. **Fixed-alternative questions** contain a limited choice of answers, such as "Yes," "No," or "Sometimes." **Scale questions**—also called *attitude scales*—measure the respondent's level of agreement or disagreement with specific issues:

> "Flag burning should be outlawed":
> Strongly Agree _____ Agree _____ Undecided _____
> Disagree _____ Strongly Disagree _____

Scale questions can be used to measure how important listeners judge something to be and how frequently they engage in a particular behavior:

> "How important is religion in your life?"
> Very Important _____ Important _____
> Moderately Important _____
> Of Minor Importance _____ Unimportant_____

Open-ended questions allow respondents to elaborate as much as they wish:

> "How do you feel about using the results of DNA testing to prove innocence or guilt in criminal proceedings?"

A mix of open- and closed-ended questions can reveal a fairly clear picture of the backgrounds and attitudes of the members of your audience. Closed-ended questions are especially helpful in uncovering the shared attitudes, experiences, and knowledge of audience members. Open-ended questions are particularly useful for probing beliefs and opinions.

Consult Published Sources

Yet another way to learn about audience members is through published sources. Organizations of all kinds publish information describing their missions, operations, and achievements. Sources include Web sites and related online articles, brochures, newspaper and magazine articles, and annual reports.

Although *published opinion polls* won't specifically reflect your particular listeners' responses, they can provide valuable insight into how a representative state, national, or international sample feels about the issue in question. Consider consulting these and other polling organizations:

- Pew Research Center for the People & the Press: people-press.org
- National Opinion Research Center (NORC): www.norc.uchicago.edu
- Roper Center for Public Opinion Research: ropercenter.uconn.edu
- Gallup: www.gallup.com

Assess the Speech Setting and Context

As important as analyzing the audience is assessing (and then preparing for) the setting in which you will give your speech—size of audience; location; time; length of speech; and rhetorical situation:

1. Where will the speech take place?
2. How long am I expected to speak?
3. How many people will attend?
4. Will I need a microphone?
5. How will any equipment I plan to use in my speech, such as an LCD projector, function in the space?
6. Where will I stand or sit in relation to the audience?
7. Will I be able to interact with the listeners?
8. Who else will be speaking?
9. Are there special events or circumstances of concern to my audience that I should acknowledge (the rhetorical situation)?

7 Selecting a Topic and Purpose

One of the first tasks in preparing any speech is to select a topic and purpose for speaking that are appropriate to the audience and occasion. Even if the topic is assigned, as often happens in the classroom and workplace, you must still adapt it to suit the unique audience and speech situation.

Decide Where to Begin

Selecting a topic, whether for a classroom speech or another venue, can be approached from a variety of angles. You can start by making an inventory of your own expertise and life experiences, from favorite hobbies to causes you care about. Perhaps you volunteer as a mentor or serve on a student group. Alternatively, you can begin by focusing on social issues of national or global consequence, such as foreign policy or the health of the oceans. Wherever you choose to begin, pick a general topic you are drawn to and want to know more about. Ask yourself: Does the topic benefit my listeners and align with their expectations? Does it suit the speech occasion?

IDENTIFYING TOPICS

PERSONAL INTERESTS	CURRENT EVENTS AND CONTROVERSIAL ISSUES
• Volunteering • Sports and exercise • Fashion • Travel • Outdoor life • Service in the armed forces • Home repair • Video games	• Energy policy • Foreign aid and national security • Public-employee unions • National debt • Immigration reform • Prison reform • Fuel-efficiency standards • Pending legislation—crime bills, new tax proposals, land use

VALUES AND GOALS	SPECIFIC SUBJECT INTERESTS
• Community service • Learning more about religion and spirituality • Political activism • Attending graduate or professional school • Being fit	• Local or ancient history • Health and medicine • Art • Religion • Science

GRASSROOTS ISSUES	NEW AND UNUSUAL ANGLES
• Land development vs. conservation • Local organizations • School issues	• Unsolved crimes • Unexplained disappearances • Scandals

Steer Clear of Overused and Trivial Topics

To avoid boring your classmates and instructor, stay away from tired issues, such as drunk driving and gun control, as well as trite topics such as "how to change a tire." Instead, consider a subject that is underserved by other speakers that yields fresh insight. As one source of ideas, consult your favorite print or online publications. Beware, however, of choosing highly charged topics for which people have deeply held beliefs, such as abortion or prayer in school. People rarely respond to persuasion directed at their core values, so speeches on such topics are likely to accomplish little except to raise tension in the classroom.

QUICK TIP

Explore Topics on CQ Researcher
*Librarians often refer students to two related publications—
CQ Researcher (published weekly) and CQ Global Researcher
(published monthly)—for trustworthy background information on pressing social, political, environmental, and regional
issues. Available online as part of your library's electronic
holdings, they include, for each topic, an overview and
assessment of the current situation; pro/con statements from
representatives of opposing positions; and bibliographies of
key sources.*

Try Brainstorming to Generate Ideas

To generate ideas for topics, try **brainstorming** by word association and topic (mind) mapping.

To brainstorm by **word association,** write down a single topic that might interest you and your listeners. Next, write down the first thing that comes to mind. Continue this process until you have a list of fifteen to twenty items. Narrow the list to two or three, and then select the best topic:

health → alternative medicine → naturopathy → homeopathy

To brainstorm by **topic (mind) mapping,** put a poten-
tial topic in the middle of a piece of paper. As related ideas come to you, write them down, as shown in Figure 7.1. Mind

FIGURE 7.1 A Topic Map

mapping allows you to visualize relationships among ideas and spurs creative thinking.

Identify the General Purpose of Your Speech

Once you have an idea for a topic, you'll need to refine and adapt it to your general speech purpose. The **general speech purpose** for any speech answers the question, "What is my objective in speaking on this topic to this audience on this occasion?" Public speakers typically seek to accomplish one of three general purposes: to inform, to persuade, or to mark a special occasion.

— Do you aim primarily to educate or inform listeners about your topic? The general purpose of an informative speech is *to increase the audience's awareness by imparting knowledge.*

— Is your goal to persuade listeners to accept your position on a topic and perhaps to take action? The general purpose of the persuasive speech is *to influence the attitudes, beliefs, values, and behaviors of audience members.*

— Are you there to mark a special occasion, such as an awards ceremony? The general purpose of the special occasion speech will be variously *to entertain, celebrate, commemorate, inspire, or set a social agenda.*

The speech occasion itself often suggests an appropriate general speech purpose. For example, a town activist, invited to address a civic group about installing solar panels in town buildings, may choose a *persuasive purpose* to encourage the group to get behind the effort. If invited to describe the initiative to the town finance committee, the activist may choose an *informative purpose*, in which the main goal is to help the committee understand project costs. If asked to speak at an event celebrating the project's completion, the speaker will choose a *special occasion purpose.* Addressing the same topic, the speaker selects a different general speech purpose to suit the audience and occasion.

Narrow Your Topic

Once you've settled on a topic and have established a general speech purpose, you'll need to narrow your focus to align with audience expectations, time constraints, and the nature of the occasion. (See "From Source to Speech: Narrowing Your Topic to Fit Your Audience," pp. 52–53):

- Consider what your listeners are likely to know about the subject and what they will want to learn.
- Consider what aspects of the topic are most relevant to the occasion. Restrict your focus to what you can competently research and then report on in the time you are given to speak.
- Pick a discrete topic category and cover it well.
- Restrict your main points to between two and five.

Just as brainstorming can be used to discover a topic, it can also be helpful in narrowing one. One way of doing this is to brainstorm by category (e.g., subtopic). Say your general topic is video games. Some related categories are platform (handheld, arcade), type (racing, roleplaying), or operating system (Linux, Macintosh, Windows). To brainstorm topics by category online, consider browsing a subject (Web) directory, such as that found on Yahoo! A subject directory provides a searchable listing of topic categories such as "Science," "Health," and "Business and Economy." Each subject category links to subtopics; each subtopic links to its own subcategories, and so on (for more on subject directories, see Chapter 10).

Form a Specific Speech Purpose

The **specific speech purpose** lays out precisely what you want the audience to get from the speech. It goes beyond the general goal of informing or persuading or marking a special occasion. To determine the specific purpose, ask yourself: What do you want the audience to learn/do/reconsider/agree with? Be specific about your aim, and then state this aim in action form, as in the following, written for an informative speech:

GENERAL TOPIC:	Consolidating Student Loans
NARROWED TOPIC:	Understanding when and why consolidating student loans makes sense
GENERAL PURPOSE:	To inform
SPECIFIC PURPOSE:	To inform my audience about the factors to consider when deciding whether or not to consolidate student loans

The specific purpose statement is seldom articulated in the speech itself. Its importance lies in implanting in your mind exactly what you want your speech to accomplish.

Compose a Thesis Statement

After narrowing your topic and forming your specific purpose, your next step is to formulate a thesis statement. The **thesis statement** (also called *central idea*) is the theme of the speech, stated in the form of a single, declarative sentence. It concisely expresses what you will attempt to demonstrate or prove in your speech. The main points, the supporting material, and the conclusion all relate to the thesis.

The thesis statement and the specific purpose are closely linked. Both state the speech topic, but in different forms. *The specific purpose describes in action form what you want to achieve with the speech; the thesis statement concisely identifies, in a single idea, what the speech is about.* The specific purpose does not have to be stated in the speech itself. However, the thesis must be clearly stated because the entire speech rests on it. The difference can be seen in the specific purpose

From Source to Speech

Narrowing Your Topic to Fit Your Audience

How do you narrow a topic to fit the audience and the speech occasion? Consider the following case study.

A Case Study

Jenny is a member of the campus animal rights club and a student in a public speaking class. She is giving two persuasive speeches this semester: one to her public speaking class and one to the student council, as a representative of her club. For both presentations, Jenny plans to speak on the broad topic of animal rights. But she must narrow this topic considerably to fit each audience and speech occasion.

First, Jenny draws a topic map to generate ideas.

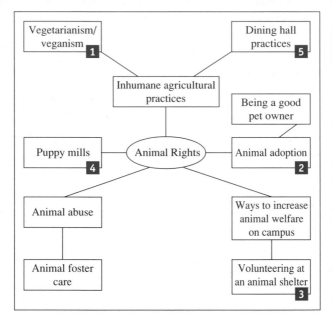

For each presentation, Jenny narrows her topic after considering her audience and the speech occasion.

PUBLIC SPEAKING CLASS (25–30 PEOPLE):

- Mixed ages, races, and ethnicities, and an even mix of males and females

- Busy with classes, jobs, sports, and clubs

- Half live in campus housing, where pets are not allowed

1 Jenny eliminates vegetarianism because she will be unlikely to change listeners' minds in a six-minute speech.

2 She eliminates animal adoption because it may not be feasible for many students.

3 Volunteering at an animal shelter is an option for all animal lovers, even those who are not allowed to have pets on campus. Jenny argues that students should donate an hour a week to a nearby shelter, so that busy students can still participate.

STUDENT COUNCIL (8–10 PEOPLE):

- Mixed demographic characteristics

- Similar interests: government, maintaining a rich campus life, an investment in ethics and the honor code, and an interest in keeping student affairs within budget

4 Jenny eliminates puppy mills—though the student council may agree that the mills are harmful, they are not in a position to directly address the problem.

5 Jenny zeroes in on dining hall practices, which are directly tied to campus life. Her club's proposed resolution to use free-range eggs in the campus dining hall benefits all students and requires the support of the council—an ideal topic for this audience.

and thesis statement for a persuasive speech on donating food to the local food bank:

SPECIFIC PURPOSE: To persuade the audience to donate non-perishable food to the local food bank to fight hunger in our community.

THESIS: A donation of nonperishable food to the local food bank is the best way to help needy community members stave off hunger.

Postpone Development of Main Points

Whether the speech is informative or persuasive, the thesis statement proposes that the statement made is true or is believed. The speech is then developed from this premise; it presents facts and evidence to support the thesis as true. Thus, postpone the development of main points or the consideration of supporting material until you have formulated the speech purpose and thesis (see Chapter 12).

In a persuasive speech, the thesis statement represents what you are going to *prove* in the address. All the main points in the speech are arguments that develop the thesis:

GENERAL PURPOSE: To persuade

SPECIFIC PURPOSE: To persuade my audience to back legislation calling for fuel-efficiency standards of 60 miles per gallon by 2017.

THESIS: Mandating fuel-efficiency standards of 60 miles per gallon by 2017, as outlined in Bill X, is a necessary step in combating climate change and decreasing dependence on foreign oil.

Notice that, after you read the thesis, you find yourself asking "Why?" or saying "Prove it!" This will be accomplished by the main points (see Chapter 12).

In informative speaking, the thesis describes what the audience will *learn*:

GENERAL PURPOSE: To inform

SPECIFIC PURPOSE: To inform my audience of three benefits of keeping a blog

THESIS: Maintaining a blog lets you sharpen your writing skills, network with persons who share similar interests, and develop basic Web site management skills.

> ☑️ **CHECKLIST: Identifying the Speech Topic, Purpose, and Thesis**
>
> ✓ Have I identified the *general speech purpose*—to inform, persuade, or mark a special occasion?
>
> ✓ Is the topic appropriate to the occasion?
>
> ✓ Will the topic appeal to my listeners' interests and needs?
>
> ✓ Will I be able to offer a fresh perspective on the topic?
>
> ✓ Have I identified what the audience is most likely to know about the subject and what they are most likely to want to learn?
>
> ✓ Have I considered how much I can competently research and then report on in the time I am given to speak?
>
> ✓ Does my thesis statement sum up in a single sentence what my speech is about?
>
> ✓ Is it restricted to a single idea?
>
> ✓ Does it make the claim I intend to make about my topic?

QUICK TIP

Use the Thesis Statement to Stay Focused

As you develop the speech, use the thesis statement to keep yourself on track. Review your research materials to determine whether they contribute to the thesis or stray from it. When you actually draft your speech, work your thesis statement into it and restate it where appropriate. Doing so will encourage your audience to understand and accept your message.

---

8 Developing Supporting Material

Good speeches contain accurate, relevant, and interesting **supporting material** in the form of examples, narratives, testimony, facts, and statistics. These are the building blocks that give substance to your speech points. As you conduct your research, focus on alternating among the different types of supporting materials.

Offer Examples

Examples illustrate, describe, or represent things. Their purpose is to aid understanding by making ideas, items, or events more concrete. Examples are particularly helpful when they are used to describe or explain things with which the audience is unfamiliar. **Brief examples** offer a single illustration of a point. In a speech titled "The Coming Golden Age of Medicine," Richard F. Corlin offers the following brief example to illustrate what American medicine can do:

> We often hear about the problems of the American health care delivery system, but just think what it can do. My 88-year-old father who needed a hip replacement got it— the week it was discovered that he needed it. That couldn't happen in any other country in the world.[1]

Sometimes it takes more than a brief example to effectively illustrate a point. **Extended examples** offer multifaceted illustrations of the idea, item, or event being described, thereby getting the point across and reiterating it effectively.

Jonathan Drori uses an extended example to illustrate how pollen can link criminals to their crimes:

> Pollen forensics . . . [is] being used now to track where counterfeit drugs have been made, where banknotes have come from. . . . And murder suspects have been tracked using their clothing. . . . Some of the people were brought to trial [in Bosnia] because of the evidence of pollen, which showed that bodies had been buried, exhumed, and then reburied somewhere else.[2]

In some speeches, you may need to make a point about something that could happen in the future if certain events were to occur. Since it hasn't happened yet, you'll need a **hypothetical example** of what you believe the outcome might be. Republican Representative Vernon Ehlers of Michigan offered the following hypothetical example when he spoke at a congressional hearing in support of a bill to ban human cloning:

> What if in the cloning process you produce someone with two heads and three arms? Are you simply going to euthanize and dispose of that person? The answer is no. We're talking about human life.[3]

Share Stories

One of the most powerful means of conveying a message is through a **story** (also called **narrative**). Stories help us make sense of our experience.[4] They tell tales, both real and imaginary, about practically anything under the sun. Common to all stories are the essential elements of a plot, characters, setting, and some sort of time line.

Stories can be brief and simple descriptions of incidents worked into the speech, or relatively drawn-out accounts that constitute most of the presentation. In either case, a successful story will strike a chord and create an emotional connection between speaker and audience members. For example, in 2008, then presidential candidate Barack Obama opened his remarks to members of the Ebeneezer Baptist Church with a **parable**—a story illustrating a moral or religious lesson—from the Bible:

> The Scripture tells us that when Joshua and the Israelites arrived at the gates of Jericho, they could not enter. The walls of the city were too steep for any one person to climb; too strong to be taken down with brute force. And so they sat for days, unable to pass on through.
>
> But God had a plan for his people.[5]

Many speakers, whether they're ministers at the Sunday morning pulpit or high-tech entrepreneurs rallying the troops, liberally sprinkle their speeches with **anecdotes**—brief stories of interesting and often humorous incidents based on real life.

QUICK TIP

Give the Story Structure

Speaking expert Earle Gray offers solid storytelling advice: A good story has structure: a blunt beginning that sets the situation ("Let me tell you a story about the importance of higher education . . ."), a rounded middle, and a sharp end. It should be no more than two minutes in a typical talk.[6]

Draw on Testimony

Consider quoting or paraphrasing people who have an intimate knowledge of your topic. **Testimony** is firsthand findings, eyewitness accounts, and people's opinions; **expert testimony** includes findings, eyewitness accounts, or opinions from professionals trained to evaluate a given topic. **Lay**

testimony, or testimony by nonexperts such as eyewitnesses, can reveal compelling firsthand information that may be unavailable to others.

Supply the name and qualifications of the person whose testimony you use, and inform listeners when and where the testimony was offered. It isn't always necessary to cite the exact date (though do keep a written record of it); in the oral presentation, terms such as "recently" and "last year" are fine. The following is an example:

> In testimony before the U.S. House Subcommittee on Human Rights and Wellness last week, Derek Ellerman (co-executive director of the Polaris Project) said, "Many people have little understanding of the enormity and the brutality of the sex trafficking industry in the United States. When they think of sex slavery, they think of Thailand or Nepal—not a suburban house in the DC area, with $400,000 homes and manicured lawns...."[7]

QUICK TIP

Use a Variety of Supporting Materials
Listeners respond most favorably to a variety of supporting materials derived from multiple sources to illustrate each main point.[8] Alternating among different types of supporting material—moving from a story to a statistic, for example— will make the presentation more interesting and credible while simultaneously appealing to your audience members' different learning styles.

Provide Facts and Statistics

Most people (especially in Western society) require some type of evidence, usually in the form of facts and statistics, before they will accept someone else's claims or position.[9] **Facts** represent documented occurrences, including actual events, dates, times, people, and places. Listeners expect the speaker to provide independent verification of facts, so check that you back up factual statements with credible evidence. **Statistics** are quantified evidence that summarizes, compares, and predicts things.

Use Statistics Accurately

Statistics add precision to speech claims, *if* you know what the numbers actually mean and use terms that describe them accurately.

USE FREQUENCIES TO INDICATE COUNTS   A **frequency** is simply a count of the number of times something occurs:

> On the midterm exam there were 8 A's, 15 B's, 7 C's, 2 D's, and 1 F.

Frequencies can help listeners understand comparisons between two or more categories, indicate size, or describe trends:

- According to *Census 2010,* the total population of the State of Rhode Island was comprised of 508,400 males and 544,167 females.[10] *(compares two categories)*
- Inside the cabin, the Airbus A380 has room for at least 400 passengers—and as many as 800.[11] *(shows size)*
- According to the American Lung Association, U.S. consumption of cigarettes has declined by more than 100 billion cigarettes over the past decade.[12] *(describes a trend)*

USE PERCENTAGES TO EXPRESS PROPORTION   A **percentage** is the quantified portion of a whole. Percentages help audience members easily grasp comparisons between things, such as the unemployment rate in several states:

> In April 2011, Nevada had the highest rate of unemployment, at 12.1 percent. The figure for Alabama was 9.6 percent; for Connecticut, 9.1 percent; and for Wyoming, 6 percent.[13]

Describing the number of males and females in the 2010 Rhode Island population in percentages, rather than in counts (as in the previous section), shows more clearly and quickly the relationship between the two amounts: 48 percent male and 52 percent female.

QUICK TIP

Use Statistics Selectively—and Memorably

Rather than overwhelm the audience with statistics, select a few figures, put into context, that will make your message most compelling. For example, instead of citing the actual number of persons belonging to Facebook by country, use a simple ratio to drive home the company's enormous reach: "Today, at least one out of every fourteen people in the world has a Facebook account."[14]

USE AVERAGES TO DESCRIBE TYPICAL CHARACTERISTICS   An **average** describes information according to its typical characteristics. Usually we think of the average as the sum of the scores divided by the number of scores. This is the *mean*, the arithmetic average. But there are two other kinds of averages—the *median* and the *mode*.

Consider a teacher whose nine students scored 5, 19, 22, 23, 24, 26, 28, 28, and 30, with 30 points being the highest possible grade. The following illustrates how she would calculate the three types of averages:

- The **mean** score is 22.8, the *arithmetic average*, the sum of the scores divided by 9.

- The **median** score is 24, *the center-most score in a distribution* or the point above and below which 50 percent of the nine scores fall.

- The **mode** score is 28, the *most frequently occurring score* in the distribution.

The following speaker, claiming that a rival organization misrepresented the "average" tax rate, illustrates how the inaccurate use of averages can distort reality:

> The Tax Foundation determines an *average* [*mean*] tax rate for American families simply by dividing all taxes paid by the total of everyone's income. For example, if four middle-income families pay $3,000, $4,000, $5,000, and $6,000, respectively, in taxes, and one very wealthy family pays $82,000 in taxes, the *average* [*mean*] tax paid by these five families is $20,000 ($100,000 in total taxes divided by five families). But four of the five families [actually] have a tax bill equaling $6,000 or less. . . .[Many] analysts would define a *median* income family—a family for whom half of all families have higher income and half have lower income—to be the "typical family" and describe the taxes paid by such a median-income family as the taxes that typical middle-class families owe.[15]

Present Statistics Ethically

Offering listeners inaccurate statistics is unethical. Following are steps you can take to reduce the likelihood of using false or misleading statistics:

Use only reliable statistics. Include statistics from the most authoritative source you can locate, and evaluate the methods used to generate the data. The more information that is available about how the statistics came about, the more reliable the source is likely to be.

Present statistics in context. Inform listeners of when the data were collected, the method used to collect the data, and the scope of the research:

> These figures represent data collected during 2011 from questionnaires distributed to all public and private schools in the United States with students in at least one of grades 9–12 in the fifty states and the District of Columbia.

Avoid confusing statistics with "absolute truth." Even the most recent data available will change the next time data are collected. Nor are statistics necessarily any more accurate than the human who collected them. Offer data as they appropriately represent your point, but refrain from declaring that these data are definitive.

QUICK TIP

Avoid Cherry-Picking

When you search for statistics to confirm an opinion or a belief you already hold, you are probably **cherry-picking—** selectively presenting only those statistics that buttress your point of view while ignoring competing data.[16] Locating statistical support material is not a trip through a buffet line to select what looks good and discard what doesn't. Present statistics in context or not at all.

Refer Orally to Your Sources

Clearly identify the source of your information and provide enough context (including approximate date of publication) to accurately interpret it. For guidelines on orally citing your sources, see Chapter 11, "Citing Sources in Your Speech."

✓ **CHECKLIST:** Evaluating Your Research Needs

Do you need . . .

✓ Examples to illustrate, describe, or represent your ideas?

✓ A story or an anecdote to drive your point home?

✓ Firsthand findings, in the form of testimony, to illustrate your points or strengthen your argument?

✓ Relevant facts, or documented occurrences, to substantiate your statements?

✓ Statistics to demonstrate relationships?

Finding the right mix of supporting material (e.g., examples, facts, statistics, opinions, stories, and testimony) for your speech requires selecting among primary and secondary sources. **Primary sources** provide firsthand accounts or direct evidence of events, objects, or people (as found, for example, in diaries and photographs).[1] **Secondary sources** provide analysis or commentary about things not directly observed or created. These include the vast world of "secondhand" information found in books, articles, and a myriad of sources other than the original.

QUICK TIP

Mix It Up with Both Primary and Secondary Sources

Many speeches can benefit from a mix of both primary and secondary sources. The firsthand nature of a primary source can build trust and engage audience members emotionally. Secondary sources can help listeners put the topic in perspective. A speech on an oil spill, for example, can command more attention if it includes testimony by oil riggers and other eyewitnesses (primary sources) along with analyses of the spill from magazines and newspapers (secondary sources).

Locate Secondary Sources

The most likely sources of secondary research include books, newspapers, periodicals, government publications; reference works such as encyclopedias, almanacs, books of quotations, and atlases; and Internet sources such as blogs and social news sites. As you gather these materials, consider how you can use them to generate interest, illustrate meaning, and add solid evidence to assertions.

Books

Books by credible authors provide detail and perspective and can serve as an excellent source of supporting material. To locate a book in your library's holdings, refer to the library's online catalog. To search the titles of all books currently in print in the United States, refer to *Books in Print* at www.booksinprint.com. Alternatively, log on to Amazon.com or another online bookseller and key in your topic.

Newspapers and Periodicals

Newspapers contain a mix of eyewitness accounts, in-depth analyses of local and world events, and human-interest feature stories of all kinds. Three comprehensive databases for searching news articles include 50states.com (to search U.S. newspapers by state), World-Newspapers.com (to search world newspapers), and NewspaperArchive.com (to research historical newspapers from 1753 to the present).

A **periodical** is a regularly published magazine or journal. Periodicals can be excellent sources because they generally include all types of supporting material. Periodicals include general-interest magazines such as *Time* and *Newsweek*, as well as the thousands of specialized magazines, newsletters, and refereed journals. Articles in *refereed journals* are evaluated by experts before being published and supply sources for the information they contain. Articles in *general-interest magazines* rarely contain citations and may or may not be written by experts on the topic.

Many general-interest magazines are available in *Infotrac Online* and *General OneFile*; to locate both general periodicals and scholarly journals, see *Academic Search Premier* and *Academic Search Elite*. There are also an ever-increasing number of databases devoted to individual disciplines, such as business, health, education, and psychology (see Table 10.2, p. 74).

Government Publications

Nearly all the information contained in government documents comes from primary sources and is therefore highly credible. Get started by logging on to USA.gov, the official portal to all government information and services, with links to millions of Web pages from federal, local, and tribal governments as well as to nations around the world. The site also includes links to reliable statistics of every kind.

Digital Collections

Digital collections, including oral histories, letters, old newspapers, photographs, and audio and video recordings, can provide a rich source of primary materials. The Library of Congress offers an online gateway to a treasury of digitized images, recordings, and documents. Nearly all libraries now offer digital collections, which are generally organized by subject, time period, or geographic area.

Reference Works

Reference works include, but are not limited to, encyclopedias, almanacs, biographical resources, books of quotations, poetry collections, and atlases.

ENCYCLOPEDIAS   **Encyclopedias** summarize knowledge that is found in original form elsewhere. Their usefulness lies in providing an overview of subjects. *General encyclopedias* attempt to cover all important subject areas of knowledge. The most comprehensive of the general encyclopedias is the *Encyclopaedia Britannica.* For a more in-depth look at a topic, consult a specialized encyclopedia devoted to it. *Specialized encyclopedias* delve deeply into one subject area, such as religion, science, art, sports, or engineering.

Online, Wikipedia is the world's largest experimental free encyclopedia, written collaboratively and often anonymously by anyone who wishes to contribute to it. Though Wikipedia's instant accessibility and vast range make it tantalizingly easy to consult, be warned that information may or may not be accurate at any given moment, as people edit material at will. As with any encyclopedia, Wikipedia may provide an initial overview of a topic but should never serve as more than a jumping-off point for further research.[2] Further, references cited in a Wikipedia article can serve as research leads—as long as you follow the links and evaluate the information for trustworthiness (See "From Source to Speech: Evaluating Web Sources," pp. 76–77). Be sure to compare the information in the article to credible sources *not* supplied in the entry itself, and do not offer Wikipedia—or any encyclopedia entry—as a source to audience members.

ALMANACS   **Almanacs** and **fact books**, published annually, contain interesting facts and statistics on many subjects from notable Supreme Court decisions to vital statistics for all nations of the world. One of the most comprehensive sources is the *World Almanac and Book of Facts.* Other helpful almanacs include the *Information Please Almanac, People's Almanac,* and *Guinness World Records.*

BIOGRAPHICAL RESOURCES   For information about famous or noteworthy people, the *Biography and Genealogy Master Index* is an excellent starting point. For analyses and criticism of the published works of individuals you may be speaking about, see *Current Biography* or *Dictionary of American Biography.* Countless *specialized biographies* feature everything from *African American Inventors* to *Famous Hispanics in the World and History* (access is free at coloquio.com/famosos/).

BOOKS OF QUOTATIONS   Public speakers often use quotations in the introductions and conclusions of speeches. *Bartlett's Familiar Quotations* contains passages, phrases, and proverbs traced to their sources. Many books are targeted specifically at public speakers; others are devoted to specific topics.

POETRY COLLECTIONS   Lines of poetry, if not entire poems, are often used by speakers both to introduce and conclude speeches and to illustrate points in the speech body. *The Columbia Granger's World of Poetry* indexes poems by author, title, and first line and is available in print and online. The Library of Congress Poetry Resources Web Guide offers links to poetry resources. Poets.org is the Web site of the Academy of American Poets.

ATLASES   An **atlas** is a collection of maps, text, and accompanying charts and tables. As well as helping you find a particular locale and learn about its terrain and demographics, many atlases use maps to explore other subjects, such as art history and human anatomy. For straightforward geographic atlases, consult *National Geographic Atlas of the World* and the *Rand McNally Commercial Atlas and Marketing Guide*. Online, go to the National Geographic Web site. To learn about what atlases offer beyond geography, conduct a search of atlases related to your topic, e.g., "art AND atlas."

✓ CHECKLIST: Finding Speeches Online

Online, you can find numerous video and audio files of speeches. These can be useful as research and as models of speeches.

✓ *American Rhetoric* (www.americanrhetoric.com/) contains 5,000+ speeches.

✓ *Gifts of Speech* (http://gos.sbc.edu/) features speeches by women from 1848 to the present.

✓ The Wake Forest University's Political Speeches gateway (http://www.wfu.edu/~louden/Political%20Communication/Class%20Information/SPEECHES.html) offers links to collections of political speeches.

✓ The United States Senate Web site (www.senate.gov) includes speeches by U.S. senators.

✓ *Vital Speeches of the Day* (vsotd.com) features current speeches delivered in the United States and is published monthly.

From Source to Speech

Recording and Citing Books

When using a book as a source, locate and record the following citation elements:

1 Title

4 City of Publication

2 Author

5 Year of Publication

3 Publisher

6 Page Number

1

predictably
irrational

revised
and expanded
edition

*The Hidden Forces
That Shape Our Decisions*

2

Dan Ariely

3

HARPER ● PERENNIAL

NEW YORK

© 2010

4

5

funerals. By 1785 it ap
ary, attached to margin

We don't know the
secretions, but we have
really had nothing to
is that Gerbi believed
of his patients.

Of course, Gerbi's w
in the market. Before re
placebos. Eye of the to
mercury, mineral water
were all touted as suita
Lincoln lay dying acros
said that his physician applied a bit of "mummy paint" to the
wounds. Egyptian mummy, ground to a powder, was believed to be a remedy for epilepsy, abscesses, rashes, frac-
tures, paralysis, migraine, ulcers, and many other things. As
late as 1908, "genuine Egyptian mummy" could be ordered
through the E. Merck catalog—and it's probably still in use
somewhere today.[14]

Mummy powder wasn't the most macabre of medicines,
though. One seventeenth-century recipe for a "cure all"
medication advised: "Take the fresh corpse of a red-haired,

229

6

Record Notes

When taking notes, create a separate heading for each idea and record each of the citation elements (author, title, and so forth). Indicate whether the material is a *direct quotation* (statements made word-for-word); a *paraphrase* (restatement of someone else's ideas); or a *summary* (brief overview of someone else's ideas) of the information (for more on these, see Chapter 4).

Following is a sample note for a paraphrase (see also sample notes for summaries, p. 69, and quotations, p. 81).

NOTES FOR A PARAPHRASE:

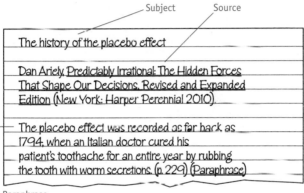

Subject   Source

The history of the placebo effect

Dan Ariely, *Predictably Irrational: The Hidden Forces That Shape Our Decisions, Revised and Expanded Edition* (New York: Harper Perennial 2010).

The placebo effect was recorded as far back as 1794, when an Italian doctor cured his patient's toothache for an entire year by rubbing the tooth with worm secretions. (p. 229) (Paraphrase)

Paraphrase

Orally Cite Sources in Your Speech

In your speech, alert the audience to the source of any ideas not your own.

SPEECH EXCERPT INDICATING A PARAPHRASE:

> **According to Dan Ariely's 2010 book *Predictably Irrational*,** the placebo effect was recorded as early as 1794, when an Italian doctor cured his patient's toothache for an entire year by rubbing the tooth with, of all things, worm secretions.

You can find more information on oral citation in Chapter 11.

For guidelines on various citation styles including *Chicago*, APA, MLA, CSE, and IEEE, see Appendix A.

From Source to Speech

Recording and Citing Articles from Periodicals

When using an article as a source, locate and record the following citation elements:

1 Author

2 Article Title

3 Periodical Title

4 Date of Publication

5 Page Number

TRANSPORTATION

Emerging technologies could make
the internal-combustion engine
substantially more fuel-efficient,
even as green vehicles make inroads

BETTER MILEAGE
NOW
BY BEN KNIGHT

KEY CONCEPTS

- Hardware and software changes to the internal-combustion engine in cars can make it much more fuel-efficient.
- New rules due soon from the Environmental Protection Agency governing greenhouse gas emissions and from the Department of Transportation on fuel economy will force the efficiency of cars, SUVs and pickups to rise 4.4 percent a year from 2012 through 2016 and probably more in later years.
- Technologies such as direct gasoline injection, variable valve timing and cylinder deactivation can reduce the major sources of energy lost in engines: waste heat and engine friction.

—*The Editors*

Demand for automobiles is rising worldwide. So is concern about greenhouse gas emissions. In response, scientists and engineers are working diligently to perfect new power plants for future vehicles, including battery and hydrogen fuel-cell electric cars. Although these and other alternatives show great promise for the long term, perhaps the single greatest way to reduce fossil-fuel consumption in the near term is to further improve today's dominant transportation power plant: the gasoline internal-combustion (IC) engine.

Fortunately, efficiency can be raised in a number of ways, notably, better control over the air-fuel mixture entering the combustion chamber, over the way gasoline is ignited there, and over the mechanical systems that harness that energy. These can improve traditional automobiles as well as gasoline-electric hybrid models.

Rapidly rising fuel prices in the latter half of 2008 began steering many consumers toward vehicles offering the best fuel efficiency, but recent price declines have hurt demand for them. Strict new fuel economy and greenhouse gas emissions regulations, about to go into force, should reverse this trend, however, and drive even more significant advancements to the technology that will be under the hood of your next new car.

The modern IC engine powers all but a hand-

ful of the world's automobiles, trucks, motorcycles and motorboats. Its greatest advantage is its use of a fuel—gasoline—that is still relatively abundant, inexpensive and energy-dense. Its greatest drawback is its mediocre efficiency. The most efficient gasoline spark-ignition engines in mass-produced automobiles today convert only 20 to 25 percent of the fuel's chemical energy into work. A modern diesel or gasoline-electric hybrid power train can reach 25 to 35 percent, but at substantially higher cost. In contrast, hydrogen fuel-cell electric cars—such as Honda's FCX Clarity, now in limited production—convert about 60 percent of the energy in gaseous hydrogen into motive power.

Despite the IC engine's reputation as old and outmoded technology, however, it continues to improve. A recent Environmental Protection Agency study showed that the fuel efficiency of engines in U.S. automobiles rose by roughly 1.4 percent a year from 1987 to 2006. The increases came through incremental gains in combustion (thermal) efficiency, reductions in engine and drivetrain friction, more advanced transmissions and reduced losses in accessory systems. Most of these gains, however, did not help drivers consume less gasoline. Instead they went to meet market demand for larger, more powerful and better-equipped vehicles.

New Rules Prompt Gains

Impending regulations will help ensure that future power train efficiency gains go primarily toward actual fuel economy. The EPA is finalizing stringent new greenhouse gas standards for automobiles, and the Department of Transportation is finishing tougher corporate average fuel economy (CAFE) standards. The agencies must issue a final ruling that incorporates both

50 SCIENTIFIC AMERICAN

February 2010

The modern IC engine powers all but a handful of the world's automobiles, trucks, motorcycles and motorboats. Its greatest advantage is its use of a fuel—gasoline—that is still relatively abundant, inexpensive and energy-dense. Its greatest drawback is its mediocre efficiency.

Impending regulations will help ensure that future power train efficiency gains go primarily toward actual fuel economy. The EPA is finalizing stringent new greenhouse gas standards for automobiles, and the Department of Transportation is finishing tougher corporate average fuel economy (CAFE) standards. The agencies

Record Notes

When taking notes, create a separate heading for each idea and record each of the citation elements (author, title, and so forth). Indicate whether the material is a direct quotation, a paraphrase, or a summary of the information. Following is a sample note for a summary (see also sample notes for paraphrases, p. 67, and quotations, p. 81).

NOTES FOR A SUMMARY:

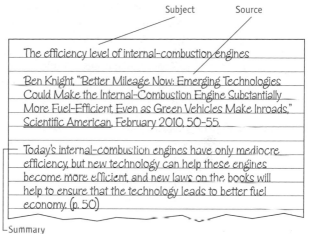

Subject   Source

The efficiency level of internal-combustion engines

Ben Knight, "Better Mileage Now: Emerging Technologies Could Make the Internal-Combustion Engine Substantially More Fuel-Efficient, Even as Green Vehicles Make Inroads," Scientific American, February 2010, 50–55.

Today's internal-combustion engines have only mediocre efficiency, but new technology can help these engines become more efficient, and new laws on the books will help to ensure that the technology leads to better fuel economy. (p. 50)

Summary

Orally Cite Sources in Your Speech

In your speech, alert the audience to the source of any ideas not your own:

SPEECH EXCERPT INDICATING A SUMMARY:

> **According to Ben Knight's article "Better Mileage Now," in the February 2010 issue of *Scientific American*,** there may be a greener future for the internal-combustion engine: technological innovations can help this engine become more efficient, and new legislation will help to ensure that these innovations lead to real increases in fuel economy.

You can find more information on oral citation in Chapter 11.

For guidelines on various citation styles including *Chicago*, APA, MLA, CSE, and IEEE, see Appendix A.

Weblogs and Social News Sites

Blogs and social news sites can provide up-to-the-minute information and opinions on certain speech topics, *if the source is reputable.* A **blog** is a site containing journal-type entries maintained by individuals or groups. Newest entries appear first. A **social news site** allows users to submit news stories, articles, and videos to share with other users of the site. The most popular items win more visibility.

Use these sources of supporting material with extreme care, referencing only those that are affiliated with reputable (local, regional, or national) news agencies and media outlets, or by well-known bloggers. See Chapter 10, "Finding Credible Sources on the Internet" for information on locating blogs and news sites.

Generating Primary Sources: Interviews and Surveys

You may wish to produce your own primary sources by conducting interviews and surveys. These tools can provide valuable information to support and enliven a speech.

Conduct Interviews

Oftentimes you can gain considerably more insight into a topic, and obtain more interesting material, by speaking personally to someone who has expertise on the subject.

- *Prepare questions for the interview* in advance of the interview date.
- *Word questions carefully*:
  - Avoid *vague questions,* those that don't give the person being interviewed enough to go on. Vague questions waste the interviewee's time and reflect the interviewer's lack of preparation.
  - Avoid *leading questions,* those that encourage, if not force, a certain response and reflect the interviewer's bias (e.g., "Like most of us, are you going to support candidate X?"). Likewise, avoid *loaded questions,* those that are phrased to reinforce the interviewer's agenda or that have a hostile intent (e.g., "Isn't it true that you've never supported school programs?").
  - Aim to create *neutral questions,* those that don't lead the interviewee to a desired response. Usually, this will consist of a mix of open, closed, primary, and secondary questions (see Chapter 6, p. 45).

- *Begin by establishing a spirit of collaboration*:
  - Acknowledge the interviewee and express respect for his or her expertise.
  - Briefly summarize your topic and informational needs.
  - State a (reasonable) goal—what you would like to accomplish in the interview—and reach agreement on it.
  - Establish a time limit for the interview and stick to it.
- *Use active listening strategies.* Listen to what the subject is saying, not just to what you want to hear:
  - Don't break in when the subject is speaking or interject with leading comments.
  - *Paraphrase* the interviewee's answers where appropriate in order to establish understanding.
  - Ask for *clarification* and *elaboration* when necessary.
- End the interview by rechecking and confirming:
  - Check that you have covered all the topics (e.g., "Does this cover everything?").
  - Briefly offer a positive summary of important things you learned in the interview.
  - Offer to send the interviewee the results of the interview.

Conduct Surveys

Like interviews, a *survey* is useful both as a tool to investigate audience attitudes and as primary source material. Surveys are an especially effective source of support for speech topics focused on the attitudes and behavior of people in your immediate environment, such as students' study or leisure habits. (For information on creating surveys, refer to Chapter 6.)

Evaluate Sources for Trustworthiness

It is vital to critically evaluate sources before using them. Whether you are reviewing a book, a newspaper article, or any other source, consider the following:

- What is the author's background—experience, training, and reputation—in the field of study?
- How credible is the publication? Who is the publisher? Is the person or organization reputable? What

other publications has the author or organization published?

- How reliable are the data, especially the statistical information? Generally, statistics drawn from government documents and scientific and academic journals are more reliable than those reported in the popular press (e.g., general-interest magazines).
- How recent is the reference? As a rule, it is best to be familiar with the most recent source you can find, even when the topic is historical.

Record References as You Go

To avoid losing track of sources, maintain a working bibliography as you conduct your research. For visual guidelines on keeping track of sources, see the "From Source to Speech" sections on citing books (p. 66), periodicals (p. 68) and Web sources (p. 80). See Appendix A for guidance on preparing an end-of-speech bibliography.

10 Finding Credible Sources on the Internet

As with conducting research in a physical library, the key to a productive search on the Internet lies in a well-thought-out research strategy, a grasp of how to use search tools effectively, and an understanding of how to select trustworthy information.

Use a Library Portal to Access Credible Sources

Easy access to the Internet may lead you to rely heavily or even exclusively on popular search engines such as Google, Bing, and even YouTube to locate supporting material. In doing so, however, you risk overlooking key sources not found on those sites and finding false and/or biased information. To circumvent this, begin your search at your school's or town's **library portal**, or electronic entry point into its holdings (e.g., its home page).

As with its shelved materials, a library's e-resources are built through careful and deliberate selection processes by trained professionals.[1] When you select a speech source from a library's print or electronic resources, you can be assured that an information specialist has vetted that source for reliability and credibility. No such standards exist for popular Web search engines. Not only that, but libraries purchase access to proprietary databases and other resources that form part of the **deep Web**—the large portion of the Web that general search engines cannot access because the information is licensed and/or fee-based. For a list of resources typically found on library portals, see Table 10.1.

TABLE 10.1 • TYPICAL RESOURCES FOUND ON LIBRARY PORTALS

- Full-text databases (newspapers, periodicals, journals)
- General reference works (dictionaries, encyclopedias, quotation resources, fact books, directories)
- Books and monographs
- Archives and special collections (collected papers, objects and images, and scholarly works unique to the institution)
- Digital collections (primary documents, e-books, image collections)
- Video collections

Access Journal Articles

A key benefit of beginning your research at a library portal is the ability to access scholarly research articles and peer-reviewed journals, which contain some of the most cutting edge and reliable research on almost any topic. To see what's available, begin with a general database such as *Academic Search Complete*; *Academic OneFile*; *Academic Search Premier*; and *LexisNexis Academic*. (Your library portal may also offer a combination search option that allows you to search several general databases simultaneously.) For more targeted searches, proceed to a subject-specific database, such as those listed in Table 10.2.

Access Books

To locate books at your college library or other libraries, use *Worldcat*, which searches library collections in the United States and worldwide. Another resource is Google Books, which permits you to search and preview millions of books.

TABLE 10.2 • SUBJECT-SPECIFIC DATABASES	
SUBJECT AREA	**DATABASES**
Business	• *ABI/INFORM* covers journals and news in business, management, economics, and related fields.
Science	• *Web of Science* indexes science articles and some engineering journals.
Medicine and allied health	• *PubMed* is the U.S. National Library of Medicine's database of citations for biomedical literature from MEDLINE, life science journals, and online books. • *CINAHL* searches nursing and allied health literature. • *Alt HealthWatch* focuses on contemporary, holistic, and integrated approaches to health care and wellness.
Public affairs	• *PAIS International* (Public Affairs Information Service) holds political science and public policy articles, books, and government documents. • *iPoll Databank* (Roper Center for Public Opinion Research) searches polling data from 1935 to the present.
Ethnic and minority-specific viewpoints and research	• *Ethnic NewsWatch* covers newspapers, magazines, and academic journals of the ethnic, minority and native press.

Access Popular Magazines

To find general-interest publications and newspapers, try *General OneFile, InfoTrac* (which also searches scholarly publications), or your library's equivalent databases. For the kinds of information available in journals, books, and popular magazines, see Chapter 9.

Be a Critical Consumer of Information

Anyone can post material on the Web, and with a little bit of design savvy, make it look professional. Determining the accuracy of online content is not always so easy. Search engines such as Google cannot discern the quality of information; only a human editor can do this. Each time you examine a document, especially one that has not been evaluated by credible editors, ask yourself, "Who put this information here, and why did they do so? What are the source's qualifications? Where is similar information found? When was the information posted, and is it timely?" (See "From Source to Speech: Evaluating Web Sources," pp. 76–77).

Distinguish among Information, Propaganda, Misinformation, and Disinformation

One way to judge a source's trustworthiness is to ask yourself: Is it reliable *information,* or is it *propaganda, misinformation,* or *disinformation*?[2]

- **Information** is data that are presented in an understandable context. *Data* are raw and unprocessed facts; information makes sense of data. For example, a patient's vital signs (temperature, blood pressure, pulse, etc.) are data. Interpreting the vital signs in the context of health status is information.

- **Propaganda** is information represented in such a way as to provoke a desired response. The purpose of propaganda is to instill a particular attitude—to encourage you to think a particular way. Military posters that encourage you to enlist are an example of propaganda.

- **Misinformation** always refers to something that is not true. One common form of misinformation on the

---

QUICK TIP

Use Watchdog Sites to Check the Facts

Our most trustworthy elected officials occasionally make false assertions, and even the most reliable news sources publish errors of fact or omission. So whom should you believe— Congresswoman X's dire predictions regarding Social Security or Senator Y's rosier assessment? To check the factual accuracy of information offered by key political players and major journalistic outlets, consult these Web sites (bearing in mind that they too are not infallible).

- *FactCheck.org, sponsored by the Annenberg Public Policy Center*
- *PolitiFact.com, sponsored by the St. Petersburg Times*
- *The Fact Checker, a blog sponsored by the Washington Post.*

From Source to Speech
Evaluating Web Sources

Check the Most Authoritative Web Sites First

Seek out the most authoritative Web sites on your topic. If your speech explores the NBA draft, investigate the NBA's official Web site first. Check government-sponsored sites such as www.usa.gov. Government-sponsored sites are free of commercial taint and contain highly credible primary materials.

Evaluate Authorship and Sponsorship

1 *Examine the **domain** in the Web address*—the suffix at the end of the address that tells you the nature of the site: educational (.edu), government (.gov), military (.mil), nonprofit organization (.org), business/commercial (.com), and network (.net). A tilde (~) in the address usually indicates that it is a personal page rather than part of an institutional Web site. Make sure to assess the credibility of each site, whether it is operated by an individual, a company, a governmental agency, or a nonprofit group.

2 *Look for an "About" link that describes the organization or a link to a page that gives more information.* These sections can tell a great deal about the nature of a site's content. Be wary of sites that do not include such a link.

3 *Identify the creator of the information.* If an individual operates the site, does the document provide relevant biographical information, such as links to a résumé or a listing of the author's credentials? Look for contact information. A source that doesn't want to be found, at least by e-mail, is not a good source to cite.

Check for Currency

4 *Check for a date that indicates when the page was placed on the Web and when it was last updated.* Is the date current? Web sites that do not have this information may contain outdated or inaccurate information.

Check That the Site Credits Its Sources and That Sources Are Trustworthy

5 *Check that the Web site documents its sources.* Reputable Web sites document the sources they use. Follow any links to these sources, and apply the same criteria to them that you did to the original source document. Verify the information you find with two other independent and reputable sources.

Check the Web Site for Objectivity

6 *Evaluate the information for bias.* Look for fallacies in reasoning, distorted data, and oversimplification of information. Check that opinions are backed by reliable sources and that important information is not missing. Look for signs of conflict of interest, such as whether the information is advertiser-driven.

Internet is the *urban legend*—a fabricated story passed along by unsuspecting people.

• **Disinformation** is the deliberate falsification of information. Doctored photographs and falsified profit-and-loss statements are examples of disinformation in action. Unfortunately, disinformation thrives on the Internet.

Make the Most of Internet Search Tools

Your research efforts will be most effective if you understand the features of search engines and subject (Web) directories and know how to use them to locate what you need.

Distinguish among Types of Search Engines

Search engines use software robots (called "spiders" or "crawlers") to index the contents of the Web, automatically scanning up to billions of documents that contain the keywords and phrases you command them to search. Then, using a set of rules unique to the engine, a software program ranks the results from most to least relevant, though criteria for relevance vary.

General search engines (such as Google and Yahoo!) compile their own databases of Web pages. *Specialized search engines* let you conduct narrower but deeper searches into a particular field. Examples include Google Scholar, which searches scholarly books and articles; THOMAS (thomas.loc.gov), a federal legislation search engine—see Figure 10.1; and Scirus.com, a scientific information search engine. To find a search engine geared specifically to your topic, type in the topic term with the keywords "search engine." For example, a search for internships AND "search engine" will lead you to various specialized sites, including AfterCollege.com and Idealist.org.

Blogs can be an important source of information about unfolding events and new trends and ideas, and with well over one hundred million English-language blogs out there, *blog-specific search engines* can help you find what you need. Technorati lets you search all of its blogs for posts on your topic or only those blogs devoted entirely to the topic. Technorati also ranks the most influential blogs on a variety of topics. It assigns each blog an "authority score" from 1 to 1,000 based on variables such as linking behavior (how often the blog is referenced by other sites); blogs' rankings rise and fall according to its authority score. Google Blog Search also searches by post and by blog; main results always link to most recent posts.

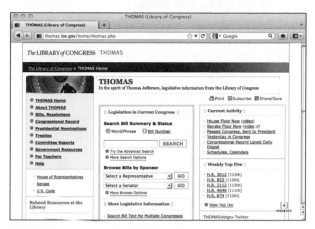

FIGURE 10.1 Home Page for THOMAS at the Library of Congress

Consult Subject (Web) Directories

A **subject (Web) directory** (also called a "subject guide") is a searchable catalog of Web sites organized by a human editor, into subject categories such as "Science," "Reference," or "Arts and Humanities." Subject directories allow you to progressively narrow your searches. If your speech is on some aspect of baseball teams, for example, you would follow these links until you find what you want:

sports → baseball → amateur → leagues → teams

Two of the most reliable academic subject directories are ipl2 (www.ipl2.org) and Infomine (http://infomine.ucr.edu). Among popular directories, Yahoo! Directory is among the most comprehensive and trustworthy.

Use Search Engines and Subject Directories for Different Purposes

Search engines and subject directories are best used for somewhat different purposes. Subject directories are most useful for learning about and narrowing a general topic, such as photography. If you are looking for a list of reputable sites on the same subject, use an academic subject directory such as ipl2, or one provided by a library; these will be free of commercial interests.

Because search engines index so many documents and scan the full text rather than just the title, first few pages, or

From Source to Speech

Recording and Citing Web Sources

When using a Web document as a source, locate and record the following citation elements:

1 Author of the Work

2 Title of the Work

3 Title of the Web Site

4 Date of Publication/Last Update

5 Site Address (URL) and Date Accessed

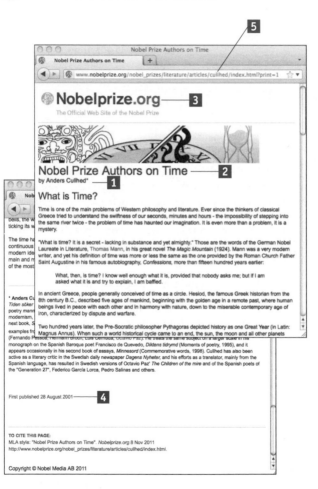

Record Notes

When taking notes, create a separate heading for each idea and record the citation elements from your sources. Indicate whether the material is a direct quotation, a paraphrase, or a summary of the information. Following is a sample note for a quotation (see also sample notes for paraphrases, p. 67, and summaries, p. 69).

NOTES FOR A QUOTATION:

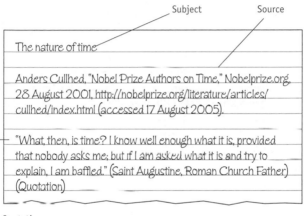

Subject   Source

The nature of time

Anders Cullhed, "Nobel Prize Authors on Time," Nobelprize.org, 28 August 2001, http://nobelprize.org/literature/articles/cullhed/index.html (accessed 17 August 2005).

"What, then, is time? I know well enough what it is, provided that nobody asks me; but if I am asked what it is and try to explain, I am baffled." (Saint Augustine, Roman Church Father) (Quotation)

Quotation

Orally Cite Sources in Your Speech

In your speech, alert the audience to the source of any ideas not your own.

QUOTATION:

> **In an article on the nature of time posted on the Web site Nobelprize.org, professor of comparative literature Anders Cullhed notes** how difficult it is to understand the nature of time. For example, **he quotes Saint Augustine, who said,** "What, then, is time? I know well enough what it is, provided that nobody asks me; but if I am asked what it is and try to explain, I am baffled."

You can find more information about oral citation in Chapter 11.

For guidelines on various citation styles including *Chicago*, APA, MLA, CSE, and IEEE, see Appendix A.

URL address, they will find information not listed in subject directories. Search engines are the tool of choice when you need to find emerging information that may not yet appear in a subject directory, as well as specific terms, facts, figures, or quotations that may be buried within documents.

Beware of Commercial Factors

When researching your topic outside of a library portal, be alert to unwanted commercial influences on your search results—specifically, whether a listing appears merely because an advertiser has paid to put it there.

Some engines and directories accept fees from companies in exchange for a guaranteed higher ranking within results (called **paid placement**). Others accept fees to include companies in the full index of possible results, without a guarantee of ranking (called **paid inclusion**).[3] For tips on identifying paid listings, see the following checklist.

CHECKLIST: Identifying Paid Listings in Search Results

✓ Look for a heading labeled "Sponsored Links" or "Sponsored Results" at the top, side, or bottom of the main page. This indicates a paid-placement listing.

✓ Use multiple search engines and compare the results.

✓ Click beyond the first page of your search results to find relevant sites.

✓ Read the fine print on a search engine's disclosure pages to find its policy on paid inclusion.

Conduct Smart Searches

You can research a topic by keyword or by subject (as well as by other fields, such as *author*, *title*, and *date*); see the Help section of the search tools you select for the fields to use. The most effective means of retrieving information with a general search engine is by *keyword*; for library catalogs and databases, as well as Web directories, *subject searching* often yields the best results.

Create Effective Keywords

Keywords are words and phrases that describe the main concepts of topics. Search engines such as Google index information by keywords tagged within documents. Queries using keywords that closely match those tagged in the document will therefore return the most relevant results.

When using a general search engine, follow these tips to create effective keyword queries:

Use more rather than fewer words. Single-word queries (e.g., "cars") will produce too many results; use more (descriptive) words to find what you need (e.g., "antique cars OR automobiles"). Try to use nouns and objects, and avoid articles ("the," "a") and pronouns ("you," "her") as these do not help narrow or target your results.

Use quotation marks. Quotation marks allow you to find exact phrases (e.g., "white wine").

Use Boolean operators. Use words placed between keywords (e.g., AND, OR, NOT) to specify how keywords are related.

Use nesting. Use parentheses ( ) and OR to search for synonymous terms, for example, *"graduate school" and (employment OR jobs)*; or to retrieve two separate searches simultaneously, for example, *"archaeological dig" AND "summer school" (Kenya OR California)*.

Use truncation. To retrieve different forms of a word, affix an asterisk to it: *Run** (retrieves, e.g., *running, ran, runners...*). You can also combine a truncated search with another term: *Run* AND marathon*.

Consult the Search Tips section. Every search engine and database has a Help or Search Tips section. Review tips for use before searching.

Search by Subject Heading

Keyword searches, while most efficient when using general search engines, may yield unsatisfactory results in a library catalog or database. Here the tool of choice is the **subject heading**—a term selected by information specialists (such as librarians) to describe and group related materials in a library catalog, database, or subject directory (e.g., "cookery" for cooking-related articles). Identifying the correct heading is the key to an effective subject search. If you use the wrong term in a catalog or database (such as keying in "Lou Gehrig's Disease" rather than the medical term "Amyotrophic lateral sclerosis") no results may appear, when in fact a wealth of sources exists, organized under another subject heading.

QUICK TIP

Find the Right Subject Headings
Librarians agree that searching by subject headings is the most precise way to locate information in library databases.[4] But how to identify the right subject headings? One tack is to check whether the database includes a thesaurus of subject headings. Another option is to do a keyword search of important terms related to your topic in a general search engine. Then try these in your subject search of your library's databases.

Use Advanced Search

The "Advanced Search" function of many search engines and databases allows you to go beyond basic search commands and narrow results even more (see Figure 10.2). Advanced search includes (at least) the following fields:

- *Keywords.* "All," "exact phrase," "at least one," and "without" filter results for keywords in much the same way as basic search commands.

- *Language* includes search results in the specified language.

- *Country* searches results originating in the specified country.

- *File format* returns results in document formats such as Microsoft Word (.doc), Adobe Acrobat (.pdf), Power-Point (.ppt), and Excel (.xls).

- *Domain* limits results to specified Internet domains (e.g., .com, .edu, .gov, .org, etc.).

- *Date* searches focus on a specified range of time.

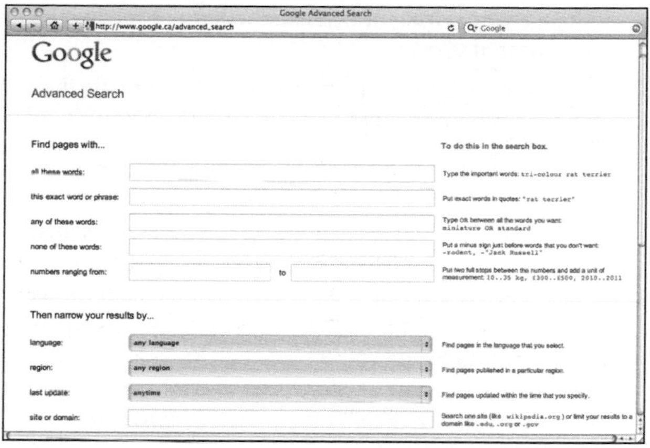

FIGURE 10.2 Google's Advanced Search Page

Record Internet Sources

Because Internet sites often change, be sure to keep track of your speech sources. Record source information as you use it, either by creating footnotes with your word-processing program or with citation tools provided by the database or with programs such as NoodleBib. Refer to the "From Source to Speech" visual guides on citing books (p. 66), periodicals (p. 68), and Web sources (p. 80) for help with keeping track of your speech sources. Also see Appendix A for instructions on maintaining a written bibliography.

11 Citing Sources in Your Speech

Acknowledging sources is a critical aspect of delivering a speech or presentation. When you credit speech sources, you:

- Demonstrate the quality and range of your research to audience members.
- Demonstrate that reliable sources support your position.
- Avoid plagiarism and gain credibility as an ethical speaker who acknowledges the work of others.

- Enhance your own authority and win more support for your point of view.
- Enable listeners to locate your sources and pursue their own research on the topic.

As described in Chapter 4 (pp. 26–28), ethically you are bound to attribute any information drawn from other people's ideas, opinions, and theories, as well as any facts and statistics gathered by others, to their original sources. Remember, you need not credit sources for ideas that are *common knowledge*— established information likely to be known by many people and described in multiple places (see pp. 26–27).

Alert Listeners to Key Source Information

An **oral citation** credits the source of speech material that is derived from other people's ideas. For each source, plan on briefly alerting the audience to the following:

1. The *author* or *origin of the source* ("documentary film-maker *Ken Burns*…"; or "On the *National Science Foundation Web site*…")
2. The *type of source* (magazine, book, personal interview, Web site, blog, online video, etc.)
3. The *title* or a *description of the source* ("In the book *Endangered Minds* . . ."; or "In *an article on sharks*…")
4. The *date of the source* ("The article, published in the *October 10th, 2012,* issue…" or "According to a report on cheating on the SAT, posted online September 28, 2012, on the *Daily Beast* . . .")

Spoken citations need not include a complete bibliographic reference (exact title, full names of all authors, volume, and page numbers); doing so will interrupt the flow of your presentation and unnecessarily divert listeners' attention. However, do keep a running list of source details for a bibliography to appear at the end of your speech draft or outline. (For guidelines on creating a written bibliography for your speeches, see Appendix A.) In place of bibliographic details, focus on presenting sources in a rhetorically effective manner.

Establish the Source's Trustworthiness

Too often, inexperienced speakers credit their sources in bare-bones fashion, offering a rote recitation of citation elements. For example, they might cite the publication name and date but leave out key details, such as that the source is a leading authority in his or her field, that could convince the audience to accept the source as reliable and its conclusions as true. But discerning listeners will accept as legitimate the supporting materials you offer for your claims—examples, stories, testimony, facts, and statistics (see Chapter 8)—only if they believe that the sources are reliable and accurate, or credible.

Source reliability refers to our level of trust in a source's credentials and track record for providing accurate information. If you support a scientific claim by crediting it to an unknown student's personal blog, for example, listeners won't find it as reliable as if you credited it to a scientist affiliated with a reputable institution.

While a source that is reliable is usually accurate, this is not always so.[1] Sometimes we have information that contradicts what we are told by a reliable source. For example, a soldier might read a news article in the *Wall Street Journal* about a battle in which he or she participated. The soldier knows the story contains inaccuracies because the soldier was there. In general, however, the soldier finds the *Wall Street Journal* a reliable source. Since even the most reliable source can sometimes be wrong, it is always better to offer a variety of sources, rather than a single source, to support a major point. This is especially the case when your claims are controversial.

To demonstrate a source's trustworthiness, offer a **source qualifier**, or brief description of the source's qualifications to address the topic. Briefly mention relevant affiliations and credentials that will help listeners put the source in perspective and establish credibility (e.g., "researcher at the Mayo Clinic," "columnist for the *Wall Street Journal*"). "From Source to Speech" on p. 88 illustrates how you can orally cite your sources in a way that listeners will accept them.

QUICK TIP

Consider Audience Perception of Sources

Not every trustworthy source is necessarily appropriate for every audience. For example, a politically conservative audience may reject information from a liberal publication. Thus, audience analysis should factor in your choice of sources. In addition to checking that your sources are reliable, consider whether they will be seen as credible by your particular audience.[2]

From Source to Speech
Demonstrating Your Sources' Reliability and Credibility

How Can I Lead the Audience to Accept My Sources as Reliable and Credible?

- If a source has relevant credentials that would inspire trust, note the credentials.
- If citing a source or study linked to a reputable institution, identify the institution.
- If citing statistics, reveal how they were derived (mention method and scope of research) and put them into context (make them meaningful).

In the following excerpt from a speech on the social consequences of texting among young cell phone users, the speaker leaves out information that would help convince the audience that the sources of her evidence are trustworthy:

> In a 2011 phone survey of 2,277 people, conducted by the Pew Research Center, young adult cell phone owners exchange an average of 109 text messages a day.
>
> Sherry Turkle, author of a book on texting, suggests that all this texting makes teens less empathetic....

Below we see a much more convincing use of the same sources.

> In a 2011 **nationally representative phone survey of 2,277 adults**, conducted by the **nonprofit, nonpartisan** Pew Internet & American Life Project, cell phone owners between the ages of 18 and 24 exchange an average of 109 text messages a day. **This is more than double the average messages for 25 to 34 year olds.** —**3**
>
> **1**
>
> **2**
>
> **4**
>
> Sherry Turkle, **director of the Initiative on Technology and Self at MIT,** and author of the book *Alone Together: Why We Expect More from Technology and Less From Each Other,* suggests that all this texting is making teens less empathetic.

1 The speaker reveals the method and scope of the research.

2 The speaker wisely identifies the sponsoring institution as "nonprofit and nonpartisan" to signal reliability for her evidence.

OUR MISSION

The Pew Internet & American Life Project is one of seven projects that make up the Pew Research Center, a nonpartisan, nonprofit "fact tank" that provides information on the issues, attitudes and trends shaping America and the world. The Project produces reports exploring the impact of the internet on families, communities, work and home, daily life, education, health care, and civic and political life.

Read More>>

---

3 The speaker puts the statistic into context by offering a comparison to another age group.

4 The speaker signals the source's credibility by noting her position and affiliation with a respected academic institution.

Sherry Turkle

Abby Rockefeller Mauzé Professor of the Social Studies of Science and Technology
Director, MIT Initiative on Technology and Self
Program in Science, Technology, and Society
Massachusetts Institute of Technology
E51-296C
Cambridge, MA 02139

sturkle@media.mit.edu

Sherry Turkle is Abby Rockefeller Mauzé Professor of the Social Studies of Science and Technology in the Program in Science, Technology, and Society at MIT and the founder (2001) and current director of the MIT Initiative on Technology and Self. Professor Turkle received a joint doctorate in sociology and personality psychology from Harvard University and is a licensed clinical psychologist.

Avoid a Mechanical Delivery

Acknowledging sources need not interrupt the flow of your speech. On the contrary, audience members will welcome information that adds backing to your assertions. The key is to avoid a formulaic, or mechanical, delivery. These strategies can help:

VARY THE WORDING   Avoid a rote delivery of sources by varying your wording. For example, if you introduce one source with the phrase, "According to . . . ," switch to another construction, "As reported by . . . ," for the next. Alternating introductory phrases, such as "In the words of . . ."; " *Baltimore Sun* reporter Jonathan X writes that . . ."; and so forth contributes to a natural delivery and provides the necessary aural variety.

LEAD WITH THE CLAIM   Another means of varying how you cite sources is to discuss a claim first—for example, "Caffeine can cause actual intoxication"—before elaborating on and acknowledging the source of it—for example, "A report in the July 5, 2013, issue of the *New England Journal of Medicine has found . . . .*" Much as transitions help listeners follow along, summarizing and previewing evidence can help listeners process it better.

Overview of Source Types with Sample Oral Citations

Following is an overview of common types of sources cited in a speech, the specific citation elements to mention, and examples of how you might refer to these elements in a presentation. Note that each example includes a source qualifier describing the source's qualifications to address the topic ("Pulitzer Prize–winning author," "pioneering researcher"). Including a source qualifier can make the difference between winning or losing acceptance for your supporting material.

BOOK

If a book has *two* or *fewer* authors, state first and last names, source qualifier, title, and date of publication. If *three* or *more* authors, state first and last name of first author and "coauthors."

> *Example:* In the book *1948: The First Arab-Israeli War*, published in *2008*, noted *Israeli historian* Benny Morris claims that . . .

> *Example:* In *The Civic Potential of Video Games,* published in 2009, Joseph Kahne, *noted professor of education and director*

of the Civic Education Research Group at Mills College, and his *two coauthors, both educators,* wrote that . . .

REFERENCE WORK

For a reference work (e.g., atlas, directory, encyclopedia, almanac), note title, date of publication, author or sponsoring organization, and source qualifier.

Example: According to *2012 Literary Marketplace, the foremost guide to the U.S. book publishing industry, Karen Hallard and her coeditors* report that . . .

PRINT ARTICLE

When citing from a print article, use the same guidelines as you do for a book.

Example: In an article published in the May 2010 edition of *Atlantic Monthly* magazine, Marc Ambider, a *journalist* and *political editor* of the *Atlantic Monthly,* outlines the epidemic of obesity in the United States and describes his own decision to have bariatric surgery. . . .

ONLINE-ONLY MAGAZINE, NEWSPAPER, JOURNAL

Follow the same guidelines as for a book, and identify the publication as "online magazine," "online newspaper," or "online journal."

Example: *Environmental columnist* Nina Shen Rastogi, writing on the socioeconomic arguments against genetically modified crops in the *May 18, 2010,* edition of the online magazine *Slate* . . .

ORGANIZATION WEB SITE

Name the Web site, source qualifier, and section of Web site cited (if applicable), and last update.

Example: On its Web site, *last updated September 10, 2012,* the *Society of Interventional Radiology* explains that radio waves are harmless to healthy cells. . . .

If Web site content is undated or not regularly updated, review the site for credibility before use, using the criteria listed on pp. 76–77.

WEBLOG ("BLOG")

Name the blogger, source qualifier, affiliated Web site (if applicable), and date of posting.

Example: In a *July 8, 2011,* posting on *Talking Points Memo, a news blog that specializes in original reporting on government and politics, editor* Josh Marshall notes that...

TELEVISION OR RADIO PROGRAM

Name the program, segment, reporter, source qualifier, and date aired.

Example: Judy Woodruff, *PBS Newshour co-anchor*, described in a segment on the auto industry *aired on June 2, 2011*...

ONLINE VIDEO

Name the online video source, program, segment, source qualifier, and date aired (if applicable).

Example: In a session on "What's Next for Mindfulness" delivered at the *University of California, Berkeley's Greater Good Science Center* on *April 20, 2010,* and *broadcast on YouTube,* Jon Kabat-Zinn, *scientist, renowned author, and founding director* of the Stress Reduction Clinic...

TESTIMONY (LAY OR EXPERT)

Name the person, source qualifier, context in which information was offered, and date information was offered.

Example: On *August 3, 2011,* in *congressional testimony* before the *Committee on Foreign Relations Subcommittee on African Affairs,* Nancy E. Lundborg, *USAID Assistant Administrator, Bureau for Democracy, Conflict, and Humanitarian Assistance,* addressed the humanitarian crisis in the Horn of Africa.

INTERVIEW AND OTHER PERSONAL COMMUNICATION

Name the person, source qualifier, and date of the interview/correspondence/e-mail/memorandum.

Example: In an interview I conducted *last week,* Tim Zeutenhorst, *Chairman* of the *Orange City Area Health System Board*, at Orange City Hospital in Iowa, said...

Example: In a June 23 e-mail/letter/memorandum from Ron Jones, a *researcher at the Cleveland Institute* ...

For examples of how to cite different types of supporting materials, including facts and statistics, see Table 11.1.

TABLE 11.1 • TYPES OF SUPPORTING MATERIALS AND SAMPLE ORAL CITATION	
TYPES OF SUPPORTING MATERIALS	**SAMPLE ORAL CITATION**
EXAMPLES (real or hypothetical)	"One example of a fiscally effective charity is Lance Armstrong's Livestrong Foundation. According to the Foundation's Annual Report, in 2012 the Livestrong Challenge events raised..."
STORIES	"In J. R. R. Tolkien's classic trilogy, *The Lord of the Rings*, a young Hobbit boy named Frodo..."
TESTIMONY (expert or lay)	"Dr. Mary Klein, a stem-cell researcher from the Brown University School of Medicine, echoed this sentiment when she spoke last Monday at the Public Health Committee meeting..."
FACTS	"According to the *Farmer's Almanac*, published every year since 1818, originally the phrase 'blue moon' referred to the second of two full moons appearing in a single month."
STATISTICS	"Data from the *U.S. Census Bureau*, which produces national population estimates annually using the latest available data on births, deaths, and international migration, indicates that in 2012, there was one birth every..."

QUICK TIP

Credit Sources in Presentation Aids

Just as you acknowledge the ideas of others in the verbal portion of your speech, be sure to credit such material used in any accompanying presentation aids. When reproducing copyrighted material, such as a table or photograph, clearly label it with a copyright symbol (©) and the source information. Even if it is not copyrighted, supporting material listed on a visual aid may require citation. You may cite this material orally, print the citation unobtrusively on the aid, or both.

Properly Citing Quoted, Paraphrased, and Summarized Information

As discussed in Chapter 4, information not your own may be cited in the form of a *direct quotation* (statements by someone else cited verbatim), *paraphrase* (a restatement of someone else's ideas, opinions, or theories in the speaker's own words), or *summary* (a brief overview of someone else's ideas, opinions, or theories).

For examples of how to cite quotations, paraphrases, and summaries, see Chapter 4, pp. 27–28, and Visual Guides on pp. 67, 69, and 81.

Part 3
Organization

12. Organizing the Speech 96
13. Selecting an Organizational Pattern 105
14. Outlining the Speech 112

A speech structure is simple, composed of just three general parts: an introduction, a body, and a conclusion. The **introduction** establishes the purpose of the speech and shows its relevance to the audience. The **body** of the speech presents main points that are intended to fulfill the speech purpose. Main points are developed with supporting material to fulfill this purpose. The **conclusion** brings closure to the speech by restating the purpose, summarizing main points, and reiterating why the thesis is relevant to the audience. In essence, the introduction of a speech tells listeners where they are going, the body takes them there, and the conclusion lets them know they have arrived.

Chapter 15 focuses on how to create effective introductions and conclusions. In this chapter, we explore the body of the speech. It consists of three elements: *main points, supporting points*, and *transitions*.

Use Main Points to Make Your Claims

Main points express the key ideas of the speech. Their function is to represent each of the main elements or claims being made in support of the speech thesis. To create main points, identify the central ideas and themes of the speech. What are the most important ideas you want to convey? What is the thesis? What key ideas emerge from your research? Each of these ideas or claims should be expressed as a main point.

Use the Purpose and Thesis Statements as Guides

Main points should flow directly from your speech purpose and thesis, as in the following example:

SPECIFIC PURPOSE:	(what you want the audience to learn or do as a result of your speech): To show my audience, through a series of easy steps, how to meditate.
THESIS:	(the central idea of the speech): When performed correctly, meditation is an effective and easy way to reduce stress.
MAIN POINTS:	I. The first step of meditation is the "positioning."
	II. The second step of meditation is "breathing."
	III. The third step of meditation is "relaxation."

Note that some topics suggest natural divisions indicating main points, such as in the sequential steps involved in meditation.

Restrict the Number of Main Points

Research has shown that audiences can comfortably take in only between two and seven main points.[1] For most speeches, and especially those delivered in the classroom, between two and five main points should be sufficient. If you have too many main points, further narrow your topic (see Chapter 7) or check the points for proper subordination (see p. 99).

Restrict Each Main Point to a Single Idea

A main point should not introduce more than one idea. If it does, split it into two (or more) main points:

INCORRECT:	I.	West Texas has its own Grand Canyon, and South Texas has its own desert.
CORRECT:	I.	West Texas boasts its own Grand Canyon.
	II.	South Texas boasts its own desert.

Main points should be mutually exclusive of one another. If they are not, consider whether a main point more properly serves as a subpoint.

Express each main point as a *declarative sentence* (one that states a fact or an argument). This emphasizes the point and alerts audience members to the main thrusts of your speech. For example, if one of your main points is that children need more vitamin D, offer the declarative statement, "According to the nation's leading pediatricians, children from infants

---

QUICK TIP

Save the Best for Last—or First

Listeners have the best recall of speech points made at the beginning of a speech, a phenomenon termed the "primacy effect," and at the end of a speech (the "recency effect") than of those made in between (unless the ideas made in between are much more striking than the others).[2] If it is especially important that listeners remember certain ideas, introduce those ideas near the beginning of the speech and reiterate them at the conclusion.

to teens should double the recommended amount of vitamin D." As shown in the example about West Texas and South Texas, strive to state your main points (and supporting points; see below) in **parallel form**—that is, in similar grammatical form and style (see p. 139 on parallelism). This strategy helps listeners understand and retain the points (by providing consistency) and lends power and elegance to your words.

Use Supporting Points to Prove Your Claims

Supporting points represent the supporting material or evidence you have gathered to justify the main points. Generate them with the supporting material you've collected in your research—examples, narratives, testimony, facts, and statistics (see Chapter 8).

In an outline, supporting points appear in a subordinate position to main points. This is indicated by **indentation**. As with main points, supporting points should be arranged in order of their importance or relevance to the main point. The most common format is the **roman numeral outline**. Main points are enumerated with uppercase roman numerals (I, II, III ...), while supporting points are enumerated with capital letters (A, B, C ...), Arabic numerals (1, 2, 3 ...), and lowercase letters (a, b, c ...), as seen in the following:

I. Main point

   A. Supporting point

      1. Sub-supporting point

         a. Sub-sub-supporting point

         b. Sub-sub-supporting point...

Here is an example (in phrase outline form; see p. 113) from a speech about using effective subject lines in business-related e-mails:

I. Subject line most important, yet neglected part of e-mail.

   A. Determines if recipient reads message

      1. Needs to specify point of message

      2. Needs to distinguish from spam

   B. Determines if recipient ignores message

      1. May ignore e-mail with missing subject line

      2. May ignore e-mail with unclear subject line

II. Use proven techniques for effective subject lines
   A. Make them informative
      1. Give specific details
      2. Match central idea of e-mail
      3. Be current
   B. Check for sense
      1. Convey correct meaning
      2. Reflect content of message
   C. Avoid continuing subject line in text
      1. May annoy the reader
      2. May be unclear
         a. Could be confused with spam
         b. Could be misinterpreted

QUICK TIP

Spend Time Organizing Speech Points
Don't skimp on organizing speech points. Listeners' under-standing of a speech is directly linked to how well it is orga-nized,[3] and audience attitudes plummet when the speech is disorganized.[4] Listeners also find speakers whose speeches are well organized more believable than those who present poorly organized ones.[5]

Pay Close Attention to Coordination and Subordination

Outlines are based on the principles of **coordination and subordination**—the logical placement of ideas relative to their importance to one another. Ideas that are *coordinate* are given equal weight; **coordinate points** are indicated by their parallel alignment. An idea that is *subordinate* to another is given relatively less weight; **subordinate points** are indicated by their indentation below the more important points. For an example, see the outline shown earlier on using effective subject lines in business-related e-mails: Coordinate points are aligned with one another, while subordinate points are indented below the points that they substantiate. Thus Main Point II is coordinate with Main Point I, Subpoint A is subordinate to Main Point I, Subpoint B is coordinate with Subpoint A, and so forth.

Strive for a Unified, Coherent, and Balanced Organization

A well-organized speech is characterized by unity, coherence, and balance. Try to adhere to these principles as you arrange your speech points.

A speech exhibits *unity* when it contains only those points implied by the purpose and thesis statements. Each main point supports the thesis, and each supporting point provides evidence for the main points. Each sub-supporting point supports each supporting point. Finally, each point should focus on a single idea.

A speech exhibits *coherence* when it is organized clearly and logically, using the principles of coordination and subordination to align speech points in logical progression (see Table 12.1). In addition, the speech body should follow logically from the introduction, and the conclusion should follow logically from the body. Within the body of the speech itself, main points should follow logically from the thesis statement, and supporting points should follow logically from the main points. Transitions serve as logical bridges that help establish coherence.

Inexperienced speakers may give overly lengthy coverage to one point and insufficient attention to others; or they might provide scanty evidence in the speech body after presenting an impressive introduction. The principle of *balance* suggests that appropriate emphasis or weight be given to each part of the speech relative to the other parts and to the theme. The body of a speech should always be the longest part, and the introduction and conclusion should be of roughly the same length. Stating the main points in parallel form is one aspect of balance. Assigning each main point at least two supporting points is another. If you have only one subpoint, consider how you might incorporate it into the superior point. Think of a main point as a body and supporting points as legs; without at least two legs, the body cannot stand.

TABLE 12.1 • PRINCIPLES OF COORDINATION AND SUBORDINATION

- Assign equal weight to ideas that are coordinate.
- Assign relatively less weight to ideas that are subordinate.
- Indicate coordinate points by their parallel alignment.
- Indicate subordinate points by their indentation below the more important points.
- Every point must be supported by at least two points or none at all (consider how to address one "dangling" point in the point above it).

> ✓ **CHECKLIST: Reviewing Main and Supporting Points**
>
> ✓ Do the main points flow directly from the speech goal and thesis?
>
> ✓ Do the main points express the key points of the speech?
>
> ✓ Is each main point truly a main point or a subpoint of another main point?
>
> ✓ Is each main point substantiated by at least two supporting points—or none?
>
> ✓ Do you spend roughly the same amount of time on each main point?
>
> ✓ Are the supporting points truly subordinate to the main points?
>
> ✓ Does each main point and supporting point focus on a single idea?
>
> ✓ Are your main and supporting points stated in parallel form?

Use Transitions to Give Direction to the Speech

Transitions are words, phrases, or sentences that tie the speech ideas together and enable the speaker to move smoothly from one point to the next. Considered the "neurosystem" of speeches, transitions provide consistency of movement from one point to the next and cue the audience that a new point will be made. Transitions can take the form of full sentences, phrases, or single words.

Use Transitions between Main Points

When moving from one main point to another, **full-sentence transitions** are especially effective. For example, to move from Main Point I in a speech about sales contests ("*Top management should sponsor sales contests to halt the decline in sales over the past two years*") to Main Point II ("*Sales contests will lead to better sales presentations*"), the speaker might use the following transition:

> Next, let's look at exactly what sales contests can do for us.

Very often, a speaker will transition from one point to the next by first restating the points just covered and then previewing the material to be covered next in what's called a **restate-forecast transition**:

> Now that we've established a need for sales contests (*restatement*), let's look at what sales contests can do for us (*forecast*).

From Point to Point

Using Transitions to Guide Your Listeners

Transitions direct your listeners from one point to another in your speech. At a bare minimum, plan on using transitions to move between:

- The introduction and the body of the speech
- The main points
- Key subpoints
- The body of the speech and the conclusion

Introduction

I. Today I'll explore the steps you can take to create a greener campus . . .

(**Transition:** Let's begin by considering what "going green" actually means.)

Body

I. "Going green" means taking action to promote and maintain a healthy environment.

   (**Transition:** So how do you go green?)

   A. Get informed—understand what is physically happening to the planet.

   (**Transition:** Understanding the issues is only part of going green, however. Perhaps most important . . .)

   B. Recognize that change starts here, on campus, with you . . . .

While transitions help guide your listeners from point to point, they can also do a lot more, including:

- Introduce propositions (major speech points)
- Illustrate cause and effect
- Signal explanations and examples
- Emphasize, repeat, compare, or contrast ideas
- Summarize and preview information
- Suggest conclusions from evidence

Following is an excerpt from a working outline on a speech about campuses going green. Note how the student edits himself to ensure that he (1) uses transitions to help listeners follow along and retain his speech points and (2) uses transitions strategically to achieve his goal of persuading the audience.

1 — (**Transition:** Why are environmentalists targeting college campuses?)
  I. College campuses generate the waste equivalent of many large towns . . .

2 — (**Transition:** As a result . . .)
   A. Colleges face disposal issues, especially of electronics . . .
   B. Administrators face decisions about mounting energy costs . . .

3 — (**Transition:** Following are some ideas to create a greener campus. First . . .)
  II. Promote a campus-wide recycling program

4 — (**Transition:** For example . . .)
   A. Decrease the availability of bottled water and dis-posable . . .
   B. Insist on recycling bins at all residence halls . . .
   C. Encourage computer centers to recycle . . .

5 — (**Transition:** Recycling is a critical part of going green.) Decreasing the consumption of plastic and paper, installing recycling bins, and responsibly disposing of print cartridges will make a huge difference. Another aspect of going green is using sustainable energy . . .

  III. Lobby administrators to investigate solar, wind, and geothermal . . .
   A. Make an argument for "eco-dorms". . .
   B. Explore alternative heating . . .

6 — (**Transition:** So far, we've talked about practical actions we can take to encourage a greener lifestyle on campus, but what about beyond the campus?)

  IV. Get involved at the town government level
   A. Town-grown committees . . .
   B. Speak up and voice your concerns . . .

7 — (**Transition:** As you can see, we have work to do . . .)
  Conclusion
  I. If we want our children and our children's children to live to see a healthy earth, we must take action now . . .

---

1 Student inserts a transition (**rhetorical question**) to introduce a new proposition (e.g., main point).

2 Student realizes he needs to insert this transitional phrase to signal a **cause-effect relationship**.

3 Student uses a transition to **move to the next proposition**.

4 This transitional phrase **introduces additional examples**.

5 Student inserts an **internal summary** to help listeners retain information and transition to the next main point.

6 Student inserts an **internal preview** to move to the next main point.

7 Student inserts a transition to signal a **shift to his concluding point**.

Another frequently used full-sentence transition is the **rhetorical question**. Rather than inviting actual responses, rhetorical questions stimulate listeners to anticipate answers from the speaker:

> Will contests be too expensive? Well, actually...

Use Transitions between Supporting Points

Transitions between supporting points can also be handled with full sentences, or with phrases or single words. For example, to move from Supporting Point A (*"Sales personnel will be motivated by competition"*) to Supporting Point B (*"Contests are relatively inexpensive"*), the speaker might use the following transition:

> Another way that sales competitions will benefit us is by their relative cost effectiveness.

Conjunctions or phrases (also called **signposts**) such as the following can be just as effective:

> Next...
> First...(second, third, and so forth)
> We now turn...
> Finally, let's consider...
> If you think that's shocking...
> Similarly...

TRANSITIONAL WORDS AND PHRASES

To show comparisons: Similarly; In the same way; Likewise; Just as

To contrast ideas: On the other hand; And yet; At the same time; In spite of; However; In contrast

To illustrate cause and effect: As a result; Hence; Because; Thus; Consequently

To illustrate sequence of time or events: First, second, third...; Following this; Later; Earlier; At present; In the past

To indicate explanation: For example; To illustrate; In other words; To simplify; To clarify

To indicate additional examples: Not only; In addition to; Let's look at

To emphasize significance: Most important; Above all; Remember; Keep in mind

To summarize: In conclusion; In summary; Finally; Let me conclude by saying

Use Previews and Summaries as Transitions

Previews are transitions that tell the audience what to expect next. In speech introductions, a **preview statement** briefly introduces the main points of the speech (see Chapter 15). Within the body itself, **internal previews** can be used to alert audience members to a shift from one main point or idea to another:

> Victoria Woodhull was a pioneer in many respects. Not only was she the first woman to run her own brokerage firm, she was also the first to run for the presidency of the United States, though few people know this. Let's see how she accomplished these feats.

Similar to the internal preview, the **internal summary** draws together important ideas before the speaker proceeds to another speech point. Internal summaries help listeners review and evaluate the thread of the theme thus far:

> It should be clear that the kind of violence we've witnessed in the schools and in our communities has a deeper root cause than the availability of handguns. Our young children are crying out for a sense of community, of relatedness and meaning, that they just aren't finding in the institutions that are meant to serve them.

See Chapter 14, "Outlining the Speech," to learn how to include transitions in the outline of your speech.

13 Selecting an Organizational Pattern

Successful speeches follow a clear structure whose purpose is twofold: to help the audience follow the speaker's ideas, and to arrange those ideas to optimum effect.[1] A good time to select an organizational pattern is after you've gathered the supporting materials and prepared preliminary main points.

Speeches make use of at least a dozen different organizational arrangements of main and supporting points. Here we look at six commonly used patterns: chronological, spatial, causal (cause-effect), problem-solution, topical, and narrative. In Chapter 24, you will find three additional patterns of organization designed specifically for persuasive speeches: *Monroe's motivated sequence, refutation,* and *comparative advantage.*

Arranging Speech Points Chronologically

Some topics lend themselves well to the arrangement of main points according to their occurrence in time relative to one another. A **chronological pattern of arrangement** (also called a *temporal pattern*) follows the natural sequential order of the main points. A speaker might describe events leading to the adoption of a peace plan, for example, or explain how to install solar panels. A speech describing the development of the World Wide Web, for example, calls for a chronological, or time-ordered, sequence of main points:

THESIS STATEMENT: The Internet evolved from a small network designed for military and academic scientists into a vast array of networks used by billions of people around the globe.

MAIN POINTS: I.   The Internet was first conceived in 1962 as the ARPANET to promote the sharing of research among scientists in the United States.

II.   In the 1980s, a team created TCP/IP, a language that could link networks, and the Internet as we know it was born.

III.   At the end of the Cold War, the ARPANET was decommissioned, and the World Wide Web constituted the bulk of Internet traffic.[2]

QUICK TIP

Blend Organizational Patterns

The pattern of organization for your subpoints need not always follow the pattern you select for your main points. Do keep your main points in one pattern—this will be the predominant pattern for the speech—but feel free to use other patterns for subpoints when it makes sense to do so. For instance, for a speech about the history of tattooing in the United States, you may choose a chronological pattern to organize the main points but use a cause-effect arrangement for some of your subpoints regarding why tattooing is on the rise today.

Arranging Speech Points Using a Spatial Pattern

When speaking about the physical arrangement of a place, an object, or an event, logic suggests that the main points can be arranged in order of their physical proximity or direction relative to one another. This calls for a **spatial pattern of arrangement**. For example, you can select a spatial arrangement when your speech provides the audience with a "tour" of a particular place:

THESIS STATEMENT: El Morro National Monument in New Mexico is captivating for its variety of natural and historical landmarks.

MAIN POINTS:
I. Visitors first encounter an abundant variety of plant life native to the high-country desert.

II. Soon visitors come upon an age-old watering hole that has receded beneath the 200-foot cliffs.

III. Beyond are the famous cliff carvings made by hundreds of travelers over several centuries of exploration in the Southwest.

In a speech describing a geothermal heating and cooling company's market growth across regions of the country, a speaker might use the spatial arrangement as follows:

THESIS STATEMENT: Sales of geothermal systems have grown in every region of the country.

MAIN POINTS:
I. Sales are strongest in the Eastern Zone.

II. Sales are growing at a rate of 10 per-cent quarterly in the Central Zone.

III. Sales are up slightly in the Mountain Zone.

Arranging Speech Points Using a Causal (Cause-Effect) Pattern

Some speech topics represent cause-effect relationships. Examples include (1) events leading to higher interest rates, (2) reasons students drop out of college, and (3) causes of spousal abuse. The main points in a **causal (cause-effect) pattern of arrangement** usually take the following form:

I. Cause

II. Effect

Sometimes a topic can be discussed in terms of multiple causes for a single effect, or a single cause for multiple effects:

MULTIPLE CAUSES FOR A SINGLE EFFECT: REASONS STUDENTS DROP OUT OF COLLEGE	**SINGLE CAUSE FOR MULTIPLE EFFECTS: RESULTS OF DROPPING OUT OF COLLEGE**
I. Cause 1 (lack of funds)	I. Cause (lack of funds)
II. Cause 2 (unsatisfactory social life)	II. Effect 1 (lowered earnings over lifetime)
III. Cause 3 (unsatisfactory academic performance)	III. Effect 2 (decreased job satisfaction over lifetime)
IV. Effect (drop out of college)	IV. Effect 3 (increased stress level over lifetime)

Some topics are best understood by presenting listeners with the effect(s) first and the cause or causes subsequently. For example, in an informative speech on the 1988 explosion of Pan Am Flight 103 over Lockerbie, Scotland, a student speaker arranges his main points as follows:

THESIS STATEMENT:	The explosion of Pan Am Flight 103 over Lockerbie, Scotland, killed 270 people and resulted in the longest-running aviation investigation in history.
MAIN POINTS:	I. (Effect) Two hundred and fifty-nine passengers and crew members died; an additional eleven people on the ground perished.
MAIN POINTS:	II. (Effect) Longest-running aviation investigation in history.
	III. (Cause) Court found cause of explosion was a terrorist act, a bomb planted by Libyan citizen Al Megrahi.
	IV. (Cause) Some people believe that Megrahi did not act alone, if he acted at all.

Arranging Speech Points Using a Problem-Solution Pattern

The **problem-solution pattern of arrangement** organizes main points to demonstrate the nature and significance of a problem and to provide justification for a proposed solution.

This type of arrangement, most often used in persuasive speeches, can be as general as two main points:

I. Problem (define what it is)
II. Solution (offer a way to overcome the problem)

But many problem-solution speeches require more than two points to adequately explain the problem and to substantiate the recommended solution:

I. The nature of the problem (identify its causes, incidence, etc.)
II. Effects of the problem (explain why it's a problem, for whom, etc.)
III. Unsatisfactory solutions (discuss those that have not worked)
IV. Proposed solution (explain why it's expected to work)

The following is a partial outline of a persuasive speech about cyberbullying arranged in a problem-solution format (for more on the problem-solution pattern, see Chapter 24).

THESIS STATEMENT: To combat cyberbullying, we need to educate the public about it, report it when it happens, and punish the offenders.

MAIN POINT:
I. Nature of cyberbullying
  A. Types of activities involved
    1. Name-calling, insults
    2. Circulation of embarrassing pictures
    3. Sharing private information
    4. Threats
  B. Incidence of bullying
  C. Profile of offenders

MAIN POINT:
II. Effects of cyberbullying on victims
  A. Acting out in school
  B. Feeling unsafe in school
  C. Skipping school
  D. Experiencing depression

MAIN POINT:	III. Unsuccessful attempts at solving cyberbullying
	A. Let offenders and victims work it out on their own
	B. Ignore problem, assuming it will go away
MAIN POINT:	IV. Ways to solve cyberbullying
	A. Educate in schools
	B. Report incidents to authorities
	C. Suspend or expel offenders

Arranging Speech Points Topically

When each of the main points is a subtopic or category of the speech topic, try the **topical pattern of arrangement** (also called *categorical pattern*). Consider an informative speech about choosing Chicago as a place to establish a career. You plan to emphasize three reasons for choosing Chicago: the strong economic climate of the city, its cultural variety, and its accessible public transportation. Since these three points are of relatively equal importance, they can be arranged in any order without affecting one another or the speech purpose negatively. For example:

THESIS STATEMENT:	Chicago is an excellent place to establish a career.
MAIN POINTS:	I. Accessible transportation
	II. Cultural variety
	III. Economic stability

This is not to say that, when using a topical arrangement, you should arrange the main points without careful consideration.

QUICK TIP

Find Freedom with the Topical Pattern

Topical arrangements give you the greatest freedom to structure main points according to the way you wish to present your topic. You can approach a topic by dividing it into two or more categories, for example. You can lead with your strongest evidence or leave your most compelling points until you near the conclusion. If your topic does not call out for one of the other patterns described in this chapter, be sure to experiment with the topical pattern.

Any number of considerations can factor in your ordering of points, not least of which should be the audience's most immediate needs and interests.

Arranging Speech Points Using the Narrative Pattern

Storytelling is often a natural and effective way to get your message across. In the **narrative pattern of arrangement**, the speech consists of a story or series of short stories, replete with character, settings, plot, and vivid imagery.

In practice, a speech built largely upon a story (or series of stories) is likely to incorporate elements of other designs. For example, you might organize the main points of the story in an effect-cause design, in which you first reveal why something happened (such as a drunken driving accident) and then describe the events that led up to the accident (the causes).

Whatever the structure, simply telling a story is no guarantee of giving a good speech. Any speech should include a clear thesis, a preview, well-organized main points, and transitions, so be certain to include these elements as you organize the speech.

✔️ **CHECKLIST: Choosing an Organizational Pattern**

Does your speech . . .

- ✓ Describe a series of developments in time or a set of actions that occur sequentially? Use the *chronological pattern of arrangement*.

- ✓ Describe or explain the physical arrangement of a place, a scene, or an object? Use the *spatial pattern of arrangement*.

- ✓ Explain or demonstrate a topic in terms of its underlying causes or effects? Use the *causal (cause-effect) pattern of arrangement*.

- ✓ Demonstrate the nature and significance of a problem and justify a proposed solution? Use the *problem-solution pattern of arrangement*.

- ✓ Stress natural divisions in a topic, in which points can be moved to emphasize audience needs and interests? Use a *topical pattern of arrangement*.

- ✓ Convey ideas through a story, using character, plot, and settings? Use a *narrative pattern of arrangement*, perhaps in combination with another pattern.

14 Outlining the Speech

Once you've selected a pattern for organizing your main points, the next step is to outline the speech. Outlines are critical to organizing a speech, revealing any weaknesses in its underlying logic and providing a blueprint for presentation.

Plan on Creating Two Outlines

As you develop a speech, you will actually create two outlines: a working outline (also called a *preparation* or *rough outline*) and a speaking, or delivery, outline. The purpose of the **working outline** is to organize and firm up main points and, using the research you've gathered, to develop supporting points to substantiate them. Completed, the working outline should contain your entire speech, organized and supported to your satisfaction.

The **speaking outline** (also called a *delivery outline*) is the one you will use when you are practicing and actually presenting the speech. Speaking outlines, which contain your ideas in condensed form, are much briefer than working outlines. Figure 14.1 provides an overview of the steps involved in organizing and outlining a speech.

Create the Main Speech Points

↓

Note Any Obvious Subpoints

↓

Select an Organizational Pattern
for the Main Points

↓

Create a Working Outline

↓

Organize Main Points and Subpoints

↓

Check Main Points and Subpoints
for Coordination and Subordination

↓

Transfer the Working Outline to a Speaking Outline

FIGURE 14.1 Steps in Organizing and Outlining the Speech

Use Sentences, Phrases, or Key Words

Speeches can be outlined in complete sentences, phrases, or key words. Working outlines typically contain full sentences, reflecting much of the text of the speech; speaking outlines use phrases or key words.

In a **sentence outline**, each main and supporting point is stated in sentence form as a declarative statement (one that makes an assertion about a subject). The following is an excerpt of a working outline in sentence format from a speech by Mark B. McClellan on keeping prescription drugs safe:[1]

I. The prescription drug supply is under unprecedented attack from a variety of increasingly sophisticated threats.

    A. Technologies for counterfeiting—ranging from pill molding to dyes—have improved across the board.

    B. Inadequately regulated Internet sites have become major portals for unsafe and illegal drugs.

A **phrase outline** uses partial construction of the sentence form of each point. Phrase outlines encourage you to become so familiar with your speech points that a glance at a few words is enough to remind you of exactly what to say. McClellan's sentence outline would appear as follows in phrase outline form:

I. Drug supply under attack

    A. Counterfeiting technologies more sophisticated

    B. Unregulated Internet sites

The **key-word outline** uses the smallest possible units of understanding to outline the main and supporting points.

I. Threats

    A. Counterfeiting

    B. Internet

The type of outline you select will affect how well you deliver the speech. The less you rely on your outline notes, the more eye contact you can have with audience members—an essential aspect of a successful speech.

For this reason, many speaking experts recommend using key-word or phrase outlines over sentence outlines for delivery, with the more succinct key-word outline often being the preferred format. Key-word outlines permit not only the greatest degree of eye contact but also greater freedom of movement and better control of your thoughts and actions than either sentence or phrase outlines. With sufficient practice, the key words will jog your memory so that the delivery of your ideas becomes more natural.

It is important to remember that outlining requirements differ among instructors. Be sure you understand your instructor's specific outlining and formatting requirements before you begin outlining your speech.

Create a Working Outline First

Begin with a working outline (many experts and instructors suggest using full sentences) before transferring its ideas to a speaking outline that uses key words or phrases. Creating a working outline will give you confidence that you've satisfactorily fleshed out your speech points and that they follow in a logical and compelling progression.

- Prepare the body of the speech before the introduction or conclusion, keeping the introduction and conclusion *separate from* the main points (see sample outlines in this chapter).

- Clearly indicate to yourself where speech points require credit, and link to references. Once you complete the outline, prepare a bibliography. For guidelines on what to include in a source note, see "From Source to Speech" guides in Chapters 9, 10, and 11, and Appendix A for individual citation styles.

- Assign the speech a title, one that informs people of its subject in a way that invites them to listen to or read it.

CHECKLIST: Steps in Creating a Working Outline

✓ Write out your topic, general purpose, specific speech purpose, and thesis.

✓ Establish your main points (optimally two to five).

✓ Flesh out supporting points.

✓ Check for correct subordination and coordination; follow the numbering system shown on p. 98.

✓ Label each speech part (i.e., "Introduction," "Body," and "Conclusion").

✓ Write out each speech point in sentence format.

✓ Label and write out transitions.

✓ Note sources for the bibliography.

✓ Assign the speech a title.

SAMPLE WORKING OUTLINE

The following outline is from a speech delivered by John Coulter at Salt Lake Community College. It uses the sentence format and includes labeled transitions as well as the wording John will use to cite his sources. John briefly notes his sources in parentheses (e.g., FTC, "Quick Facts") for ease in assembling a required bibliography.

Staying ahead of Spyware

JOHN COULTER
Salt Lake Community College

TOPIC:	Problems and solutions associated with spyware
SPECIFIC PURPOSE:	To inform my audience of the dangers of spyware so that they may take steps to prevent infection
THESIS STATEMENT:	Computer and mobile device users must understand the evolving nature of spyware and what it can do in order to take the necessary steps to protect themselves.

INTRODUCTION

I. Do you worry about identity theft online?

II. Are you anxious about the security of your passwords and credit card numbers? *(Attention getter)*

III. Many of you are aware of software known as spyware that can install itself on your computer and smartphone and harvest sensitive information without your knowledge.

IV. Spyware is constantly evolving, however, and to stay safe, we need to stay on top of new developments and arm ourselves against the threats spyware poses. *(Thesis statement)*

V. Today, I'll talk about what forms spyware takes, how it gets into your computer and phone, the harm it causes, and how to keep from becoming infected by it. *(Preview)*

TRANSITION: So, what's the state of spyware today?

BODY

I. Spyware is a type of privacy invasion "malware," or "malicious software" that installs itself on a computer or mobile device, gathers data from it, and sends it back to a remote computer *without your consent*. (FTC, "Quick Facts")

A. Some types of spyware track your Web-browsing habits, selling this information to marketers.

B. Some spyware programs capture passwords and other sensitive information, leading to identity theft.

C. One particularly spooky type of spyware can secretly record everything you type or text.

TRANSITION: Many people are confused about the differences between spyware, adware, and another type of malware—the computer virus.

D. *Adware* refers to programs that display ads on your computer. (*PC Magazine*, "Nine Ways")

1. Adware may be annoying, but it doesn't contain software that can track you.

2. Spyware, on the other hand, does what its name suggests—it sends your stolen data to "the lair of its evil creator," as tech writer Neil Rubenking so aptly puts it. ("Nine Ways")

E. Unlike spyware, viruses are designed to replicate themselves.

1. Individuals generally write viruses in order to brag about causing damage, whereas spyware often is written by corporate teams to make money. (CNET Video)

2. Viruses are illegal, whereas legislation outlawing spyware, such as the Internet Spyware Prevention Act, has thus far failed passage, according to GovTrack.us, a Web site that tracks the status of federal legislation. (GovTrack.us, "I-SPY")

TRANSITION: You may be wondering how spyware gains a foothold in your computer.

II. Spyware takes various routes into your computer depending on what it's programmed to do, from tracking your Internet browsing habits to stealing your identity.

A. Spyware often "piggybacks" onto downloadable programs, such as free file-sharing applications and games.

B. Links in pop-up ads and the "unsubscribe" button in spam are known sources.

    C. Legitimate-seeming antispyware protection programs, called "scareware," promise to fix your problems, but install spyware when downloaded. (Microsoft, "Fake Virus")

    D. Keystroke logging software can capture your keystrokes, enabling actual spying as well as identity theft.

        1. Some people deliberately install keystroke loggers to spy on spouses, children, employees, or students.

        2. Reporting in the June 29, 2010 edition of *Newsweek*, Jessica Ramirez writes that keystroke loggers can be attached to smartphone apps. (*Newsweek*: Spying on Your Cellphone")

TRANSITION: Spyware even lurks on social networking sites such as Facebook and Twitter.

    E. Clicking on pop-up ads on social media sites or accepting invitations to take certain quizzes or join certain groups can activate spyware.

III. The symptoms and problems associated with spyware are fairly easy to recognize.

    A. One sign of infiltration, according to Google's Web search help page, is a constant stream of pop-up ads. (Google, "Help")

    B. Strange toolbars may appear on the desktop.

    C. Browser settings may be hijacked, forcing users to strange Web pages.

    D. The computer may behave sluggishly, files may disappear, or the computer may crash.

TRANSITION: Now for the good news. You can protect yourself from spyware.

IV. Prevention is the best way to avoid spyware's harmful and potentially dangerous effects.

    A. There are some good antispyware programs on the market.

        1. Microsoft now distributes *Windows Defender* with its operating systems and offers a free program called *Microsoft Security Essentials*.

        2. *PC Magazine*'s Editor's Choice for stand-alone malware protection is *Spyware Doctor with*

Antivirus; its choice for security suite is *Norton Internet Security.* (*PC Magazine,* "Free Virus and Spyware Protection")

3. Be aware that free antispyware software, according to *PC Magazine,* doesn't do as thorough a job as rated commercial software, and some free programs actually contain spyware.

TRANSITION: Along with the antispyware software you can install, what else can you do?

B. Keep your browser up-to-date to take advantage of security updates.

C. Don't install any software without reading the fine print, or first checking for reviews of it.

D. Download free software or any smartphone apps only from sites you know and trust.

E. Don't click on links in pop-up windows.

F. Don't reply to or even open spam or e-mail that isn't from someone you know.

G. Don't hit the "unsubscribe" button in spam because spyware is known to lurk here.

H. Use the maximum security level settings on social media sites.

I. As suggested on the Web site Identity Theft 911, use strong passwords that can't be easily guessed and don't set up your smartphone to automatically remember them. (ID Theft 911, "Smartphones")

CONCLUSION

I. The makers of spyware are in it for the money, so the problem is likely to be long-lasting. *(Signals close of speech)*

II. Spyware appears in various guises in order to use personal information stored on computers or smartphones without your consent, but taking the right steps can help you avoid unwanted intrusions. *(Summarizes main points)*

III. One final suggestion is to stay abreast of developments related to spyware and malware by consulting reputable Web sites such as Stopbadware.org and StaySafe-Online.org. *(Leaves audience with something to think about)*

IV. Be vigilant, stay safe, and good luck! *(Memorable close)*

Works Cited

Federal Trade Commission. "Spyware: Quick Facts."
   OnGuardOnline.gov Web site. March 2010. http://www
   .onguardonline.gov/topics/spyware.aspx.

"H.R. 1525: Internet Spyware (I-SPY) Prevention Act of 2007."
   GovTrack.us. http://www.govtrack.us/congress/bill
   .xpd?bill=h110-1525.

Identity Theft 911. "Get Wise about Smartphones." August
   2010 Newsletter. http://identitytheft911.org/newsletters/
   newsletter.ext?sp=11291.

Ramirez, Jessica. "Is Someone Spying on Your Cellphone Calls?"
   Newsweek, June 29, 2010, 16.

Rubenking, Neil. "Free Virus and Spyware Protection: What's Right
   for You?" *PC Magazine,* July 6, 2010. http://www.pcmag
   .com/article2/0,2817,2356509,00.asp.

---. "Nine Ways to Wipe Out Spyware." *PC Magazine*, February 5, 2008.
   http://www.pcmag.com/article2/0,2817,2255854,00.asp.

"Suspicious Results and Strange Behavior: Strange Pop-Ups and
   Other Malware." Google Web Search Help. Accessed August
   30, 2010. http://www.google.com/support/websearch/bin/
   answer.py?hl=en&answer=809.

"Virus vs. Spyware." CNET.com. Videos section. September 1,
   2010. http://cnettv.cnet.com/?tag=hdr;snav.

"Watch Out for Fake Virus Alerts." Microsoft Security Web site.
   Accessed August 25, 2010. www.microsoft.com/security/
   antivirus/rogue.aspx.

Prepare a Speaking Outline for Delivery

Using the same numbering system as the working outline, condense the full sentences into key words or phrases, including just enough words to jog your memory. Place the speaking outline on large (at least 4 × 6-inch) notecards or 8.5 × 11-inch sheets of paper. Print large enough so that you can see the words at a glance.

QUICK TIP

Sometimes Only Exact Wording Will Do
Even though the delivery outline should contain key words or phrases almost exclusively, when exact wording is critical to an accurate representation of your speech material (as in conveying quotations verbatim or when the issue is highly controversial or emotion-laden and precise wording is needed to make the point as clear as possible), you may want to write it out in full sentences.

Indicate Delivery Cues

Include any **delivery cues** that will be part of the speech. To ensure visibility, capitalize the cues, place them in parentheses, and/or highlight them.

DELIVERY CUE	EXAMPLE
Transitions	(TRANSITION)
Timing	(PAUSE) (SLOW DOWN)
Speaking Rate/Volume	(SLOWLY) (LOUDER)
Presentation Aids	(SHOW MODEL) (SLIDE 3)
Source	(ATLANTA CONSTITUTION, August 2, 2005)
Statistic	(2010, boys to girls = 94,232; U.S. Health Human Services)
Quotation	Eubie Blake, 100: "If I'd known I was gonna live this long, I'd have taken better care of myself."
Difficult-to-Pronounce or -Remember Names or Words	Eowyn (A-OH-win)

> ✓ **CHECKLIST: Tips on Using Notecards or Sheets of Paper**
>
> ____ 1. Leave some blank space at the margins. This will help you find your place as you glance at the cards.
>
> ____ 2. Number your notecards or sheets so that you can follow them with ease.
>
> ____ 3. Instead of turning the cards or sheets, slide them under one another.
>
> ____ 4. Do not staple notes or sheets together.
>
> ____ 5. If you use a lectern, place the notes or sheets near eye level.
>
> ____ 6. Do not use the cards or sheets in hand gestures, as they become distracting pointers or flags.

Practice the Speech

The key to the successful delivery of any speech, particularly when using a key-word outline, is practice. The more you rehearse your speech, the more comfortable you will become when you speak. For more information on practicing the speech, see Chapter 19, "Using the Body."

SAMPLE SPEAKING OUTLINE

Staying ahead of Spyware

JOHN COULTER
Salt Lake Community College

INTRODUCTION

I.   Worry, identity?

II. Anxious, security? *(Attention getter)*

III. Aware spyware install, without knowledge, harvest sensitive, steps, protect

IV. Evolving, stay safe, arm against *(Thesis statement)*

V.   Today, forms spyware, harm, keep infected *(Preview)*

(TRANSITION: So, state...?)
        [PAUSE]

BODY

I. Type privacy invasion, *malware,* installs, gathers, sends *without consent* (FTC, "Quick Facts")

 A. Some, Web-browsing habits, sell

 B. Capture passwords, identity theft

 C. Spooky, strokes, records

(**TRANSITION:**   Many confused . . . differences spyware, adware, malware, virus.)

 D. *Adware* display ads (*PC Magazine,* "Nine Ways")

  1. Annoying, no track you

  2. Spyware, stolen data, "the lair of its evil creator," Neil Rubenking ("Nine Ways")

 E. Viruses replicate

  1. Individuals, brag; spyware written corporate teams, make money (CNET Video)

  2. Viruses illegal, spyware legislation, failed passage (GovTrack.us, "I SPY")

(**TRANSITION:**   May be wondering . . . gains foothold . . .)

II. Different routes, programmed, browsing to theft

 A. Installs silently, "piggybacking" downloadable, free file-sharing, games

 B. Links, pop-ups, "unsubscribe" spam, known sources

 C. Legitimate antispyware, scareware, promise fix, install (Microsoft, "Fake Virus")

 D. Keystroke, spying, identity theft [SHOW SLIDE]

  1. Deliberately

  2. June 29, 2010, *Newsweek,* Jessica Ramirez, Smart-phone apps

(**TRANSITION:**   . . . Spyware lurks, social networking sites . . .)

 E. Clicking pop-ups, quizzes, groups, activate spyware

III. Symptoms, problems easy

 A. Sign infiltration, Google's Web search help page, stream, pop-up ads (Google, "Help")

 B. Strange toolbars [SHOW SLIDE]

 C. Browser settings hijacked, forcing strange Web

 D. Behave sluggishly, files, displaced, disappear, crash

(TRANSITION: Good news ... protect ...)

IV. Prevention, best way, harmful, potentially dangerous
    A. Good antispyware
        1. Microsoft, *Windows Defender* operating systems; free *Microsoft Security Essentials*
        2. *PC Magazine* Editor's Choice stand-alone malware protection *Spyware Doctor with Antivirus*; security suite *Norton Internet Security* (*PC Magazine*, "Free Virus and Spyware Protection")
        3. Free antispyware, *PC Magazine:* doesn't do thorough job; contains spyware

(TRANSITION: So along with antispyware software, else?)

    B. Browser up-to-date, security updates
    C. Don't install, fine print, check reviews
    D. Software, smartphone apps, know, trust
    E. Don't click links pop-up
    F. Reply, open spam, e-mail
    G. "Unsubscribe" spam, lurk here
    H. Maximum security, social media
    I. Strong passwords easily guessed; not smartphone automatically remember (ID Theft 911) [PAUSE]

CONCLUSION

I. Money, problem long-lasting
II. Spyware guises use personal stored computers, smartphones without consent, right steps, unwanted intrusions
III. Final, stay abreast, consult Stopbadware.org, StaySafeOnline.org
IV. Be vigilant, stay safe, luck!

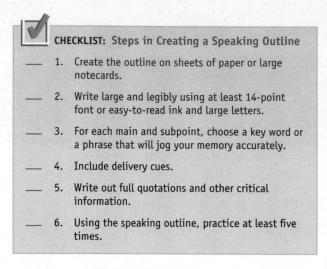

CHECKLIST: Steps in Creating a Speaking Outline

___ 1. Create the outline on sheets of paper or large notecards.

___ 2. Write large and legibly using at least 14-point font or easy-to-read ink and large letters.

___ 3. For each main and subpoint, choose a key word or a phrase that will jog your memory accurately.

___ 4. Include delivery cues.

___ 5. Write out full quotations and other critical information.

___ 6. Using the speaking outline, practice at least five times.

Part 4
Starting, Finishing, and Styling

15. Developing the Introduction and Conclusion 126
16. Using Language 133

15 Developing the Introduction and Conclusion

The introduction and conclusion, although not more important than the body of the speech, are equally essential to its success. A good opening previews what's to come in a way that engages listeners in the topic and establishes a tone of goodwill. An effective conclusion ensures that the audience remembers the speech and reacts in a way that the speaker intends.

Any kind of supporting material—examples, stories, testimony, facts, or statistics—can be used to open and conclude a speech as long as it accomplishes these objectives.

Preparing the Introduction

The choices you make about the introduction can affect the outcome of the entire speech. In the first several minutes (one speaker pegs it at ninety seconds),[1] audience members will decide whether they are interested in the topic of your speech, whether they will believe what you say, and whether they will give you their full attention.

A good introduction serves to:

- Arouse the audience's attention and willingness to listen.
- Introduce the topic and purpose.
- Establish your credibility to speak on the topic.
- Preview the main points.
- Motivate the audience to accept your speech goals.

CHECKLIST: Guidelines for Preparing the Introduction

✓ Prepare the introduction after you've completed the speech body so you will know exactly what you need to preview.

✓ Keep the introduction brief—as a rule, no more than 10 to 15 percent of the entire speech.

✓ Practice delivering your introduction until you feel confident you've got it right.

Gain Audience Attention

An introduction must first of all win the audience's attention. Some time-honored techniques include sharing a compelling quotation or story, posing a question, providing

126

unusual information, using humor, acknowledging the audience, and referring to the occasion.

USE A QUOTATION   A Czech proverb says, "Do not protect yourself by a fence but rather by your friends." A quotation that elegantly and succinctly expresses a theme of the speech will draw the audience's attention. Quotations can be culled from literature, poetry, and film, or directly from people you know.

TELL A STORY   Noted speechwriter and language expert William Safire once remarked that stories are "surefire attention getters."[2] Stories personalize issues by encouraging identification and making ideas relevant. And they are, importantly, entertaining. Speeches that begin with brief stories of interesting, humorous, or real-life incidents both motivate the audience to listen and promote greater understanding and retention of the speaker's message.[3]

POSE QUESTIONS   "Are you concerned about student loans?" Posing a question such as this can be an effective way to draw the audience's attention to what you are about to say. Questions can be real or rhetorical. **Rhetorical questions** do not invite actual responses. Instead, they make the audience think

OFFER UNUSUAL INFORMATION   "Virtually no one is having babies anymore in parts of Western Europe." Surprising audience members with startling or unusual facts and statistics is one of the surest ways to get their attention. Speakers frequently base their startling statements on statistics, a powerful means of illustrating consequences and relationships that can quickly bring points into focus.

USE HUMOR   Handled well, humor can build rapport and set a positive tone for the speech. Used ineffectively, however, humor can backfire. Simply telling a series of unrelated jokes without making a relevant point will detract from your purpose. And few things turn an audience off more quickly than tasteless humor. Strictly avoid humor or sarcasm that belittles others—whether on the basis of race, sex, ability, or otherwise. A good rule of thumb is that speech humor should always match the audience, topic, purpose, and occasion.

REFER TO THE AUDIENCE   Audiences are won over when speakers express interest in them and show that they share in the audience's concerns and goals. This creates goodwill and a feeling of common ground (or *identification;* see also Chapter 6). Finding common ground helps overcome the natural human divisions that separate people.[4] Use your knowledge of the audience to touch briefly on areas of shared experience.

REFER TO THE OCCASION   Introductions that include references to the speech occasion and to any relevant facts about the audience make listeners feel recognized as individuals. People appreciate the direct reference to the event, and they are interested in the meaning the speaker assigns to it.

Preview the Topic and Purpose

Once you've gained the audience's attention, use the introduction to alert listeners to the speech topic and purpose (see the Quick Tip below for exceptions to this rule). Declare what your speech is about and what you hope to accomplish.

Topic and purpose are clearly revealed in this introduction to a speech by Marvin Runyon, former postmaster general of the United States:

> This afternoon, I want to examine the truth of that statement—"Nothing moves people like the mail, and no one moves the mail like the U.S. Postal Service." I want to look at where we are today as a communications industry, and where we intend to be in the days and years ahead.[5]

QUICK TIP

When Not to Preview Your Topic
Usually, in the introduction you should inform the audience of your topic and purpose. However, when your purpose is to persuade, and the audience is not yet aware of this purpose, "forewarning" may predispose listeners in the opposite direction and thwart your persuasive goal. However, when the audience knows of your persuasive intent, previewing the topic and purpose can enhance understanding.[6]

Establish Credibility as a Speaker

During the introduction, audience members make a decision about whether they are interested not just in your topic but also in you. They want to know why they should believe you. To build credibility, make a simple statement of your qualifications for speaking on the topic. Briefly emphasize some experience, knowledge, or perspective you have that is different from or more extensive than that of your audience.

Preview the Main Points

Once you've revealed the topic and purpose and established your credibility, briefly preview the main points of the speech. This helps audience members mentally organize the speech as they follow along. Introductory previews are straightforward. You simply tell the audience what the main points will be and in what order you will address them. Save your in-depth discussion of each one for the body of your speech.

Robert L. Darbelnet effectively introduces his topic, purpose, and main points with this preview statement:

> My remarks today are intended to give you a sense of AAA's ongoing efforts to improve America's roads. Our hope is that you will join your voices to ours as we call on the federal government to do three things:
>
> Number one: Perhaps the most important, provide adequate funding for highway maintenance and improvements.
>
> Number two: Play a strong, responsible, yet flexible role in transportation programs.
>
> And number three: Invest in highway safety.
>
> Let's see what our strengths are, what the issues are, and what we can do about them.[7]

Motivate the Audience to Accept Your Goals

A critical function of the introduction is to motivate the audience to care about your topic and believe that it is relevant to them. One way to do this is to address your topic's practical implications and what the audience stands to gain by listening to you. Another is to convince audience members that your speech purpose is consistent with their motives and values. A student speech about the value of interview training shows how this can be accomplished:

> Let me start by telling you why you need interview training. It boils down to competition. As in sports, when you're not training, someone else is out there training to beat you. All things being equal, the person who has the best interviewing skills has got the edge.

> **QUICK TIP**
>
> **When Establishing Credibility Is Especially Key**
> Although it is always important to establish your credibility
> in the introduction, it is particularly so when the audience
> does not know you well and you must clearly establish your
> expertise.[8] In these situations, be sure to stress the reasons
> why audience members should trust you and believe what you
> have to say.

 CHECKLIST: How Effective is Your Introduction?

Does your introduction . . .

___ 1. Capture the audience's attention?

___ 2. Alert listeners to the speech purpose and topic?

___ 3. Establish your credibility?

___ 4. Indicate the main points of the speech?

___ 5. Motivate listeners to accept your speech goals?

Preparing the Conclusion

Conclusions give you the opportunity to drive home your
purpose, leaving the audience with ideas to think about and
even to act upon. The conclusion consists of several elements
that end the speech effectively. Conclusions serve to:

- Signal that the speech is coming to an end and provide
  closure.
- Summarize the key points.
- Reiterate the central idea of the speech.
- Challenge the audience to respond.
- End the speech memorably.

Signal the End of the Speech and Provide Closure

People who listen to speeches are taking a journey of sorts,
and they want and need the speaker to acknowledge the
journey's end. They look for logical and emotional closure.

One signal that a speech is about to end is a transitional
word or phrase: *finally, looking back, in conclusion, let me*

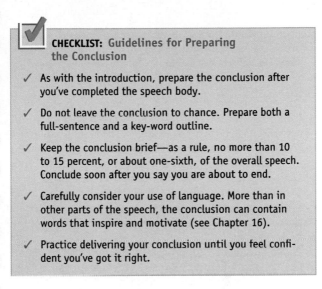

CHECKLIST: Guidelines for Preparing the Conclusion

✓ As with the introduction, prepare the conclusion after you've completed the speech body.

✓ Do not leave the conclusion to chance. Prepare both a full-sentence and a key-word outline.

✓ Keep the conclusion brief—as a rule, no more than 10 to 15 percent, or about one-sixth, of the overall speech. Conclude soon after you say you are about to end.

✓ Carefully consider your use of language. More than in other parts of the speech, the conclusion can contain words that inspire and motivate (see Chapter 16).

✓ Practice delivering your conclusion until you feel confident you've got it right.

close by saying (see Chapter 12). You can also signal closure by adjusting your manner of delivery; for example, you can vary your tone, pitch, rhythm, and rate of speech to indicate that the speech is winding down.

Once you've signaled the end of your speech, conclude in short order (though not abruptly).

Summarize the Key Points

One bit of age-old advice for giving a speech is "Tell them what you are going to tell them (in the introduction), tell them (in the body), and tell them what you told them (in the conclusion)." The idea is that emphasizing the main points three times will help the audience to remember them. A restatement of points in the conclusion brings the speech full circle and gives the audience a sense of completion.

Reiterate the Topic and Speech Purpose

The conclusion should reiterate the topic and speech purpose— to imprint it on the audience's memory. In the conclusion to a persuasive speech about the U.S. immigration debate, Elpidio Villarreal reminds his listeners of his central idea:

> Two paths are open to us. One path would keep us true to our fundamental values as a nation and a people. The other would lead us down a dark trail; one marked by 700-mile-long fences, emergency detention centers and vigilant border

patrols. Because I really am an American, heart and soul, and because that means never being without hope, I still believe we will ultimately choose the right path. We have to.[9]

Challenge the Audience to Respond

A strong conclusion challenges audience members to put to use what the speaker has shared with them. In an *informative speech*, the speaker challenges audience members to use what they've learned in a way that benefits them. In a *persuasive speech*, the challenge usually comes in the form of a **call to action**. Here the speaker challenges listeners to act in response to the speech, see the problem in a new way, or change both their actions and their beliefs about the problem.

Hillary Rodham Clinton makes a strong call to action in her conclusion to an address presented to the United Nations World Conference on Women:

> We have seen peace prevail in most places for a half century. We have avoided another world war. But we have not solved older, deeply rooted problems that continue to diminish the potential of half the world's population. *Now it is time to act on behalf of women everywhere.* If we take bold steps to better the lives of women, we will be taking bold steps to better the lives of children and families too.... Let this conference be our—and the world's—call to action.[10]

Make the Conclusion Memorable

A speech that makes a lasting impression is one that listeners are most likely to remember and act on. To accomplish this, make use of the same devices for capturing attention described for use in introductions—quotations, stories, questions, startling statements, humor, and references to the audience and the occasion.

QUICK TIP

Bring Your Speech Full Circle
Picking up on a story or an idea you mentioned in the introduction can be a memorable way to close a speech and bring the entire presentation full circle. You can provide the resolution of the story ("what happened next?") or reiterate the link between the moral (lesson) of the story and the speech theme.

> ☑️ **CHECKLIST: How Effective Is Your Conclusion?**
>
> Does your conclusion...
>
> _____ 1. Alert the audience that the speech is ending?
>
> _____ 2. Actually come to an end soon after you say you will finish?
>
> _____ 3. Last no more than about one-sixth of the time spent on the overall speech?
>
> _____ 4. Reiterate the main points?
>
> _____ 5. Remind listeners of the speech topic and purpose?
>
> _____ 6. Challenge the audience to respond to your ideas or appeals?
>
> _____ 7. Provide a sense of closure and make a lasting impression?

16 Using Language

In public speaking, choosing the right words is crucial to creating a dynamic connection with your audience and helping listeners understand, believe in, and retain your message.[1] **Style** is the specific word choices and **rhetorical devices** (techniques of language) speakers use to express their ideas. A speaker's style can make a speech colorful and convincing or bland and boring.

Prepare Your Speeches for the Ear

Whereas readers who fail to understand something can reread a passage or pause to look up an unfamiliar word, listeners have only one chance to get the message. Speeches should therefore be prepared for the ear, using familiar words, easy-to-follow sentences, repetition, and a direct form of address.

Strive for Simplicity

When selecting between two synonyms, choose the simpler term. Try to use fewer rather than more words, and shorter, rather than longer sentences. Translate **jargon**—the specialized, "insider" language of a given profession—into commonly understood terms. As speechwriter Peggy Noonan notes in her book *Simply Speaking*:

> Good hard simple words with good hard clear meanings are good things to use when you speak. They are like pickets in a fence, slim and unimpressive on their own but sturdy and effective when strung together.[2]

Make Frequent Use of Repetition

Good speeches, even very brief ones, often repeat key words and phrases. Repetition adds emphasis to important ideas, helps listeners follow your logic, and imbues language with rhythm and drama.

QUICK TIP

Experiment with Phrases and Sentence Fragments
To make your speech come alive, experiment with using phrases and sentence fragments in place of full sentences. This speaker, a physician, demonstrates how they can add punch to a speech: "I'm just a simple bone-and-joint guy. I can set your broken bones. Take away your bunions. Even give you a new hip. But I don't mess around with the stuff between the ears.... That's another specialty."[3]

Use Personal Pronouns

The direct form of address, using personal pronouns such as *we*, *us*, *I*, and *you*, draws the audience into the message and makes them feel recognized. Note how the following speaker uses personal pronouns to encourage involvement in his message:

> My talk today is about you. Each one of you personally. I know you hear many presentations. For the most part, they tend to be directed mostly to others with very little for you. My presentation today is different; the topic and the information will be important to every one of you.... I'm going to show and tell each of you how to become a verbal visionary.[4]

Following are some ways you can incorporate personal pronouns into your speeches:

"*I* am indebted to the ideas of…"

"Those of *us* who have lived during a world war…"

"To *me,* the truly great lessons…"

"Some of *you* will recall…"

Choose Concrete Words and Vivid Imagery

Concrete words and vivid imagery engage audience members' senses and encourage involvement. **Concrete language** is specific, tangible, and definite. Words such as "mountain," "spoon," "dark," and "heavy" describe things we can physically sense (see, hear, taste, smell, and touch). In contrast, abstract language is general or nonspecific, leaving meaning open to interpretation. Abstract words, such as "peace," "freedom," and "love," are purely conceptual; they have no physical reference. Politicians use abstract language to appeal to mass audiences, or to be noncommittal: "We strive for peace." In most speaking situations, however, listeners will appreciate concrete nouns and verbs.

Experiment with concrete imagery to clarify key speech points. Trade weak and mundane verbs with those that are strong and colorful. Rather than "walk," you can say "saunter"; in place of "look," use "gaze."

Offer Vivid Imagery

Imagery is concrete language that brings into play the senses of smell, taste, sight, hearing, and touch to paint mental pictures. Speeches containing ample imagery elicit more positive responses than those that do not.[5]

Create vivid images by modifying nouns with descriptive adjectives. President Franklin D. Roosevelt used this technique when he portrayed the Japanese bombing of Pearl Harbor as "the dark hour,"[6] conveying with one simple adjective the gravity of the attack.

Use Figures of Speech

Figures of speech, including similes, metaphors, and analogies, make striking comparisons between the unfamiliar and the known, allowing listeners to more quickly grasp meaning. A **simile** explicitly compares one thing to another, using *like* or *as*: "He works like a dog," and "The old woman's hands were as soft as a baby's." A **metaphor** also compares two things, but does so by describing one thing as actually *being* the other: "Time is a thief."

An **analogy** is simply an extended metaphor or simile that compares an unfamiliar concept or process to a more familiar one. Analogies help emphasize or explain key ideas or processes to an audience. For example, note how African American minister Phil Wilson used metaphoric language when he preached to his congregation in Los Angeles about the dangers of AIDS:

> Our house is on fire! The fire truck arrives, but we won't come out, because we're afraid the folks from next door will see that we're in that burning house. AIDS is a fire raging in our community and it's out of control![7]

As useful as analogies are, they can be misleading if used carelessly—as they often are. A weak or **faulty analogy** is an inaccurate or misleading comparison suggesting that because two things are similar in some ways, they are necessarily similar in others. (See Chapter 24 for a discussion of other logical fallacies.)

QUICK TIP

Avoid Clichés and Mixed Metaphors
*Try not to use tired metaphors and similes, known as clichés. A **cliché** is a predictable and stale comparison such as "sold like hotcakes" (a clichéd simile), "pearly white teeth" (a clichéd metaphor). Beware, too, of **mixed metaphors**, those that juxtapose unlike images or expressions: for example, "burning the midnight oil at both ends" incorrectly joins two (clichéd) expressions "burning the midnight oil" and "burning the candle at both ends."*

Choose Words That Build Credibility

To gain trust and credibility, use language that is appropriate, accurate, assertive, and respectful.

Use Words Appropriately

As a rule, strive to uphold the conventional rules of grammar and usage associated with General American (GA) English, but as prepared for the ear. The more formal the occasion, the closer you will want to remain within these conventional bounds. Listeners view speakers who use General American English as more competent—though not necessarily more trustworthy or likable—than those who speak in a distinctive dialect (regional variation of speech).[8]

At times it may be appropriate to mix casual language, dialects, or even slang into your speech. Done carefully, the selective use of dialect, sometimes called **code-switching**, can imbue your speech with friendliness, humor, earthiness, honesty, and nostalgia.[9] The key is to ensure that your meaning is clear and your use is appropriate for your audience. Consider the following excerpt:

> On the gulf where I was raised, *el valle del Rio Grande* in South Texas—that triangular piece of land wedged between the river *y el golfo* which serves as the Texas–U.S./Mexican border—is a Mexican *pueblito* called Hargill. [10]

Use Words Accurately

Audiences lose confidence in speakers who misuse words. Check that your words mean what you intend, and beware of **malapropisms**—the inadvertent, incorrect uses of a word or phrase in place of one that sounds like it[11] ("It's a strange receptacle" for "It's a strange spectacle").

QUICK TIP

Avoid the "Shock Jock" Syndrome
"Shock Jock" is an informal term for a radio host who uses suggestive language, bathroom humor, and obscene references. These (ab)uses of language are never appropriate in a public speech event. Even those audience members who otherwise might not object to off-color material will react to it unfavorably.

Use the Active Voice

Speaking in the active rather than passive voice will make your statements clear and assertive instead of indirect and weak. **Voice** is the feature of verbs that indicates the subject's relationship to the action. A verb is in the *active voice* when the subject performs the action, and in the *passive voice* when the subject is acted upon or is the receiver of the action:

PASSIVE:	A test was announced by Ms. Carlos for Tuesday.
	A president is elected every four years.
ACTIVE:	Ms. Carlos announced a test for Tuesday.
	The voters elect a president every four years.

Use Culturally Sensitive and Gender-Neutral Language

Be alert to using language that reflects respect for audience members' cultural beliefs, norms, and traditions. Review and eliminate any language that reflects unfounded assumptions, negative descriptions, or stereotypes of a given group's age, class, gender, ability, geographic, ethnic, racial, or religious characteristics. Consider, too, whether certain seemingly well-known names and terms may be foreign to some listeners, and include brief explanations for them. Sayings specific to a certain region or group of people (termed **colloquial expressions** or *idioms*) such as "back the wrong horse" and "ballpark figure" can add color and richness to a speech, but only if listeners understand them.

Word your speech with gender-neutral language: Avoid the third-person generic masculine pronouns (*his, he*) in favor of inclusive pronouns such as *his or her, he or she, we, our, you, your*, or other gender-neutral terms (e.g., instead of "police/mailman," use "police officer" and "mail carrier"; replace "mankind" with "humankind" or "humans" and "anchor/chairman" with "news anchor," "chair," . . .).

Choose Words That Create a Lasting Impression

Oral language that is artfully arranged and infused with rhythm draws listeners in and leaves a lasting impression on audience members. You can create a cadenced arrangement of language through rhetorical devices such as repetition, alliteration, and parallelism.

QUICK TIP

Denotative versus Connotative Meaning

*When drafting your speech, choose words that are both deno-tatively and connotatively appropriate to the audience. The **denotative meaning** of a word is its literal, or dictionary, definition. The **connotative meaning** of a word is the special (often emotional) association that different people bring to bear on it. For example, you may agree that you are "angry," but not "irate," and "thrifty" but not "cheap." Consider how the connotative meanings of your word choices might affect the audience's response to your message, including those of non-native speakers of English.*

Use Repetition to Create Rhythm

Repeating key words, phrases, or even sentences at various intervals throughout a speech creates a distinctive rhythm and thereby implants important ideas in listeners' minds.

Repetition works particularly well when delivered with the appropriate voice inflections and pauses.

In a form of repetition called **anaphora**, the speaker repeats a word or phrase at the beginning of successive phrases, clauses, or sentences. For example, in his speech delivered in 1963 in Washington DC, Dr. Martin Luther King Jr. repeated the phrase "I have a dream" numerous times, each with an upward inflection followed by a pause. Speakers have made use of anaphora since earliest times. For example, Jesus preached:

> Blessed are the poor in spirit....
>
> Blessed are the meek....
>
> Blessed are the peacemakers....[12]

Repetition can help to create a thematic focus for a speech. Speakers often do this by using both anaphora and *epiphora* in the same speech. Rather than at the beginning of successive statements, in **epiphora** (also called *epistrophe*) the repetition of a word or phrase appears at the end of them. In a speech to his New Hampshire supporters, Barack Obama used both anaphora and epiphora to establish a theme of empowerment (italics added):

> *It was* a creed written into the founding documents that declared the destiny of a nation: *Yes we can.*
>
> *It was* whispered by slaves and abolitionists as they blazed a trail toward freedom through the darkest of nights: *Yes we can.*
>
> *It was* sung by immigrants as they struck out from distant shores and pioneers who pushed westward against an unforgiving wilderness: *Yes we can.*[13]

Use Alliteration for a Poetic Quality

Alliteration is the repetition of the same sounds, usually initial consonants, in two or more neighboring words or syllables. Alliteration lends speech a poetic, musical rhythm. Classic examples of alliteration in speeches include phrases such as Jesse Jackson's "Down with dope, up with hope" and former U.S. Vice-President Spiro Agnew's disdainful reference to the U.S. press as "nattering nabobs of negativism."

Experiment with Parallelism

The arrangement of words, phrases, or sentences in a similar form is known as **parallelism**. Parallel structure can help the speaker emphasize important ideas, and can be as simple as orally numbering points ("first, second, and third"). Like repetition, it also creates a sense of steady or building rhythm.[14] Speakers often make use of three parallel elements, called a *triad*:

> ...of the people, by the people, and for the people...
> —Abraham Lincoln

Parallelism in speeches often makes use of **antithesis**—setting off two ideas in balanced (parallel) opposition to each other to create a powerful effect:

> One small step for a man, one giant leap for mankind.
> —Neil Armstrong on the moon, 1969

> For many are called, but few are chosen. —Matthew 22:14

✓ CHECKLIST: Use Language Effectively

✓ Use familiar words, easy-to-follow sentences, and straightforward syntax.

✓ Root out **biased language**.

✓ Avoid unnecessary jargon.

✓ Use fewer rather than more words to express your thoughts.

✓ Make striking comparisons with *similes*, *metaphors*, and *analogies*.

✓ Use the active voice.

✓ Repeat key words, phrases, or sentences at the beginning of successive sentences (*anaphora*) and at their close (*epiphora*).

✓ Experiment with *alliteration*—words that repeat the same sounds, usually initial consonants, in two or more neighboring words or syllables.

✓ Experiment with *parallelism*—arranging words, phrases, or sentences in similar form.

Part 5
Delivery

17. Choosing a Method of Delivery 142
18. Controlling the Voice 146
19. Using the Body 150

The delivery of a speech is the moment of truth. For most of us, delivery makes us feel anxious because this is the moment when all eyes are upon us. In fact, effective delivery rests on the same natural foundation as everyday conversation.[1] Focusing on the quality of naturalness can help you reduce the fear of delivery and make your presentations more authentic.

Strive for Naturalness and Enthusiasm

Effective **delivery** is the controlled use of voice and body to express the qualities of naturalness, enthusiasm, confidence, and directness. Audiences respond most favorably to speakers who project these characteristics during delivery.

- *Strive for naturalness.* Rather than behaving theatrically, act naturally. Think of your speech as a particularly important conversation.

- *Show enthusiasm.* Speak about what interests and excites you. Inspire your listeners by showing enthusiasm for your topic and for the occasion. An enthusiastic delivery helps you feel good about your speech, and it focuses your audience's attention on the message.

- *Project a sense of confidence.* Focus on the ideas you want to convey rather than on yourself. Inspire the audience's confidence in you by appearing confident to them.

- *Engage directly with audience members.* Demonstrate your interest and concern for listeners by establishing eye contact, using a friendly tone of voice, and smiling whenever it is appropriate. Consider positioning yourself so that you are physically close to the audience.

Select a Method of Delivery

For virtually any type of speech or presentation, you can choose from four basic methods of delivery: speaking from manuscript; speaking from memory; speaking impromptu; and speaking extemporaneously.

Speaking from Manuscript

When **speaking from manuscript**, you read a speech *verbatim*—that is, from prepared written text that contains the entire speech, word for word. As a rule, speaking from manuscript restricts eye contact and body movement, and may also limit expressiveness in vocal variety and quality. Watching a speaker read a speech can be monotonous and boring for the audience.

There are times, however, when it is advisable or necessary to read a speech—for example, when you must convey a very precise message, when you will be quoted and must avoid misinterpretation, or when you must address an emergency and need to convey exact descriptions and directions (see Chapter 34 on crisis communication).

If you must read from a prepared text, do what you can to deliver the speech naturally:

- Vary the rhythm of your words (see Chapter 18).

- Become familiar enough with the speech so that you can establish some eye contact.

- Use a large font and double- or triple-space the manuscript so that you can read without straining.

- Consider using some compelling presentation aids (see Chapter 20).

Speaking from Memory

The formal name for **speaking from memory** is **oratory**. In oratorical style, you put the entire speech, word for word, into writing and then commit it to memory. In the United States, speaking from memory rarely occurs anymore, though this form of delivery is common in other parts of the world.[2]

Memorization is not a natural way to present a message. True eye contact with the audience is unlikely, and memorization invites potential disaster during a speech because there is always the possibility of a mental lapse or block. Some kinds of brief speeches, however, such as toasts and introductions, can be well served by memorization. Sometimes it's helpful to memorize a part of the speech, especially when you use direct quotations as a form of support. If you do find an occasion to use memorization, learn that portion of your speech so completely that in actual delivery you can convey enthusiasm and directness.

Speaking Impromptu

Speaking impromptu, a type of delivery that is unpracticed, spontaneous, or improvised, involves speaking on relatively short notice with little time to prepare. Many occasions require that you make some remarks on the spur of the moment. An instructor may ask you to summarize key points from an assignment, for example, or a fellow employee who was scheduled to speak on a new project may be sick and your boss invites you to take his or her place.

Try to anticipate situations that may require you to speak impromptu, and prepare some remarks beforehand. Otherwise, maximize the time you do have to prepare on the spot:

- Think first about your listeners. Consider their interests and needs, and try to shape your remarks accordingly. For example, who are the people present, and what are their views on the topic?

- Listen to what others around you are saying. Take notes in a key-word or phrase format and arrange them into main points from which you can speak.

- If your speech follows someone else's, acknowledge that person's statements. Then make your points.

- Stay on the topic. Don't wander off track.

- Use transitions such as "first," "second," and "third," both to organize your points and to help listeners follow them.

As much as possible, try to organize your points into a discernible pattern. If addressing a problem, for example, such as a project failure or glitch, consider the problem-solution pattern—state problem(s), then offer solution(s); or the cause-effect pattern of organizational arrangement—state cause(s) first, then address effect(s); see Chapter 13 for various ways of using these patterns. If called upon to defend one proposal as superior to another, consider using the comparative advantage pattern to illustrate various advantages of your favored proposal over the other options (see Chapter 24, p. 206).

Speaking Extemporaneously

Speaking extemporaneously falls somewhere between impromptu and written or memorized deliveries. In an extemporaneous speech, you prepare well and practice in advance, giving full attention to all facets of the speech—content, arrangement, and delivery alike. Instead of memorizing or writing the speech word for word, you speak from an outline of key words and phrases (see Chapter 14), having concentrated throughout your preparation and practice on the ideas that you want to communicate.

More speeches are delivered by extemporaneous delivery than by any other method. Because this technique is most conducive to achieving a natural, conversational quality of delivery, many speakers prefer it among the four types of delivery. Knowing your idea well enough to present it without memorization or manuscript gives you greater flexibility in adapting to the specific speaking situation. You can modify wording, rearrange your points, change examples, or omit information in keeping with the audience and the setting. You can have more eye contact, more direct body orientation, greater freedom of movement, and generally better control of your thoughts and actions than any of the other delivery methods allow.

Speaking extemporaneously does present a possible drawback. Occasionally, even a glance at your speaking notes may fail to jog your memory on a point you wanted to cover, and you momentarily find yourself searching for what to say next. The remedy for this potential pitfall is frequent practice using a speaking outline.

METHODS OF DELIVERY AND THEIR PROBABLE USES	
WHEN...	METHOD OF DELIVERY
✓ Precise wording is called for; for instance, when you want to avoid being misquoted or misconstrued, or you need to communicate exact descriptions and directions...	Consider *speaking from manuscript* (reading part or all of your speech from fully prepared text).
✓ You must deliver a short special-occasion speech, such as a toast or an introduction, or you plan on using direct quotations...	Consider *speaking from memory* (memorizing part or all of your speech).
✓ You are called upon to speak without prior planning or preparation...	Consider *speaking impromptu* (organizing your thoughts with little or no lead time).
✓ You have time to prepare and practice developing a speech or presentation that achieves a natural conversational style...	Consider *speaking extemporaneously* (developing your speech in working outline and then practicing and delivering it with a phrase or key-word outline).

18 Controlling the Voice

Used properly in the delivery of a speech, the voice signals a speaker's confidence and credibility and communicates meaning as he or she intends.[1] With a bit of practice, you can learn to control each of the elements of vocal delivery—volume, pitch, speaking rate, pauses, vocal variety, and pronunciation and articulation—to deliver a successful speech.

Adjust Your Speaking Volume

Volume, the relative loudness of a speaker's voice while delivering a speech, is usually the most obvious vocal element we notice about a speaker, and with good reason. We need to hear the speaker at a comfortable level. *The proper volume for delivering a speech is somewhat louder than that of normal conversation.* Just how much louder depends on three factors: (1) the size of the room and of the audience, (2) whether or not you use a microphone, and (3) the level of background noise. Speaking at the appropriate volume is critical to how credible your listeners will perceive you to be, so check that audience members can hear you. Be alert to signals that your volume is slipping or is too loud and make the necessary adjustments.

QUICK TIP

Breathe from Your Diaphragm

To project your voice so that it is loud enough to be heard by everyone in the audience, breathe deeply from your diaphragm rather than more shallowly from your vocal cords. The reason? The strength of our voices depends on the amount of air the diaphragm—a large, dome-shaped muscle encasing the inner ribcage—pushes from the lungs to the vocal cords.

Vary Your Intonation

Pitch is the range of sounds from high to low (or vice versa). Vocal pitch is important in speechmaking because it powerfully affects the meaning associated with spoken words. For example, say "stop." Now, say "Stop!" Hear the difference? This rising and falling of vocal pitch across phrases and sentences, termed **intonation**, conveys two very distinct meanings.

As you speak, pitch conveys your mood, level of enthusiasm, concern for the audience, and overall commitment to the occasion. When there is no variety in pitch, speaking becomes monotonous—a death knell to any speech.

Adjust Your Speaking Rate

Speaking rate is the pace at which you convey speech. The normal rate of speech for native English speaking adults is roughly between 120 and 150 words per minute, but there is no standard, ideal, or most effective rate. If the rate is too slow, it may lull the audience to sleep. If your speech is too fast, listeners may see you as unsure about your control of the speech.[2]

Being alert to the audience's reactions is the best way to know whether your rate of speech is too fast or too slow. Some serious topics benefit from a slower speech rate; a lively pace generally corresponds with a lighter tone. An audience will get fidgety, bored, listless, perhaps even sleepy if you speak too slowly. If you speak too rapidly, listeners will appear irritated and confused, as though they can't catch what you're saying.

QUICK TIP

Control Your Rate of Speaking
To control your speaking rate, choose 150 words from your speech and time yourself for one minute as you read them aloud. If you fall very short of finishing, increase your pace. If you finish well before the minute is up, slow down. Practice until you achieve a comfortable speaking rate.

Use Strategic Pauses

Pauses enhance meaning by providing a type of punctuation, emphasizing a point, drawing attention to a thought, or just allowing listeners a moment to contemplate what is being said. In short, they make a speech far more effective than it might otherwise be. Both the speaker and the audience need pauses.

QUICK TIP

Avoid Meaningless Vocal Fillers
*Many novice speakers are uncomfortable with pauses. It's as if there were a social stigma attached to any silence in a speech. We often react the same way in conversation, covering pauses with unnecessary and undesirable **vocal fillers** such as "uh," "hmm," "you know," "I mean," and "it's like." Like pitch, however, pauses are important strategic elements of a speech. Use them purposefully, taking care to eliminate distracting vocal fillers.*

Strive for Vocal Variety

Rather than operating separately, all the vocal elements described so far—volume, pitch, speaking rate, and pauses—work together to create vocal variety. Indeed, the real key to effective vocal delivery is to vary all these elements with a tone of enthusiasm. Vocal variety comes quite naturally when you are excited about what you are saying to an audience, when you feel it is important and want to share it with them.

CHECKLIST: Practice Check for Vocal Effectiveness

___ 1. As you practice, does your voice project authority?

___ 2. Is your voice too loud? Too soft?

___ 3. Do you avoid speaking in a monotone? Do you vary the stress or emphasis you place on words to clearly express your meaning?

___ 4. Is your rate of speech comfortable for listeners?

___ 5. Do you avoid unnecessary vocal fillers, such as "uh," "hmm," "you know," and "I mean"?

___ 6. Do you use silent pauses for strategic effect?

___ 7. Does your voice reflect a variety of emotional expressions? Do you convey enthusiasm?

Carefully Pronounce and Articulate Words

Few things distract an audience more than improper pronunciation or unclear articulation of words. **Pronunciation** is the correct formation of word sounds—examples of mispronunciation include, "aks" for "asked" (*askt*), and "jen yu wine" for "genuine" (jen yu *in*). **Articulation** is the clarity or forcefulness with which the sounds are made, regardless of whether they are pronounced correctly. Incorrect pronunciation and poor articulation are largely a matter of habit. It is important to pay attention to and work on both areas.

A very common pattern of poor articulation is **mumbling**—slurring words together at a low level of volume and pitch so that they are barely audible. Sometimes the problem is **lazy speech**. Common examples are saying "fer" instead of "for" and "wanna" instead of "want to."

Like any habit, poor articulation can be overcome by unlearning the problem behavior:

- If you mumble, practice speaking more loudly and with emphatic pronunciation.

- If you tend toward lazy speech, put more effort into your articulation.

- Consciously try to say each word clearly and correctly.

- Practice clear and precise enunciation of proper word sounds. Say "articulation" several times until it rolls off your tongue naturally.

- Do the same for these words: "want to," "going to," "Atlanta," "chocolate," "sophomore," "California."

CHECKLIST: Tips on Using a Microphone

✓ Always do a sound check with the microphone before delivering your speech.

✓ When you first speak into the microphone, ask your listeners if they can hear you clearly.

✓ Speak directly into the microphone; if you turn your head or body, you won't be heard.

✓ To avoid broadcasting private statements, beware of "open" mikes.

✓ When wearing a **lavaliere microphone** attached to your lapel or collar, speak as if you were addressing a small group. The amplifier will do the rest.

✓ When using a *handheld* or *fixed microphone*, beware of *popping*. Popping occurs when you use sharp consonants such as "p," "t," and "d" and the air hits the mike. To prevent popping, move the microphone slightly below your mouth and about six inches away.[3]

Use Dialect (Language Variation) with Care

A **dialect** is a distinctive way of speaking associated with a particular region or social group. Dialects such as Cajun, Appalachian English, and Ebonics (Black English) differ from standard language patterns such as General American English (GAE) in pronunciation, grammar, or vocabulary. Although dialects are neither superior nor inferior to standard language patterns, the audience must be able to understand and relate to the speaker's language. As you practice your delivery, ensure that your pronunciation and word usage can be understood by all audience members.

REGULAR LANGUAGE PATTERNS IN SELECTED DIALECTS	
Appalachia	The *uh* sound before words ending in "ing" (She's a-fishing today)
Urban African American	The use of *be* to denote activities (She be fishing all the time)
Rural Southern	The absence of the plural *s* inflection (She ran four *mile*)[4]

19   Using the Body

Pay Attention to Body Language

As audience members listen to you, they are simultaneously evaluating the messages sent by your facial expressions, eye behavior, gestures, and general body movements. Audiences do not so much listen to a speaker's words as "read" the **body language** of the speaker who delivers them.[1]

Research confirms the importance of body language. One study suggests that when speakers talk about their feelings and attitudes, the audience derives a mere *7 percent* of the speaker's meaning from the words they utter. The balance comes from the speaker's **nonverbal communication**: 38 percent from the speaker's voice, and 55 percent from the speaker's body language and appearance.[2]

Animate Your Facial Expressions

From our facial expressions, audiences can gauge whether we are excited about, disenchanted by, or indifferent to our speech—and the audience to whom we are presenting it.

Few behaviors are more effective for building rapport with an audience than *smiling*. A smile is a sign of mutual welcome at the start of a speech, of mutual comfort and interest during the speech, and of mutual goodwill at the close of a speech. In addition, smiling when you feel nervous or otherwise uncomfortable can help you relax and gain heightened composure. Of course, facial expressions need to correspond to the tenor of the speech. Doing what is natural and normal for the occasion should be the rule.

CHECKLIST: Tips for Using Effective Facial Expressions

✓ Use animated expressions that feel natural and express your meaning.

✓ Avoid a deadpan expression.

✓ Never use expressions that are out of character for you or inappropriate to the speech occasion.

✓ In practice sessions, loosen your facial features with exercises such as widening the eyes and moving the mouth.

✓ Establish rapport with the audience by smiling naturally when appropriate.

Maintain Eye Contact

If smiling is an effective way to build rapport, maintaining eye contact is mandatory in establishing a positive relationship with your listeners. Having eye contact with the audience is one of the most, if not *the* most, important physical actions in public speaking. Eye contact does the following:

- Maintains the quality of directness in speech delivery.
- Lets people know they are recognized.
- Indicates acknowledgment and respect.
- Signals to audience members that you see them as unique human beings.

With an audience of one hundred to more than a thousand, it's impossible to look at every listener. But in most speaking situations you are likely to experience, you should be able to make the audience feel recognized by using a technique called **scanning**. When you scan an audience, you move your gaze from one listener to another and from one section to another, pausing to gaze at one person long enough to complete one thought. Be certain to give each section of the room equal attention.

Use Gestures That Feel Natural

Words alone seldom suffice to convey what we want to express. Physical gestures fill in the gaps, as in illustrating the size or shape of an object (e.g., by showing the size of it by extending two hands, palms facing each other), or expressing the depth of an emotion (e.g., by pounding a fist on a podium). Gestures should arise from genuine emotions and should conform to your personality.[3]

- Use natural, spontaneous gestures.
- Avoid exaggerated gestures, but use gestures that are broad enough to be seen by each audience member.
- Eliminate distracting gestures, such as fidgeting with pens or pencils, brushing back hair from your eyes, or jingling coins in your pockets.
- Analyze your gestures for effectiveness in practice sessions.
- Practice movements that feel natural to you.

Create a Feeling of Immediacy

In most Western cultures, listeners learn more from and respond most positively to speakers who create a perception of physical and psychological closeness, called **nonverbal immediacy**, between themselves and audience members.[4] An enthusiastic vocal delivery, frequent eye contact, animated facial expressions, and natural body movements are the keys to establishing immediacy.

Audience members soon tire of listening to a **talking head** that remains steadily positioned in one place behind a microphone or a podium. Use your physical position vis-à-vis audience members to adjust your relationship with them, establishing a level of familiarity and closeness that is appropriate to the topic, purpose, and occasion. Movement towards listeners stimulates a sense of informality and closeness; remaining behind the podium fosters a more formal relationship of speaker to audience.

QUICK TIP

Stand Straight

A speaker's posture sends a definite message to the audience. Listeners perceive speakers who slouch as being sloppy, unfocused, or even weak. Strive to stand erect, but not ramrod straight. The goal should be to appear authoritative but not rigid.

Dress Appropriately

Superficial as it may sound, the first thing an audience is likely to notice about you as you approach the speaker's position is your clothing. The critical criteria in determining appropriate dress for a speech are audience expectations and the nature of the speech occasion. If you are speaking as a representative of your business, for example, you will want to complement your company's image.[5]

An extension of dress is the possession of various objects on or around your person while giving a speech—pencil and pen, a briefcase, a glass of water, or papers with notes on them. Always ask yourself if these objects are really necessary. A sure way to distract an audience from what you're saying is to drag a briefcase or a backpack to the speaker's stand and open it while speaking, or to fumble with a pen or other object.

> ✓ **CHECKLIST:** Broad Dress Code Guidelines
>
> ✓ For a "power" look, wear a dark-colored suit.
>
> ✓ Medium or dark blue paired with white can enhance your credibility.
>
> ✓ Yellow and orange color tones convey friendliness.
>
> ✓ The color red focuses attention on you.
>
> ✓ Flashy jewelry distracts listeners.

Practice the Delivery

Practice is essential to effective delivery. The more you practice, the greater your comfort level will be when you actually deliver the speech. More than anything, it is uncertainty that breeds anxiety. By practicing your speech using a fully developed speaking outline, you will know what to expect when you actually stand in front of an audience.

> **QUICK TIP**
>
> *Learn from the Legends*
> *Apple cofounder Steve Jobs was such an effective speaker that whole books have been devoted to his techniques. As Apple CEO, Jobs delivered his presentations without notes and spoke in a conversational style, making emotional connections with his audience. But while Jobs projected an image of casualness, the time he devoted to preparation and practice is legendary.[6]*

Focus on the Message

The primary purpose of any speech is to get a message across, not to display extraordinary delivery skills. Keep this goal foremost in your mind. Psychologically, too, focusing on your message is likely to make your delivery more natural and confident.

Plan Ahead and Practice Often

If possible, begin practicing your speech at least several days before you are scheduled to deliver it.

- Practice with your speaking notes, revising those parts of the speech that aren't satisfactory, and altering the notes as you go.
- Focus on your speech ideas rather than on yourself.
- Time each part of your speech—introduction, body, and conclusion.
- Practice with any presentation aids you plan to use.
- Practice your speech several times, and then record it with a tape recorder.
- If possible, videotape yourself twice—once after several practice sessions, and again after you've worked to incorporate any changes into your speech.
- Visualize the setting in which you will speak, and practice the speech under realistic conditions, paying particular attention to projecting your voice to fill the room.
- Practice in front of at least one volunteer, and seek constructive criticism.
- Schedule your practice sessions early in the process so that you have time to prepare.

QUICK TIP

Practice Five Times
Many expert speakers recommend practicing your speech about five times in its final form. Given that few speeches are longer than twenty minutes, and most are shorter, this represents a maximum of two hours of practice time—time certainly well spent.

Part 6
Presentation Aids

20. Speaking with Presentation Aids 156
21. Designing Presentation Aids 161
22. A Brief Guide to Microsoft PowerPoint 164

Presentation aids can help listeners process and retain information, convey information in a time-saving fashion, and enhance an image of professionalism. Designed well and used with care, aids can spark interest and even make a speech memorable.

Most people process and retain information best when it is presented both verbally and visually. That is, we learn better from words and pictures than from words alone, a principle dubbed the "multimedia effect."[1] However, no matter how powerful a photograph, chart, or other presentation aid may be, the audience will be less interested in merely gazing at it than in discovering how you will relate it to a specific point. Emphasis should be on using the aids to further the audience's understanding and not on the aids themselves.[2]

Select an Appropriate Aid

Presentation aids include objects, models, pictures, graphs, charts, audio, video, and multimedia. Select the aid, or combination of aids, that will help audience members grasp information most effectively.

Props and Models

A **prop** can be any inanimate or even live object—a stone or a snake, for instance—that captures the audience's attention and illustrates or emphasizes key points. A **model** is a three-dimensional, scale-size representation of an object. Presentations in engineering, architecture, medicine, and many other disciplines often make use of models. When using a prop or model:

- In most cases, keep the prop or model hidden until you are ready to use it.
- Make sure it is big enough for everyone to see (and read, if applicable).
- Practice your speech using the prop or model.

Pictures

Pictures are two-dimensional representations and include photographs, line drawings, diagrams, maps, and posters. A *diagram* (also called a "schematic drawing") visually explains how something works or is made or operates. *Maps* help listeners visualize geographic areas and understand relationships among them; they also illustrate the proportion of one thing to something else in different areas.

Graphs and Charts

A **graph** represents relationships among two or more things. Four types of graphs are line graphs, bar graphs, pie graphs, and pictograms.

A *line graph* uses points connected by lines to demonstrate how something changes or fluctuates in value.

A *bar graph* uses bars of varying lengths to compare quantities or magnitudes; bars may be arranged either vertically or horizontally. When creating line and bar graphs:

- Label both axes and start the numerical axis at zero.
- Compare only like variables.
- Put no more than two lines of data on one line graph.

A *pie graph* depicts the division of a whole into slices. Each slice constitutes a percentage of the whole. When creating pie graphs:

- Restrict the number of pie slices to a maximum of seven.
- Identify and accurately represent the values or percentages of each pie slice.

A *pictogram* uses picture symbols (icons) to illustrate relationships and trends; for example, a generic-looking human figure repeated in a row can demonstrate increasing enrollment in college over time. When creating pictograms:

- Clearly indicate what the pictogram symbolizes.
- Make all pictograms the same size.
- Label the axes of the pictogram.

A **chart** visually organizes complex information into compact form. Several different types of charts help listeners grasp key points.

A **flowchart** diagrams the progression of a process, helping viewers visualize a sequence or directional flow.

A **table** (tabular chart) systematically groups data in column form, allowing viewers to examine and make comparisons about information quickly.

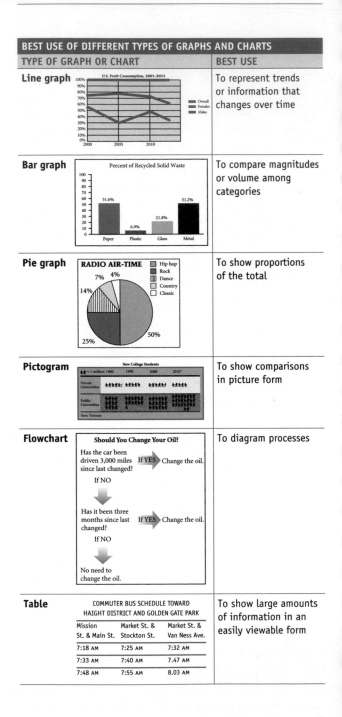

TYPE OF GRAPH OR CHART	BEST USE
Line graph	To represent trends or information that changes over time
Bar graph	To compare magnitudes or volume among categories
Pie graph	To show proportions of the total
Pictogram	To show comparisons in picture form
Flowchart	To diagram processes
Table	To show large amounts of information in an easily viewable form

Audio, Video, and Multimedia

Introducing an *audio clip*—a short recording of sounds, music, or speech—can enliven certain presentations. Similarly, *video*—including movie, television, and other recording instruments—can serve to motivate attention by helping to introduce, transition into, and clarify points.[3] (See Chapter 22 for guidelines on linking audio and video clips to PowerPoint slides.) **Multimedia**, which combines stills, sound, video, text, and data into a single production, requires more planning than other forms of presentation aids. Producing multimedia requires familiarity with presentation software programs such as Windows Live Movie Maker and Apple iMovie. When incorporating audio and video into your presentation:

- Use the audio or video clip in a manner consistent with copyright.
- Cue the audio or video clip to the appropriate segment before the presentation.
- Alert audience members to what they will be hearing or viewing before you play it back.
- Reiterate the relevance of the audio or video clip to your key points once it is over.

Decide How to Present the Aid

Many presenters create computer-generated aids shown with digital projectors or LCD displays. On the more traditional side, options for presenting the aids to the audience include overhead transparencies, flip charts, chalkboards, posters, and handouts.

Computer-Generated Aids and Displays

With software programs such as Microsoft PowerPoint and Apple Keynote, speakers can create computer-generated slides, which they project using **LCD** (liquid crystal display) **panels** and projectors or the newer **DLP** (digital light processing) **projectors**. See Chapter 22 for guidelines on using presentation software.

Overhead Transparencies

An **overhead transparency** is an image printed on clear acetate that can be viewed by projection. You can create transparencies in advance using PowerPoint, or write on the transparency during the presentation, much like a chalk-board. When using overhead transparencies:

- Check that the projector is in good order before the speech.
- Stand to the *side* of the projector and face the *audience,* not the projected image.
- Use a pointer to indicate specific sections of a transparency—point to the transparency, not to the screen.
- If writing on the transparency, use a water-soluble trans-parency pen and write clearly.
- Cover the transparencies when finished using them.

Flip Charts

A **flip chart** is simply a large (27–34 inch) pad of paper on which a speaker can write or draw. They are often prepared in advance; then, as you progress through the speech, you simply flip through the pad to the next exhibit. You can also write and draw on the pad as you speak.

QUICK TIP

Hold the Handouts

*A **handout** conveys information that either is impractical to give to the audience in another manner or is intended to be kept by audience members after the presentation. To avoid distracting listeners, unless you specifically want them to read the information as you speak,* wait until you are fin-ished before you distribute the handout. *If you do want the audience to view a handout during the speech, pass it out only when you are ready to talk about it.*

Posters

Speakers use **posters**—large paperboards incorporating text, figures, and images, alone or in combination—to illustrate some aspect of their topic; often the poster rests on an easel. See Chapter 30 for guidelines on using posters in presenta-tions called *poster sessions.*

✓ **CHECKLIST:** Incorporating Presentation Aids into Your Speech

✓ Practice with the aids until you are confident that you can handle them without causing undue distractions.

✓ Talk to your audience rather than to the screen or object—avoid turning your back to the audience.

✓ Maintain eye contact with the audience.

✓ Place the aid to one side rather than behind you, so that the entire audience can see it.

✓ Display the aid only when you are ready to discuss it.

✓ If you decide to use a pointer, once you've indicated your point, put it down.

✓ In case problems arise, be prepared to give your presentation without the aids.

21 Designing Presentation Aids

Whether creating your presentation aids by hand or generating them electronically, focus on keeping design elements simple and consistent across all aids. Audience members can follow only one information source at a time, and aids that are crowded or difficult to decipher will divert attention from your message.[1]

Keep the Design Simple

Visuals that try to communicate too many messages will quickly overwhelm the audience. Audience members have only a few moments to view an aid, so present one major idea per aid. Use these guidelines to convey your points effectively on a slide:

• Follow the **six-by-six rule**; use no more than six words in a line and no more than six lines on one slide.

• Word your text in active verb form and parallel grammatical structure (see Chapter 16 on language).

- Create concise titles that tell viewers what to look for and that reinforce your message.
- Allow plenty of *white space*, or "visual breathing room" for viewers.[2]

QUICK TIP

Beware of "Chartjunk"
Certain kinds of information—especially statistical data and sequences of action—are best understood through visual reasoning. However, avoid what design expert Edward Tufte coined as "chartjunk"—slides jammed with too many graphs, charts, and meaningless design elements that obscure rather than illuminate information. Tufte counsels using fewer rather than more slides and only those design elements that truly enhance meaning.[3]

Use Design Elements Consistently

Apply the same design decisions you make for one presentation aid to all of the aids you display in a speech. Doing so will ensure that viewers don't become distracted by a jumble of unrelated visual elements. Carry your choice of any key design elements—color, fonts, upper- and lowercase letters, styling (boldface, underlining, italics), general page layout, and repeating elements such as titles and logos—through to each aid.

Select Appropriate Typeface Styles and Fonts

A **typeface** is a specific style of lettering, such as Arial or Times Roman. Typefaces come in a variety of **fonts**, or sets of sizes (called the point size), and upper and lower cases. Designers divide the thousands of available typefaces into two major categories: serif and sans serif. **Serif typefaces** include small flourishes, or strokes, at the tops and bottoms of each letter. **Sans serif typefaces** are more blocklike and linear; they are designed without these tiny strokes. When selecting type sizes for presentation aids, consider these guidelines:

- Check the lettering for legibility, taking into consideration the audience's distance from the presentation. On slides, experiment with 36-point type for major headings, 24-point type for subheadings, and at least 18-point type for text.

- Make sure that the lettering stands apart from the background, using either dark text on light background (for a more informal feeling) or light text on dark background (for a more formal look).

- Use a familiar typeface that is simple and easy to read, not distracting.

- Use standard upper- and lowercase type; this combination is easier to read than all capital letters.

- Pair no more than two complementary typefaces, such as Times Roman and Helvetica, in the text body, or use only one font throughout.

- Use **boldface**, <u>underlining</u>, or *italics* sparingly, to emphasize only the most important points.

QUICK TIP

Using Serif and Sans Serif Type
For reading a block of text, serif typefaces are easier on the eye. Small amounts of text, however, such as headings, are best viewed in sans serif type. Thus, consider a sans serif typeface for the heading and a serif typeface for the body of the text. If you include only a few lines of text, consider using sans serif type throughout.

Use Color Carefully

Color can set the mood of a presentation, and its selective use can make things easier to see. Conversely, poor color combinations will set the wrong mood, render an image unattractive, or make it unreadable.

- Keep the background color constant across all slides.

- Limit colors in most graphics to no more than two or three and stay within the same family of hues.

- For typeface and graphics, use colors that contrast rather than clash with or blend into the background; check for visibility when projecting.

Consider Subjective Interpretations of Color

Colors can evoke distinct associations for people, so take care not to summon an unintended meaning or mood. For example, for financial managers, blue signifies cooperation and reliability; for health-care professionals, however, it signifies death. Control engineers see red and think danger, whereas a financial manager will think unprofitability, and a health-care professional, health.

Consider, too, that the meanings associated with certain colors may differ across cultures. Western societies don black for funerals, while the Chinese use white. If you are presenting in a cross-cultural context, check the meanings of colors for the relevant countries.

✓ CHECKLIST: Apply the Principles of Simplicity and Continuity

✓ Concentrate on presenting one major idea per visual aid.

✓ Apply design decisions consistently to each aid.

✓ Use type that is large enough for audience members to read comfortably.

✓ Use color to highlight key ideas and enhance readability.

✓ Check that colors contrast rather than clash.

---

22 A Brief Guide to Microsoft PowerPoint

Various presentation software packages such as Prezi and SlideRocket—and even some free Web-based applications, such as Google Docs (docs.google.com)—offer public speakers powerful tools for creating and displaying professionally polished visual aids. The best known and most available of these programs is Microsoft's PowerPoint. Preloaded templates provide expert guidelines for font, color, and background combinations, but you can also design your own. Multimedia displays may be produced by importing video and audio into your slides.

Give a Speech, Not a Slide Show

Many speakers mistake the PowerPoint display itself for the presentation, or they believe the slide show will somehow save an otherwise poorly planned speech. Some speakers become so enamored of creating glitzy multimedia presentations that they forget their primary mission: to communicate through the spoken word and their physical presence. PowerPoint slides, like all presentation aids, can sometimes help listeners process information, but only as long as they truly work to engage your audience and achieve your speech goal.

Develop Effective Slides

The best place to begin planning your slides is with your speaking outline. Think through which points in your speech might be better explained to your audience with some kind of visual; decide what the content of your slides should be, how many slides you'll need, and how to arrange them. Ask yourself, "Are some of the points more suited to visual display than others? What features should be used for each slide?" There is no fixed formula for answering these questions, so you must rely on your own creativity and critical thinking.

✓ CHECKLIST: Using PowerPoint Presentations Effectively

✓ Don't let the technology get in the way of relating to your audience.

✓ Talk to your audience rather than to the screen. Maintain eye contact as much as possible.

✓ Have a backup plan in case of technical errors, and prepare to give the speech without slides.

✓ If you use a pointer (laser or otherwise), turn it off and put it down as soon as you have made your point. Never shine a laser pointer into anyone's eyes.

✓ Incorporate the aids into your practice sessions until you are confident that they strengthen, rather than detract from, your core message.

Avoid Technical Glitches

For all its promise, the use of PowerPoint slides can be fraught with peril. To minimize problems, do the following:

- Check for compatibility of the equipment, operating system, and software. Incompatibilities between versions can distort your graphics, audio, and video; in some cases one version may not recognize another.

- Properly save all the files associated with your presentation (e.g., images, sound files, videos) into the same folder you will use in your presentation.

- Verify that you've saved the files to a source—a flash drive, CD, DVD, Web site, or e-mail—that will be recognized by the presentation computer.

- Familiarize yourself with the layout and functioning of the presentation computer *before the speech*.

- Prepare a hard copy of your presentation as backup. Use the Handout Master and handout printing option to print out your slides for distribution.

Using Microsoft PowerPoint

PowerPoint allows you to generate slides containing text, artwork, photos, charts, graphs, tables, clip art, video, and audio. You can upload PowerPoint presentations onto the Web for viewing elsewhere, and with additional software you can stream your PowerPoint presentation online in real time. This section offers a brief overview of PowerPoint's primary features.

Presentation Options

Begin by familiarizing yourself with the toolbars and icons at the top and bottom of the main screen (see Figure 22.1). PowerPoint provides three options for composing a set of presentation slides.

THE HOME TAB This tab presents menus for inserting new slides after the first one, choosing layouts and themes for your slides, and manipulating fonts and styles. Use *Slide Layout* to choose the format you want to display a title page and section pages, headings, body text, pictures, and captions (see Figure 22.2). This layout will apply to all slides. In the left pane, you can view slides as you create them.

FIGURE 22.1 PowerPoint Toolbars

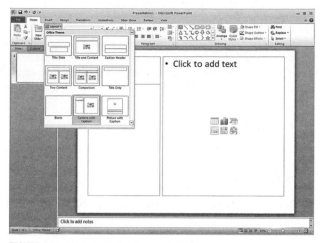

FIGURE 22.2 PowerPoint Slide Layout Options

THE DESIGN TAB This tab includes approximately forty-eight predesigned templates, called *Themes* (see Figure 22.3) Templates allow you to apply a consistent layout and color scheme to each slide in the presentation. Each template is designed to convey a certain look or feel.

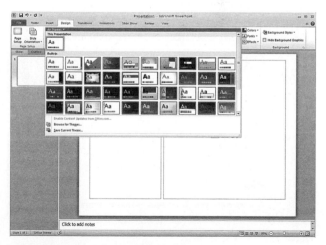

FIGURE 22.3 PowerPoint Design Templates

BLANK SLIDE LAYOUT With *Blank* slide layout, you customize color, font, type and size, organization of content, and graphics (see Figure 22.4). This option allows the greatest degree of flexibility. Once you have designed a slide with the features you want, you can set it as a template so all slides share the same features.

View Options

Current versions of PowerPoint offer three different ways to view slides as you create them: *normal view*, *slide-sorter view*, and *slide-show view*.

- *Normal view* allows you to view and edit individual slides. The left pane shows the thumbnail and outline views of the slides as they are created. Below the slide is a space to add notes.

- *Slide-sorter view* provides a graphical representation of all the slides in the order they are created. Here you can delete slides or click and drag slides to reorganize the presentation sequence.

- *Slide-show view* is the actual view to use for projecting the presentation to an audience. Each slide fills the entire screen.

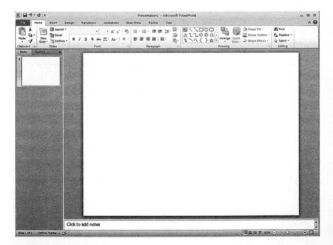

FIGURE 22.4 Blank Slide Layout

Masters

For each presentation you create using a design template, PowerPoint creates a *Slide Master* and a *Handout Master.* The Slide Master contains the elements that you want to appear on every slide, such as a logo, an image, or a line of text. The Handout Master is a page-size view depicting a number of slides per page. When printed, this view serves as a handout of the slides. To display a Master, go to the View tab and select Slide Master.

Transitions and Animation Effects

When moving from one slide to the next, or from one point to another within a single slide, you may wish to add special effects in the form of transitions and text animations. *Transitions* add motion and sound effects as you click from one slide to another. *Animation effects*—sometimes referred to as builds—allow you to reveal text or graphics within a slide during a presentation.

As a rule of thumb, your PowerPoint presentation will be just as effective without transitions and animation effects, but if you decide to include them, use them sparingly and keep them consistent throughout the entire show or within different sections.

Entering and Editing Text

Whenever you choose a slide layout other than a blank layout, you replace the sample text in a placeholder or textbox with your own text. PowerPoint text can be edited much like text in a word processor—you can apply bold, italics, and other text modifications. When you finish entering text, deselect the placeholder by clicking a blank area of the slide.

Inserting Objects

PowerPoint allows you to create or import photos, pictures, clip art, and other objects into the slides to supplement or illustrate speech points.

PICTURES Photos can be inserted from your own picture files, from a disk or portable drive, or from photo Web sites.

CLIP ART   You can select clip art from the PowerPoint Clip Art gallery and import clip art from other programs or Web sites such as Microsoft's online Clip Art page (office.microsoft.com/images).

TABLES AND WORKSHEETS   To insert a table or a worksheet into your PowerPoint presentation, follow these steps:

1. Click Insert > Table or Insert > Table > Excel Spreadsheet. A drop-down grid of cells appears.

2. Click and drag the mouse pointer across the cells in the grid to indicate how many rows or columns you want in your table or worksheet. Upon releasing the mouse button, PowerPoint inserts a special object into your slide, replacing the PowerPoint toolbars for either Word or Excel toolbars. In effect, the special object allows you to use either Word or Excel inside a PowerPoint window.

3. To create the content of the table or worksheet, use the mouse, the tab key, or the arrow keys to move from cell to cell and type in the text. When you are finished, insert the object into the slide by clicking outside the table or worksheet.

Inserting Videos and Sounds

The growing availability of amateur video on Web sites such as YouTube (www.youtube.com) and Google Video (video.google.com) and the increasing ease of transferring video to computers from portable digital devices such as iPods, pocket-size hard drives, and cell phones makes the embedding of video even simpler. To add video to a slide, follow these steps:

1. In Normal view, click the slide to which you want to add a video clip.

2. On the Insert menu, click the arrow under video.

3. Do one of the following:

   - Click Video from File, locate the folder that contains the file, and then double-click the file that you want to add. You will have to include this file in the same folder with your PowerPoint file if you display the presentation from a different computer.

   - Click Video from Web site, paste the embed code from the Web site into the text box, then click Insert (an embed code is provided with each video on sites such as YouTube).

- Click Clip Art Video, use the Clip Art task pane to find an image, and then click it to add it to the slide.

You can also access PowerPoint Help (click the white question mark in the upper right corner of the Power-Point screen) for instructions to add and play a video in a presentation. Inserting portions of a digital movie from a DVD to a PowerPoint slide requires third-party software. To insert a music track from an external source, select Audio from the Insert menu and then select the location to access the file.

Avoiding Copyright Infringement

Be certain to abide by copyright restrictions when using visual and audio materials from the Internet or other sources. Recognize when material is available under fair-use provisions (see Chapter 4, p. 29). Even if fair use applies, cite the source of the material in your presentation.

Consult your school's information technology (IT) office for statements of policy pertaining to copyrighted and fair-use materials, especially from undocumented sources such as peer-to-peer (P2P) sharing. Improper acquisition or use of a copyrighted object could lead to loss of privileges on your campus computer network or, worse, to legal consequences.

✓ CHECKLIST: Ensuring Legal Use of Media Acquired Electronically

✓ Cite the source of all copyrighted material in your presentation. For example, include a bibliographic footnote on the slide containing the material.

✓ Be wary of sites purporting to offer "royalty free" media objects; there might actually be other costs associated with the materials.

✓ When time, resources, and ability allow, create and use your own pictures, video, or audio for your presentation slides.

From Slide Show to Presentation

Getting Ready to Deliver a PowerPoint Presentation

Preparing thoroughly before delivering a speech with PowerPoint can help you take full advantage of this powerful medium and avoid technical glitches.

Check the Venue

Before your speech, take stock of the equipment and room layout. See the annotated photo below for tips on achieving a smooth delivery with digital aids.

1. **Locate power sources.** Ensure that cords can reach the presentation equipment, and consider taping them to the floor to keep them out of the way.

2. **Computer needs and compatibility.** Check that all files, from the slide show to audio and video clips, load successfully to the presentation computer. If possible, practice at least once on this computer.

3. **Internet access.** Have wireless log-in information available and/or a cable that reaches the Internet jack.

4. **Backup plan.** Create a contingency plan in case of computer failure; for example, print overhead transparencies from slide show, prepare to put information on board, or create handouts.

5. **Audio.** Determine how you will broadcast any audio aids, and check speaker volume before the speech.

Position Yourself Carefully

Choose a place to stand that gives the audience clear sightlines to you and your slide show. Stand such that you can face forward even when changing slides or gesturing toward your aids. This helps you connect with your audience, project your voice clearly, and prevents you from reading off your slides.

Placement needs improvement: This speaker's sideways stance discourages eye contact and indicates that he may be reading off his slides.

Good placement: This speaker can access the computer or gesture toward the slides without blocking the audience's sightlines.

Running the Presentation

During the presentation, you can control your slides using the commands listed in the table that follows.

COMMANDS TO RUN A POWERPOINT SLIDE SHOW	
FUNCTION	**METHOD**
Show the next slide	Click the left mouse button or press the space bar, N, right arrow, down arrow, or Page Down
Show the preceding slide	Click the right mouse button or press Backspace, P, left arrow, up arrow, or Page Up
Show a specific slide	Type the number and press Enter
Access Meeting Minder or pointers	Click the right mouse button and select the appropriate option
Toggle the mouse pointer on or off (show or hide)	Type A or the equal sign
Toggle between a black screen and a current screen	Type B or a period
Toggle between a white screen and a current screen	Type W or a comma
End the show	Press ESC, hyphen, or CTRL-Break
Pause and resume an automatic slide show	Type S or the plus sign

Part 7
Types of Speeches

23. Informative Speaking 176
24. Persuasive Speaking 189
25. Speaking on Special Occasions 219

23 Informative Speaking

To *inform* is to communicate knowledge. The goal of **informative speaking** is to impart knowledge in order to raise awareness or deepen understanding of some phenomenon.[1] Informative speeches bring new topics to light, offer new insights on familiar subjects, or provide novel ways of thinking about something. Your speech might be an analysis of an issue, a report of an event; or a physical demonstration of how something works. As long as the audience learns something, the options are nearly limitless.

QUICK TIP

Enlighten Rather Than Advocate

Whereas a persuasive speech would seek to modify attitudes or ask an audience to adopt a specific position, an informative speech stops short of this. Yet there are always elements of persuasion in an informative speech, and vice versa. Nevertheless, if you keep the focus on sharing knowledge, you will be able to deliver a speech whose primary function is to enlighten rather than to advocate.

Gain and Sustain Involvement

Audience members are not simply empty vessels into which you can pour facts and figures for automatic processing. Before your listeners retain information, they must be able to recognize, understand, and relate to it.

Use Audience Analysis

Use audience analysis to gauge the audience's existing knowledge of your topic and their likely interests and needs with respect to it (see Chapter 6). Then adjust the amount and complexity of information accordingly. Most people will recall less than half of the information you tell them, so focus on what you most want to convey and trim material that does not strongly support your central idea.[2]

Present New and Interesting Information

Audiences seek knowledge; they want to learn something new. To satisfy this drive, try to uncover information that is fresh and compelling. Seek out unusual angles, novel interpretations, moving stories, and striking examples. If a speech does not offer audience members anything new, they will feel that their time has been wasted and will rightly be offended.[3]

Help Listeners Follow Along

Audience members cannot put the speaker on "pause" in order to digest information, so help them to stay on track:

- Prepare a well-organized introduction that clearly previews main points (see Chapter 15).
- Make liberal use of transition words and phrases ("first," "next," "I"ll now turn...") to tie speech ideas together and map the logical flow of ideas.
- Use *internal previews* to forecast key points and *internal summaries* to reinforce them.
- Use rhetorical devices such as repetition and parallelism to reinforce information and drive home key ideas.
- Choose an organizational pattern to help listeners mentally organize ideas and see relationships among them.[4]

Subject Matter of Informative Speeches

Broadly speaking, informative speeches may be about *objects* or *phenomena, people, events, processes, concepts,* or *issues.* These are not hard-and-fast divisions—a speech can be about both the *process* of dance and the *people* who perform it, for example—nor are they the only way to categorize informative speeches. These categories, however, do indicate the range of potential subject matter suited to an informative purpose, as seen in the following table.

SUBJECT MATTER OF INFORMATIVE SPEECHES	SAMPLE TOPICS
Objects or Phenomena Addresses various aspects of nonhuman subjects (their history and function, for example)	• The health of Lake Michigan • Ribbon use in awareness-raising campaigns • History of graphic novels
People Addresses impact of individuals and groups on society (including athletes, authors, inventors, political leaders, refugees, soldiers, and others)	• Rahul Singh, founder, GlobalMedic • Amy Poehler, actress • Ai Weiwei, artist • You, the speaker
Current or Historical Events Addresses noteworthy occurrences, past and present	• 1937 Paris World's Fair • The fall of Libya's dictator • The Battle of Britain
Processes Demonstrates and/or explains how something is done, how it is made, or how it works	• Development of baby penguins • Visualization in sports • Operation of hybrid cars • Interviewing for a job
Concepts Addresses abstract or complex ideas, theories, or beliefs	• Responsible knowledge • Chaos theory • Free speech
Issues Addresses problems or matters of dispute to raise awareness and deepen understanding (rather than to advocate for a position)	• Impact of long-term unemployment • French ban on burkas • Obesity epidemic in the United States

---

QUICK TIP

Reveal the Backstory
*Speeches about events and those about people often rely in part on **reportage**—the who, what, where, when, and why of the facts. But more than facts, audience members want insight. One way to shed light on an event is through the **backstory**—the little-known story revealing what led up to the event. Offering "behind-the-scenes" information nearly always sparks interest.*

Decide How to Communicate Your Information

Typically, we communicate information by defining, describing, demonstrating, and/or explaining it. Some speeches rely on a single approach (e.g., they focus on *demonstrating* how something works or *explaining* what something means). Oftentimes, speakers combine strategies. As you prepare your speech, ask yourself, "How much emphasis should I give to defining my topic, describing it, demonstrating it, or explaining its meaning?"

DEFINITION When your topic is new to the audience and/or addresses a complex concept (*What is a fractal?*), pay particular attention to providing adequate definitions. To define something is to identify its essential qualities and meaning.

You can approach definition in a number of ways, including the following:

- Defining something by what it does (**operational definition**): *A computer is something that processes information.*
- Defining something by describing what it is not (**definition by negation**): *Courage is not the absence of fear.*
- Defining something by providing several concrete examples (**definition by example**): *Health professionals include doctors, nurses, EMTs, and ambulance drivers.*
- Defining something by comparing it to something synonymous (**definition by synonym**): *A friend is a comrade or a buddy.*
- Defining something by illustrating its root meaning (**definition by word origin**): *Our word* rival *derives from the Latin word* rivalis, *"one living near or using the same stream."*[5]

DESCRIPTION Whether offering your audience a "virtual tour" of the top of Mount Everest, or describing the physical ravages wrought by drug abuse, the point of speeches, or sections of speeches, relying on description is to offer a vivid portrayal of the topic. When you *describe* information, you provide an array of details that paint a mental picture for the audience. Concrete words and vivid imagery will help listeners visualize your depictions (see Chapter 16).

DEMONSTRATION Sometimes the purpose of an informative speech is to explain how something works or to actually demonstrate it. The many "how to" videos and podcasts on the Web rely on demonstration. A speech may not include an actual physical demonstration (e.g., *how to use social bookmarks*), but the speaker will nevertheless rely on a verbal demonstration of the steps involved.

EXPLANATION Certain informative speech topics are built on *explanation*—providing reasons or causes, demonstrating relationships, and offering interpretation and analysis.

The classroom lecture is a classic example of explanation in an informative context. But many kinds of speeches rely on explanation, from those that address difficult or confusing theories and processes (*What is the relationship between the glycemic index and glycemic load?*) to those that present ideas that challenge conventional thinking (*Why do researchers say that sometimes emotion makes us more rather than less logical?*). See the checklist on p. 181 for strategies for explaining complex ideas.

Take Steps to Reduce Confusion

New information can be hard to grasp, especially when it addresses a difficult concept (such as *equilibrium* in engineering), a difficult-to-envision process (such as *cash-flow management* in business), or a counterintuitive idea—one that challenges commonsense thinking (such as *drinking a glass of red wine a day can be healthy*).[6]

Useful for almost any speech, the following strategies for communicating information are especially helpful when attempting to clarify complex information.

Use Analogies to Build on Prior Knowledge

Audience members will understand a new concept more easily if the speaker uses an analogy to relate it to something that they already know.[7] For example, to explain the unpredictable paths that satellites often take when they fall to earth, you can liken the effect to dropping a penny into water: "Sometimes it goes straight down, and sometimes it turns end over end and changes direction. The same thing happens when an object hits the atmosphere."[8]

QUICK TIP

Use Analogies Accurately

Linking the unfamiliar with the familiar through analogy aids understanding. But no analogy can exactly represent another concept; at a certain point, the similarities will end.[9] To ensure accuracy, state the limits of the comparison. The statement "The heart is like a pump, except that the heart actually changes size as it pushes blood out" demonstrates that, though similar, a heart and a pump are not the same.[10]

Demonstrate Underlying Causes

Listeners may fail to understand a process because they believe that something "obviously" works a certain way when in fact it does not. To counter faulty assumptions, first acknowledge common misperceptions and then offer an accurate explanation of underlying causes.[11]

✓ CHECKLIST: Strategies for Explaining Complex Information

To explain a concept or term:

✓ Build on prior knowledge.

✓ Use analogies that link concepts to something familiar.

✓ Define terms in several ways.

✓ Simplify terminology wherever possible.

To explain a process or structure, do all of the above *and:*

✓ Make ample use of visual aids, including models and drawings.

To explain a counterintuitive idea, do all of the above *and:*

✓ Address the commonly held assumption first.

✓ Acknowledge its plausibility.

✓ Demonstrate its limitations using familiar examples.

Appeal to Different Learning Styles

People have different **learning styles**, or preferred ways of processing information. One learning theory model suggests four preferences: visual, aural, read/write, and kinesthetic[12] (see table on p. 182 on different learner types). Some of us are *multimodal learners*, in that we combine two or more preferences.

Audience analysis may give you a sense of individuals' learning styles. For example, mechanics of all types have strong spatial visualization abilities and thus would be classified as visual learners; they may also be kinesthetic learners who want to "test" things for themselves. Often, however, you may not have enough information to determine your listeners' learning style, *so plan on conveying and reinforcing information in a variety of modes.*

COMMUNICATING INFORMATION TO DIFFERENT TYPES OF LEARNERS	
TYPE	ADVICE FOR COMMUNICATING INFORMATION
Visual	Will most easily grasp ideas communicated through pictures, diagrams, charts, graphs, flowcharts, maps.
Aural	Will most easily grasp ideas communicated through the spoken word, whether in live lectures, tapes, group discussions, or podcasts.
Read/Write	Will most easily grasp ideas communicated through text-based delivery, handouts, PowerPoint with text-based slides.
Kinesthetic	Will most easily grasp ideas communicated through real-life demonstrations, simulations, and movies, and through hands-on applications.

Arrange Points in a Pattern

Our understanding of a speech is directly linked to how well it is organized.[13] Informative speeches can be organized using any of the patterns described in Chapter 13, including the topical, chronological, spatial, cause-effect, and narrative patterns. (Note that although the problem-solution pattern may be used in informative speeches, it often is a more logical candidate for persuasive speeches.) A speech about the Impressionist movement in painting, for example, could be organized *chronologically*, in which main points are arranged in sequence from the movement's early period to its later falling out of favor. It could be organized *causally* (cause-effect), by demonstrating that Impressionism came about as a reaction to the art movement that preceded it. It could also be organized *topically* (by categories), by focusing on the major figures associated with the movement, famous paintings linked to it, or notable contemporary artists who paint in the style.

In a student speech on "How to Buy a Guitar," Richard Garza organizes his main points chronologically:

GENERAL PURPOSE: Buying and caring for a guitar involve knowing what to look for when purchasing it and understanding how to maintain it once you own it.

MAIN POINTS:	I. Decide what kind of guitar you need.
	II. Inspect the guitar for potential flaws.
	III. Maintain the guitar.

In a speech on the nonmonetary uses of gold, Krista Kim organizes her main points topically, dividing her points by category:

THESIS STATEMENT:	Although its nonmonetary value is generally unknown to the population at large, gold has many applications in medicine and science.
MAIN POINTS:	I. Gold has many unique and useful qualities.
	II. Gold has many applications in medicine.
	III. Gold has several applications in the NASA space program.

✓ CHECKLIST: Possible Matches of Organizational Patterns with Speech Types

✓ Objects—spatial, topical

✓ People—chronological, topical, narrative

✓ Events—chronological, cause-effect, narrative

✓ Processes—chronological, narrative

✓ Concepts—topical, circle, cause-effect

✓ Issues—chronological, cause-effect, topical, circle

SAMPLE INFORMATIVE SPEECH

The following speech by student David Kruckenberg describes a promising new way to treat cancer. David clarifies information with definitions and analogies and uses transitions and repetition to help listeners follow along. He also cites sources wherever he offers information gathered and reported by others.

David's topic could suggest a chronological pattern of arrangement. For example, he could have arranged his main points to trace the invention from inception to ongoing trials. Instead, he uses the *topical pattern of arrangement* (see Chapter 13) to first focus on the history of the new cancer treatment and then explain key concepts related to it.

John Kanzius and the Quest to Cure Cancer

DAVID KRUCKENBERG
Santiago Canyon College

One night in 2003, Marianne Kanzius awoke to a tremendous clamor coming from downstairs. She found her husband John sitting on the kitchen floor, cutting up her good aluminum pie pans with a pair of shears.

This is David's "attention getter."

As Peter Panepento describes the scene in an article titled "Sparks of Genius," published in the May 2006 edition of *Reader's Digest,* when Marianne asked him why he was wiring the pans to his ham radio, John told her to go back to bed. So off she went, knowing that her single-minded husband wasn't the kind of person to quit until he was satisfied.

Marianne soon learned that John's late-night experiment with pie pans was an attempt to use radio waves to kill cancer cells—and to rid himself of the rare form of leukemia threatening his life. In the next five years, John Kanzius would radically modify an existing cancer treatment technique called *radiofrequency ablation,* making it potentially far more effective than existing treatments. Soon, the work of this retired TV and radio engineer might give additional hope to the 1.4 million Americans diagnosed with cancer every year, according to the 2008 American Cancer Society "Facts and Figures" section of its Web site.

David draws listeners in with an unusual story.

Thesis statement.

To understand John's discovery, we'll explore how the medical profession currently makes use of radio waves to treat cancer, learn about John's truly promising new approach, and consider the implications for the future.

David previews the main points, then moves into a transition.

But first, to understand radiofrequency energy, we need a crash course in wave physics.

Energy moves in a wave and is measured in *frequency,* how quickly it moves up and down. *High frequency waves,* like Supermans's X-ray vision—and real X-rays—move quickly and penetrate most matter, but can alter the chemical and genetic material in cells. *Low frequency waves,* such as radio waves, move slowly and don't disturb the atomic balance of matter they pass

David increases understanding using an analogy to X-ray vision, definitions of high and low frequency waves, and recognizable examples of each.

through. Radio waves are harmless to healthy cells, making them a promising tool for ablation.

Let me explain the term. *Ablation,* according to the 7
National Cancer Institute's *Dictionary of Cancer Terms,*
available on its Web site, is the medical term
for "the removal or destruction of a body David defines terms
part or tissue or its function," using hormone may not know.
therapy, conventional surgery, or radiofrequency. *Radiofrequency ablation,* or RFA, uses radiofrequency energy to "cook" and kill cancer cells, according
to the Society of Interventional Radiology. The least invasive
RFA technique practiced today is through the skin; it's also
done laparoscopically.

Here's how the Radiological Society of This transition
North America explains radiofrequency helps listeners focus
ablation on its Web site, last updated explanation.
December 17, 2008.

First, a doctor makes a small incision in the skin and 9
inserts a needle electrode or a straight hollow needle containing retractable electrodes.

The doctor guides the needle to the site of the tumor 10
using an imaging technique such as ultrasound.

The needle in turn is connected to an electric genera- 11
tor, and once in place, electrodes extend out of it and into
the tumor.

Next, contact pads, also wired to the generator, are 12
placed on the patient's skin; this completes
an electric circuit so that when the genera- Such signal words
tor is turned on, electric energy in the form help listeners follow
of radio waves pass through the body, going the procedure's
back and forth between the needles and the organized steps.
contact pads.

Here's the critical part: 13

Every time that the radio waves meet the resistance 14
of the electrodes at the treatment site, they create heat.
It's kind of like an atomic mosh pit, with
a crowd of atoms suddenly agitated by David's mosh-pit
radio waves; the electrons begin to bounce listeners understand
around and collide, creating friction and a complex concept.
thus heat. This heat gets up to 212 degrees
Fahrenheit, the temperature at which water boils. The heat
destroys the cancerous cells in the tumor, essentially cooking them, but leaving noncancerous cells alone.

In many ways, it's a great treatment option right now. 15
However, while it is called "minimally invasive" surgery,

the needles required by this method can damage tissue and even organs near the tumor site, limiting its usefulness.

Enter John Kanzius.

John was diagnosed with leukemia in 2002, and his ordeal with chemotherapy motivated him to find a better way to attack cancer cells.

This transition adds drama.

Now John had no medical training, but he had worked 18 in the radio industry for forty years, and he knew all about radio waves. He recalled that a colleague wearing wire-rimmed glasses got burned as she stood too close to a radio transmitter. As Peter Panepento describes it in *Reader's Digest,* this led Kanzius to theorize that if you could infuse cancer cells with a conductive substance, you could use a transmitter to heat them with radio waves, while avoiding invasive needles. The cells marked with the substance would act like "tiny antennas," as Panepento put it.

David is careful to credit direct quotations.

It was this chain of thought which spurred John's late-19 night kitchen experiment with the pie pans and his ham radio.

Two things were amazing about John's initial 20 experiment.

First, John was able to replicate RFA in his kitchen. 21 Second, John made a huge improvement upon the technique, alone and at home. Instead of inserting needles into a tumor, he injected tiny metal minerals into a stand-in hotdog. He then placed the hotdog between the radio transmitter and receiver so that the radio waves would pass through the meat. When he cut the hotdog open, the area around the minerals was cooked, but the rest remained raw. Kanzius later repeated the experiment with liver, then steak, obtaining the same results.

Could there really be a way to use radiofrequency without side effects, and to treat more types of cancer with it?

Here he uses a transition in the form of a rhetorical question.

As told by Charles Schmidt in the *Journal of the National Cancer Institute* on July 16, 2008, John shared his results with several leading oncologists, who immediately recognized the potential. He then filed for a patent for his RF machine.

Researchers at two prominent cancer centers decided 24 to test John's theory, starting in August 2005 with the University of Pittsburgh's Liver Cancer Center. As detailed in the University of Pittsburgh Medical Center newsletter of March 22, 2006, instead of using a hotdog, the researchers placed a thin test tube between the radio transmitter and the receiver. Inside this tube was a solution of carbon nanoparticles—actually pieces of metal about 1/75,000 times smaller than the width of a human hair. A speck of dandruff is like a mountain to a nanoparticle. When they turned on the electricity, the carbon nanoparticles successfully heated to 130 degrees Fahrenheit—the perfect temperature at which to kill cancer cells, according to Peter Panepento's *Reader's Digest* piece.

> Because the size of a nanometer is hard to visualize, David compares it to something with which listeners are familiar—a strand of hair and dandruff.

Now that I've explained John's major improvement over current RFA procedures, let's consider the implications of his discovery. 25

John's noninvasive radiofrequency cancer treatment holds tremendous promise as an alternative to existing cancer therapies. First, because RFA uses electromagnetic energy in the form of radio waves, it's much safer than chemotherapy and traditional radiation treatment. As noted, radio waves are harmless to healthy cells, as compared to X-rays. 26

Second, as explained in the January 2008 issue of the *Journal of Nanobiotechnology* by Gannon et al., the current RFA procedure can only be used in cancers that are not difficult to reach, such as liver, breast, lung, and bone; John's new method potentially can target tumors anywhere in the body. 27

> Using full oral citations supports David's credibility and allows the audience to seek further information on the topic.

Third, the current RFA procedure must be performed several times to target multiple tumors, but John's method could make it possible to target multiple tumors in just a single treatment. 28

Intensive research is now underway at the renowned M.D. Anderson Cancer Center in Houston. The goal is to find ways to make the nanoparticles target cancer cells exclusively. Success occurred in late 2007, when in a preclinical trial researchers at the M.D. Anderson Cancer Center used the technique to completely destroy liver cancer tumors in rabbits, as described in the December 2007 issue of the journal *Cancer*. 29

Another area they are trying to resolve, according to Schmidt, is the potential toxicity of nanoparticles in the bloodstream. Human trials may begin in two to three years, according to Dr. Steven Curley, lead investigator 30 on the Kanzius project at M.D. Anderson, as reported this summer by David Bruce in the *Erie Times News*.

Today we learned how a man with vision discovered how to cook a hotdog with a ham radio. We explored first the current procedure, then John's new approach, and, finally, the implications of this new hope for treating cancer.

John's cancer is in remission, and he's established the John Kanzius Cancer Research Foundation, which you can read about online. He is continuing to refine his technique and is working on clinical trials.

> David gives a clear signal of the speech's conclusion with a summary of the main points.

Marianne Kanzius was upset when she saw her husband destroying her good pie pans, but now it's clear that the loss of a few pie pans and a hotdog may soon save millions of lives.

> A return to David's opening story brings the speech full circle.

31

33

Works Cited

American Cancer Society. "Cancer Facts and Figures, 2008." www.cancer.org/docroot/STT/content/STT_1x_Cancer_Facts_and_Figures_2008.asp.

Bruce, David. "Community United behind Kanzius, Human Trials." *Erie Times-News,* July 27, 2008. doc ID: 1222E79CB5E00DA0.

Gannon, Christopher J., Chitta Ranjan Patra, Resham Bhattacharya, Priyabrata Mukherjee, and Steven A. Curley. "Intracellular Gold Nanoparticles Enhance Non-Invasive Radiofrequency Thermal Destruction of Human Gastrointestinal Cancer Cells." *Journal of Nanobiotechnology* 6, no. 2 (2008). doi:10.1186/1477-3155-6-2.

Gannon, Christopher J., et al. "Carbon Nanotube-Enhanced Thermal Destruction of Cancer Cells in a Noninvasive Radiofrequency Field." *Cancer* (Wiley), October 24, 2007. doi: 10.1002/cncr.23155.

Match (a publication of the Thomas E. Starzl Transplantation Institute). University of Pittsburgh Medical Center Web Site. March 22, 2006.

National Cancer Institute. *Dictionary of Cancer Terms.* Accessed December 15, 2008. www.cancer.gov/templates/db_alpha.aspx?expand=A.

Panepento, Peter. "Sparks of Genius: Efforts Done by John Kanzius, a Cancer Patient, to Find a Better Cure for Cancer." *Reader's Digest* (May 2006): 132–36.

Radiological Society of North America. "Radiofrequency Ablation of Liver Tumors." Accessed December 17, 2008. www.radiologyinfo.org/en/info.cfm?PG=rfa.

Schmidt, Charles. "A New Cancer Treatment from an Unexpected Source." *Journal of the National Cancer Institute* 100, no. 14 (2008): 985-86. doi:10.1093/jnci/djn246.

Society of Interventional Radiology. "Radiofrequency Catheter Ablation." Accessed June 23, 2009. http://www.sirweb.org.

24 Persuasive Speaking

To persuade is to advocate, to ask others to accept your views. The goal of **persuasive speaking** is to influence audience members' attitudes, beliefs, values, and actions (see Chapter 6). Some persuasive speeches attempt to move the audience's attitudes and values closer to the speaker's stance. Others aim for a more explicit response, as when urging listeners to donate money for a cause or to vote for a candidate.

Focus on Motivation

Success in persuasive speaking requires attention to human psychology—to what motivates listeners. Audience analysis is therefore extremely important in persuasive appeals.

Research confirms that you can increase the odds of achieving your persuasive speech goal if you:

- Use information gleaned through audience analysis to make your message personally relevant to listeners.[1]
- Demonstrate how any change you propose will benefit the audience.[2]
- Establish your credibility. Audience members' feelings toward you strongly influence their receptivity toward the message.
- Set modest goals. Expect minor rather than major changes in your listeners' attitudes and behaviors.

- Demonstrate how an attitude or a behavior might keep listeners from feeling satisfied and competent, thereby encouraging receptivity to change.

- Expect to be more successful when addressing an audience whose position differs only moderately from your own.

QUICK TIP

Expect Modest Results
Regardless of how thoroughly you have conducted audience analysis, or how skillfully you present your point of view, don't expect your audience to respond immediately or completely to a persuasive appeal. Persuasion does not occur with a single dose. Changes tend to be small, even imperceptible, especially at first.

Balance Reason and Emotion

Persuasion is a complex psychological process of reasoning and emotion, and effective persuasive speeches appeal to not one but both processes in audience members. Emotion gets the audience's attention and stimulates a desire to act; reason provides the justification for the action.

Persuasive speeches use arguments as a framework for making appeals. An **argument** is a stated position, with support, for or against an idea or issue. Appealing to reason and logic—or to what Aristotle termed **logos**—is important in gaining agreement for your argument; it is especially critical when asking listeners to reach a conclusion regarding a complicated issue or to take a specific action (see p. 195 for guidance on constructing sound arguments). To truly persuade listeners to care about your position, however, you must also appeal to their emotions—to what Aristotle termed **pathos**. Feelings such as pride, love, compassion, anger, shame, and fear underlie many of our actions and motivate us to think and feel as we do.

You can evoke pathos in a speech by using vivid imagery, telling compelling stories (especially ones that touch upon shared values such as patriotism, selflessness, faith, and hope), and using repetition and parallelism (see Chapter 16 for guidelines on using these and other techniques of language in a speech). Consider the following example from a speech by Elpidio Villarreal about the value of immigrants to the United States. In this excerpt, Villarreal movingly relates the story of the death of his uncle, an immigrant from Mexico, during combat in World War II. Villarreal's vivid imagery and reference to loyalty and sacrifice for country effectively arouse appreciation for Mexican American and other immigrant soldiers:

> On June 6, 1944, [my Uncle Lupe] landed at a place called Omaha Beach in Normandy, France. He was killed while leading an attack on an enemy Bunker.... I was privileged to walk the battlefields of Normandy, including Omaha Beach, and I visited the great American Cemetery there where lie 17,000 Americans who gave the "last full measure of devotion," as Lincoln so beautifully put it. Simple white marble crosses, interspersed with occasional Stars of David, stretch out for 70 acres....
>
> I thought about all the brave Americans buried there and of the meaning of their deaths, but I thought especially about my Uncle Lupe, the one who went to war knowing he would die for no other reason than that his country, the one that treated him as a second-class citizen, asked him to.[3]

QUICK TIP

Base Your Emotional Appeals on Sound Reasoning
Although emotion is a powerful means of moving an audience, relying solely on naked emotion will fail most of the time.[4] What actually persuades an audience is the interplay between emotion and logic. When using emotions to appeal to an audience, always do so on the basis of sound reasoning.

Stress Your Credibility

Audiences want more than logical and emotional appeals from a speaker; they want what's relevant to them from someone who cares. Aristotle termed this effect of the speaker on the audience **ethos**, or moral character. Modern-day scholars call it **speaker credibility**.

Audience members' feelings about your credibility strongly influence how receptive they will be to your proposals, and studies confirm that attitude change is related directly to the extent to which listeners perceive speakers to be truthful and competent (well prepared).[5]

The following steps will help you establish credibility:

- Emphasize your grasp of the topic; note related expertise.
- Demonstrate trustworthiness by revealing your true speech goals, establishing common ground with audience members, and expressing genuine interest in their welfare.
- Strive for a dynamic delivery.

APPLYING ARISTOTLE'S THREE PERSUASIVE APPEALS	
Appeal to Logos	Targets audience members' reasoning and logic through argument (e.g., claims, evidence, warrants).
Appeal to Pathos	Targets audience members' emotions using techniques of language such as vivid imagery, dramatic storytelling, and repetition.
Appeal to Ethos	Targets audience members' feelings about the speaker's character through demonstrations of trustworthiness, competence, and concern for audience welfare.

Target Listeners' Needs

Audience members are motivated to act on the basis of their needs; thus, one way to persuade listeners is to point to some need they want fulfilled and then give them a way to fulfill it. According to psychologist Abraham Maslow's classic **hierarchy of needs** (see Figure 24.1), each of us has a set of basic needs ranging from essential, life-sustaining ones to less critical, self-improvement ones. Our needs at the lower, essential levels (physiological and safety needs) must be fulfilled before the higher levels (social, self-esteem, and self-actualization needs) become important and motivating. Using Maslow's hierarchy to persuade your listeners to wear seat belts, for example, you would appeal to their need for safety. Critics of this approach suggest that we may be driven as much by *wants* as by needs; nevertheless, the theory points to the fact that successful appeals depend on understanding what motivates the audience.[6] Following are Maslow's five basic needs, along with suggested actions a speaker can take to appeal to them.

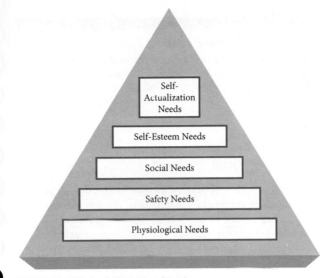

FIGURE 24.1 Maslow's Hierarchy of Needs

NEED	SPEECH ACTION
Physiological needs (to have access to basic sustenance, including food, water, and air)	• Plan for and accommodate the audience's physiological needs—are they likely to be hot, cold, hungry, or thirsty?
Safety needs (to feel protected and secure)	• Appeal to safety benefits—how wearing seat belts or voting for a bill to stop pollution will remove a threat or protect the audience members from harm.
Social needs (to find acceptance; to have lasting, meaningful relationships)	• Appeal to social benefits—if you want teenagers to quit smoking, stress that if they quit they will appear more physically fit and attractive to their peers.
Self-esteem needs (to feel good about ourselves; self-worth)	• Appeal to emotional benefits—stress that the proposed change will make listeners feel better about themselves.
Self-actualization needs (to achieve goals; to reach our highest potential)	• Appeal to your listeners' need to fulfill their potential—stress how adopting your position will help them "be all that they can be."

QUICK TIP

Show Them the Reward
*In order for change to endure, listeners must be convinced
they will be rewarded in some way. For example, to persuade
people to lose weight and keep it off, you must make them
believe that they will be healthier and happier if they do so.
Skillful persuaders motivate their listeners to help themselves.*

Encourage Mental Engagement

According to the **elaboration likelihood model of persuasion**, audience members will mentally process your persuasive message by one of two routes, depending on their degree of involvement in the message.[7] When they are motivated and able to think critically about a message, they engage in **central processing**. That is, these listeners seriously consider what your message means to them and are the ones who are most likely to act on it. When listeners lack the motivation (or the ability) to judge the argument based on its merits, they engage in **peripheral processing** of information—they pay little attention and respond to the message as being irrelevant, too complex to follow, or just plain unimportant. Even though such listeners may sometimes "buy into" your message, they will do so not on the strength of the arguments but on the basis of such superficial factors as reputation, entertainment value, or personal style. Listeners who use peripheral processing are unlikely to experience meaningful changes in attitudes or behavior.

You can encourage listeners to engage in central rather than peripheral processing (and thus increase the odds that your persuasive appeal will produce lasting changes in their attitudes and behavior) with these steps:

- Link your argument to the practical concerns of your listeners and emphasize direct consequences to them.

  "Hybrid cars may not be the best-looking or fastest cars on the market, but as gas prices continue to soar, they will save you a great deal of money."

- Present your message at an appropriate level of understanding.

  For a general audience: "The technology behind hybrid cars is relatively simple."

  For an expert audience: "To save even more gas, you can turn an EV into a PHEV with a generator and additional batteries."

- Demonstrate common bonds (i.e., foster identification).

  "It took me a while to convince myself to buy a hybrid."

- Stress your credibility to offer the claims.

  "Once I selected the car, I found I saved nearly $2,000 this year."

Construct Sound Arguments

The persuasive power of any speech is based on the quality of the arguments within it. Arguments themselves are comprised of three elements: claims, evidence, and warrants.

1. The **claim** (also called a *proposition*) states the speaker's conclusion, based on evidence. The claim answers the question, "What are you trying to prove?"[8]

2. The **evidence** substantiates the claim. Every key claim you make in a speech must be supported with evidence that provides grounds for belief (see Chapter 8).

3. The **warrant** provides reasons that the evidence is valid or supports the claim. Warrants are lines of reasoning that substantiate in the audience's mind the link between the claim and the evidence (see Figure 24.2).

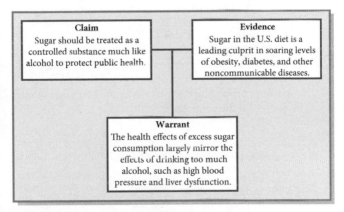

FIGURE 24.2 Core Components of Argument
Source: Robert H. Lustig, Laura A. Schmidt, and Claire D. Brindis, "Public Health: The Toxic Truth About Sugar." *Nature* 482 (February 2, 2012), doi:10.1038/482027a.

Identify the Nature of Your Claims

Depending on the nature of the issue, an argument may address three different kinds of claims: of *fact*, of *value*, and of *policy*. Each type requires evidence to support it. A persuasive speech may contain only one type of claim or, very often, consist of several arguments addressing different kinds of claims. In a persuasive speech, a claim can serve as a main point or it can be the speech thesis (if using only one claim).

- **Claims of fact** focus on whether something is or is not true or whether something will or will not happen. They usually address issues for which two or more competing answers exist, or those for which an answer does not yet exist (called a *speculative claim*). An example of the first is, "Does affirmative action discriminate against nonminority job applicants?" An example of the second is, "Will a woman president be elected in the next U.S. presidential election?"

- **Claims of value** address issues of judgment. Rather than attempting to prove the truth of something, as in claims of fact, speakers arguing claims of value try to show that something is right or wrong, good or bad, worthy or unworthy. Examples include "Is assisted suicide ethical?" and "Should late-term abortions be permitted when a woman's health is at stake?" The evidence in support of a value claim tends to be more subjective than for a fact claim.

- **Claims of policy** recommend that a specific course of action be taken or approved. Examples include "Full-time students who commute to campus should be granted reduced parking fees" and "Property taxes should be increased to fund classroom expansions in city elementary schools." Notice that in each claim the word "should" appears. A claim of policy speaks to an "ought" condition, proposing that certain better outcomes would be realized if the proposed condition were met.

✓ CHECKLIST: Structure the Claims in Your Persuasive Speech

✓ When addressing whether something is or is not true, or whether something will or will not happen, frame your argument as a *claim of fact*.

✓ When addressing issues that rely upon individual judgment of right and wrong for their resolution, frame your argument as a *claim of value*.

✓ When proposing a specific outcome or solution to an issue, frame your argument as a *claim of policy*.

Use Convincing Evidence

Every key claim must be supported with convincing *evidence*, supporting material that provides grounds for belief. Chapter 8 describes several forms of evidence: *examples*, *narratives*, *testimony*, *facts*, and *statistics*. These most common forms of evidence—called "external evidence" because the knowledge does not generate from the speaker's own experience—are most powerful when they impart new information that the audience has not previously used in forming an opinion.[9]

You can also use the *audience's preexisting knowledge and opinions*—what listeners already think and believe—as evidence for your claims. Nothing is more persuasive to listeners than a reaffirmation of their own attitudes, beliefs, and values, especially for claims of value and policy. To use this form of evidence, however, you must first identify what the audience knows and believes about the topic, and then present information that confirms these beliefs.

Finally, when the audience will find your opinions credible and convincing, consider using your own *speaker expertise* as evidence. Be aware, however, that few persuasive speeches can be convincingly built solely on speaker experience and knowledge. Offer your expertise in conjunction with other forms of evidence.

Address the Other Side of the Argument

A persuasive speech message can be either one- or two-sided. A **one-sided message** does not mention opposing claims; a **two-sided message** mentions opposing points of view and sometimes refutes them. Research suggests that two-sided messages generally are more persuasive than one-sided messages, as long as the speaker adequately refutes opposing claims.[10]

All attempts at persuasion are subject to counterargument. Listeners may be persuaded to accept your claims, but once they are exposed to opposing claims they may change their minds. If listeners are aware of opposing claims and you ignore them, you risk a loss of credibility. Yet you need not painstakingly acknowledge and refute all opposing claims. Instead, raise and refute the most important counterclaims and evidence that the audience would know about. Ethically, you can ignore counterclaims that don't significantly weaken your argument.[11]

Use Effective Reasoning

Reasoning is the process of drawing conclusions from evidence. Arguments can be reasoned inductively, deductively, or causally. Arguments using **deductive reasoning** begin with a general principle or case, followed by a specific example of the case, which then leads to the speaker's conclusion.

In a deductive line of argument, if you accept the general principle and the speaker's specific example of it, you must accept the conclusion:

GENERAL CASE ("MAJOR PREMISE"):	All men are mortal.
SPECIFIC CASE ("MINOR PREMISE"):	Socrates is a man.
CONCLUSION:	Therefore Socrates is mortal.

Reversing direction, an argument using **inductive reasoning** moves from specific cases (minor premises) to a general conclusion supported by those cases. The speaker offers evidence that points to a conclusion that *appears to be*, but *is not necessarily*, true:

SPECIFIC CASE 1:	In one five-year period, the average daily temperature (ADT) on Continent X rose three degrees.
SPECIFIC CASE 2:	In that same period, ADT on Continent Y rose three degrees.
SPECIFIC CASE 3:	In that same period, ADT on Continent Z rose three degrees.
CONCLUSION:	Globally, average daily temperatures appear to be rising by three degrees.

Arguments based on inductive reasoning can be *strong* or *weak*; that is, listeners may decide the claim is probably true, largely untrue, or somewhere in between.

Reasoning by analogy is a common form of inductive reasoning. Here, the speaker compares two similar cases and implies that what is true in one case is true in the other. The assumption is that the characteristics of Case A and Case B are similar, if not the same, and that what is true for B must also be true for A.

Arguments can also follow lines of **causal reasoning**, in which the speaker argues that one event, circumstance, or idea (the cause) is the reason (effect) for another. For example, "Smoking causes lung cancer." Sometimes a speaker can argue that multiple causes lead to a single effect, or that a single cause leads to multiple effects. (For more details on the cause-effect pattern, see Chapter 13.)

Avoid Fallacies in Reasoning

A **logical fallacy** is either a false or erroneous statement or an invalid or deceptive line of reasoning.[12] In either case, you need to be aware of fallacies in order to avoid making them in your own speeches and to be able to identify them in the speeches of others. Many fallacies of reasoning exist; the following are merely a few.

LOGICAL FALLACY	EXAMPLES
Begging the question An argument that is stated in such a way that it cannot help but be true, even though no evidence has been presented.	• "War kills." • "Intelligent Design is the correct explanation for biological change over time because we can see godly evidence in our complex natural world."
Bandwagoning An argument that uses (unsubstantiated) general opinion as its (false) basis.	• "Nikes are superior to other brands of shoes because everyone wears Nikes." • "Everybody on campus is voting for her so you should, too."
Either-or fallacy An argument stated in terms of only two alternatives, even though there may be many additional alternatives.	• "If you don't send little Susie to private school this year, she will not gain admission to college." • "Either you're with us or against us."
Ad hominem argument An argument that targets a person instead of the issue at hand in an attempt to incite an audience's dislike for that person.	• "I'm a better candidate than X because, unlike X, I work for a living." • "How can you accept my opponent's position on education when he has been divorced?"

LOGICAL FALLACY	**EXAMPLES**
Red herring An argument that relies on irrelevant premises for its conclusion.	• "The previous speaker suggests that Medicare is in shambles. I disagree and recommend that we study why the young don't respect their elders." • "I fail to see why hunting should be considered cruel when it gives pleasure to many people and employment to even more."[13]
Hasty generalization An argument in which an isolated instance is used to make an unwarranted general conclusion.	• "As shown by the example of a Labrador retriever biting my sister, this type of dog is dangerous and its breeding should be outlawed." • "My neighbor who works for K-Mart is untrustworthy; therefore, K-Mart is not a trustworthy company."
Non sequitur ("does not follow") An argument in which the conclusion is not connected to the reasoning.	• "Because she lives in the richest country in the world, she must be extremely wealthy." • "If we can send a man to the moon, we should be able to cure cancer in five years."
Slippery slope A faulty assumption that one case will lead to a series of events or actions.	• "Helping refugees in the Sudan today will force us to help refugees across Africa and worldwide." • "If we outsource jobs from the United States, then other companies will outsource jobs, and then the U.S. economy will collapse."

LOGICAL FALLACY	EXAMPLES
Appeal to tradition An argument suggesting that audience members should agree with a claim because that is the way it has always been done.	• "A marriage should be between a man and a woman because that is how it has always been." • "The president of the United States must be a man because a woman has never been president."

Address Culture

The audience's cultural orientation will significantly affect their responses to persuasion.[14]

CORE VALUES Audience members of the same culture often share core values, such as *self-reliance* and *individual achievement* (in individualist cultures such as the United States); and *interdependence* and *group harmony* (in collectivist cultures such as those of China and India). Usually, appeals that clash with core values are unsuccessful, although globalization may be leading to some cross-pollination of values.[15]

CULTURAL NORMS *Cultural norms* are a group's rules for behavior. Attempts to persuade listeners to think or do things contrary to important cultural norms usually will fail.[16] The argument that intermarriage leads to happier couples, for example, will find greater acceptance among Reform rather than Orthodox Jews, since the latter group has strong prohibitions against the practice.

CULTURAL PREMISES Listeners sharing a common culture usually hold culturally specific values about identity and relationships, called *cultural premises.* Prevalent among the Danes and Israelis, for example, is the premise of egalitarianism, the belief that everyone should be equal. A different premise exists in Korea, Japan, and other Asian societies, where status most often is aligned strictly with one's place in the social hierarchy. Bear in mind that it is difficult to challenge deeply held cultural premises.[17]

EMOTIONS Culture also influences our responses to emotional appeals. Appeals that touch on *ego-focused* emotions such as pride, anger, happiness, and frustration, for example, tend to find more acceptance among members of individual-ist cultures;[18] those that use *other-focused* emotions such as empathy, indebtedness, and shame are more apt to encourage identification in collectivist cultures.[19] Usually, it is best to appeal to emotions that lie within the audience's "comfort zone."[20] A good strategy is to avoid undue emphasis on emotions that may make certain audience members feel uncomfortable.

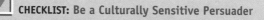

CHECKLIST: Be a Culturally Sensitive Persuader

✓ Do you appeal to any *core values* (deeply held ideas of what's important in life) that might clash with those held by audience members?

✓ Do you attempt to persuade listeners to think or do things contrary to their *norms* (rules for behavior)?

✓ Do you challenge any *cultural premises* (deeply held values about identity and relationships)?

✓ Do you appeal to emotions that lie outside of the audience's "comfort zone"?

Strengthen Your Case with Organization

Once you've developed your speech claims, the next step is to structure your speech points using one (or more) of the organizational patterns described in Chapter 13 and in this chapter. Factors to consider when selecting a pattern include the nature of your arguments and evidence; the response you want to elicit from audience members; and your target audience's attitudes toward the topic. Following are organizational patterns especially well-suited to persuasive speeches.

Problem-Solution Pattern

Some speech topics or claims clearly suggest a specific design, such as the claim that cigarettes should cost less. Implied is that the current high price of cigarettes represents a problem and that lower prices represent a solution. The **problem-solution pattern of arrangement** is a commonly used design for persuasive speeches, especially those based on *claims of policy* (see p. 196). Here you organize speech points to demonstrate the nature and significance of a problem and then to provide justification for a proposed solution:

I.   Problem (define what it is)

II. Solution (offer a way to overcome the problem)

Most problem-solution speeches require more than two points to adequately explain the problem and to substantiate the recommended solution. Thus a three-point **problem-cause-solution pattern** may be in order:

I.   The nature of the problem (explain why it's a problem, for whom, etc.)

II. Reasons for the problem (identify its causes, incidence)

III. Proposed solution (explain why it's expected to work, noting any unsatisfactory solutions)

When arguing a claim of policy, it may be important to demonstrate the proposal's feasibility. To do this, use a four-point *problem-cause-solution-feasibility pattern,* with the last point providing evidence of the solution's feasibility.

This organization can be seen in the following claim of policy about changing the NBA draft:

THESIS:

The NBA draft should be changed so that athletes like you aren't tempted to throw away their opportunity for an education.

I.   The NBA draft should be revamped so that college-age athletes are not tempted to drop out of school. (*Need/problem*)

II. The NBA's present policies lure young athletes to pursue unrealistic goals of superstardom while weakening the quality of the game with immature players. (*Reasons for the problem*)

III. The NBA draft needs to adopt a minimum age of twenty. (*Solution to the problem*)

IV. National leagues in countries X and Y have done this successfully. (*Evidence of the solution's feasibility*)

Monroe's Motivated Sequence

The **motivated sequence pattern of arrangement**, developed in the mid-1930s by Alan Monroe,[21] is a five-step sequence that begins with arousing listeners' attention and ends with calling for action. This pattern is particularly effective when you want the audience to do something—buy a product, donate to a cause, and so forth.

STEP 1: ATTENTION   The *attention step* addresses listeners' core concerns, making the speech highly relevant to them. Here is an excerpt from a student speech by Ed Partlow on becoming an organ donor:

> Today I'm going to talk about a subject that can be both personal and emotional. I am going to talk about becoming an organ donor. Donating an organ is a simple step you can take that will literally give life to others—to your husband or wife, mother or father, son or daughter—or to a beautiful child whom you've never met.
>
> There is one thing I want to acknowledge from the start. Many of you may be uncomfortable with the idea of becoming an organ donor. I want to establish right off that it's OK if you don't want to become a donor.
>
> Many of us are willing to donate our organs, but because we haven't taken the action to properly become a donor, our organs go unused. As a result, an average of eighteen people die every day because of lack of available organs.

STEP 2: NEED   The *need step* isolates the issue to be addressed. If you can show the members of an audience that they have an important need that must be satisfied or a problem that must be solved, they will have a reason to listen to your propositions. Continuing with the organ donor speech, here the speaker establishes the need for donors:

> According to statistics compiled by the U.S. Department of Health and Human Services' Organ Procurement and Transplantation Network, found on the OPTN Web site, there are nearly 73,000 people on the waiting list this day for an organ transplant. Over 50,000 are waiting for a kidney transplant alone, and the stakes are high: 90 percent of patients who receive a kidney from a living donor live at least 10 years after the transplant. One of the people on the waiting list is Aidan Malony, who graduated two years ago from this college. Without a transplant, he will die. It is agonizing for his family and friends to see him in this condition. And it is deeply frustrating to them that more people don't sign and carry organ donor cards. I have always carried my organ donor card with me, but didn't realize the extreme importance of doing so before talking to Aidan.

Every sixteen minutes another name joins that of Aidan Malony and is added to the National Transplant Waiting List.

STEP 3: SATISFACTION The *satisfaction step* identifies the solution. This step begins the crux of the speech, offering the audience a proposal to reinforce or change their attitudes, beliefs, and values regarding the need at hand. Here is an example from the speech on organ donation:

> It takes only two steps to become an organ donor. First, fill out an organ donor card and carry it with you. You may also choose to have a note added to your driver's license next time you renew it.
>
> Second and most important, tell your family that you want to become an organ donor and ask them to honor your wishes when the time arrives. Otherwise, they may discourage the use of your organs should something happen to you. Check with your local hospital to find out about signing a family pledge—a contract where family members share their wishes about organ and tissue donation. This is an absolutely essential step in making sure the necessary individuals will honor your wish to become an organ donor.

STEP 4: VISUALIZATION The *visualization step* provides the audience with a vision of anticipated outcomes associated with the solution. The purpose of this step is to carry audience members beyond accepting the feasibility of your proposal to seeing how it will actually benefit them:

> There are so many organs and such a variety of tissue that may be transplanted. One organ donor can help up to fifty people. Who can forget the story of 7-year-old American Nicholas Green, the innocent victim of a highway robbery in Italy that cost him his life? Stricken with grief, Nicholas's parents, Reg and Maggie Green, nevertheless immediately decided to donate Nicholas's organs. As a direct result of the donation, seven Italians thrive today, grateful recipients of Nicholas's heart, corneas, liver, pancreas cells, and kidneys. Today, organ donations in Italy are twice as high as they were in 1993, the year preceding Nicholas's death. The Italians call this phenomenon "The Nicholas Effect."

STEP 5: ACTION Finally, in the *action step* the speaker asks audience members to act according to their acceptance of the message. This may involve reconsidering their present way of thinking about something, continuing to believe as they do but with greater commitment, or implementing a new set of behaviors. Here, the speaker makes an explicit call to action:

> It takes courage to become an organ donor.
> You have the courage to become an organ donor.
> All you need to do is say yes to organ and tissue donation on your donor card and/or driver's license and discuss your decision with your family. You can obtain a donor card at www.organdonor.gov.
>
> Be part of "The Nicholas Effect."

Comparative Advantage Pattern

Another way to organize speech points is to show how your viewpoint or proposal is superior to one or more alternative viewpoints or proposals. This design, called the **comparative advantage pattern of arrangement**, is most effective when your audience is already aware of the issue or problem and agrees that a need for a solution (or an alternative view) exists. To maintain credibility, make sure to identify alternatives that your audience is familiar with and ones supported by opposing interests.

With the comparative advantage pattern, the main points in a speech addressing the best way to control the deer population might look like these:

THESIS: Rather than hunting, fencing, or contraception alone, the best way to reduce the deer population is by a dual strategy of hunting *and* contraception.

I. A combination strategy is superior to hunting alone because many areas are too densely populated by humans to permit hunting; in such cases, contraceptive darts and vaccines can address the problem. (*Advantage over alternative #1*)

II. A combination strategy is superior to relying solely on fencing because fencing is far too expensive for widespread use. (*Advantage over alternative #2*)

III. A dual strategy is superior to relying solely on contraception because only a limited number of deer are candidates for contraceptive darts and vaccines. (*Advantage over alternative #3*)

✔️	**CHECKLIST: Steps in the Motivated Sequence**

- ✓ *Step 1: Attention* Address listeners' core concerns, making the speech highly relevant to them.

- ✓ *Step 2: Need* Show listeners that they have an important need that must be satisfied or a problem that must be solved.

- ✓ *Step 3: Satisfaction* Introduce your proposed solution.

- ✓ *Step 4: Visualization* Provide listeners with a vision of anticipated outcomes associated with the solution.

- ✓ *Step 5: Action* Make a direct request of listeners that involves changing or strengthening their present way of thinking or acting.

Refutation Pattern

When you feel confident that the opposing argument is vulnerable, consider the **refutation pattern of arrangement**, in which you confront and then refute (disprove) opposing claims to your position. Refutation works best when you can target the audience's chief objections to the opposing argument. If done well, refutation may influence audience members who either disagree with you or are conflicted about where they stand.

Main points arranged in a refutation pattern follow a format similar to this:

MAIN POINT I:	State the opposing position.
MAIN POINT II:	Describe the implications or ramifications of the opposing claim, explaining why it is faulty.
MAIN POINT III:	Offer arguments and evidence for your position.
MAIN POINT IV:	Contrast your position with the opposing claim to drive home the superiority of your position.

Consider the speaker who argues for increased energy conservation versus a policy of drilling for oil in protected land in Alaska.

THESIS:	Rather than drilling for oil in Alaska's Arctic National Wildlife Refuge, we should focus on energy conservation

measures as a way of lessening our dependence on foreign oil.

I.   Proponents claim that drilling in the Arctic Refuge is necessary to decrease dependence on foreign oil sources and hold down fuel costs while adding jobs, and that modern drilling techniques along with certain environmental restrictions will result in little negative impact on the environment. (*Describes opposing claims*)

II. By calling for drilling, these proponents sidestep our need for stricter energy conservation policies, overlook the need to protect one of the last great pristine lands, and ignore the fact that the oil would make a negligible dent in oil imports—from 68 percent to 65 percent by 2025. (*Describes implications and ramifications of opposing claims*)

III. The massive construction needed to access the tundra will disturb the habitat of caribou, polar bear, and thousands of species of birds and shift the focus from energy conservation to increased energy consumption, when the focus should be the reverse. (*Offers arguments and evidence for the speaker's position, as developed in subpoints*)

IV. The proponents' plan would encourage consumption and endanger the environment; my plan would encourage energy conservation and protect one of the world's few remaining wildernesses. (*Contrasts the speaker's position with opposition's, to drive home the former's superiority*)

Identify the Disposition of the Audience

Where your target audience stands in relation to your topic will significantly affect how they will respond to your persuasive appeals. Are they likely to be receptive to your claims? Critical of them? Persuasion scholar Herbert Simon describes four types of potential audiences and suggests various reasoning strategies and possible organizational patterns for each.[22]

AUDIENCE TYPE	PERSUASIVE STRATEGIES
Hostile audience or those that strongly disagree	• Stress areas of agreement. • Address opposing views. • Don't expect major change in attitudes. • Wait until the end before asking the audience to act, if at all. • Reason inductively: start with evidence, leaving conclusion until last ("tuition should be raised"). • Consider the *refutation* pattern.
Critical and conflicted	• Present strong arguments and evidence. • Address opposing views, perhaps by using the *refutation* pattern.
Sympathetic audience	• Use motivational stories and emotional appeals to reinforce positive attitudes. • Stress your commonality with listeners. • Clearly tell the audience what you want them to think or do. • Consider the *narrative* (storytelling) pattern.
Uninformed, less-educated, or apathetic audience	• Focus on capturing their attention. • Stress personal credibility and "likeability." • Stress the topic's relevance to listeners.

SAMPLE PERSUASIVE SPEECH (PROBLEM-CAUSE-SOLUTION)

The following speech by college student Lisa Roth investigates the crisis in emergency room care and advocates a claim of policy—that our emergency room system should be overhauled. Note that the speech is organized in a problem-cause-solution pattern. Lisa offers a variety of types of claims, evidence, and reasoning to build her argument.

Emergency in the Emergency Room

LISA ROTH
Illinois Central College

Last year, 49-year-old Beatrice Vance began experiencing   1
some alarming symptoms—nausea, shortness of breath,
and chest pain. She called her daughter, Monique, who
raced her to the emergency room at Vista
Medical Center in Lake County, Illinois. At   This dramatic
sign-in, a nurse briefly met with Beatrice   incident serves as an
and told her to wait until she could be seen   effective attention
by a doctor. She advised the women that patients were
treated in order of severity.

Two hours later, when her name was   Lisa's vivid
finally called, Beatrice didn't respond. Hos-   description appeals
pital officials found her slumped over in   to listeners'
her chair, ten feet or so from the admitting   emotion (pathos)
station, unconscious and without a pulse.   problem exists.
According to an ABC *Nightly News* report
on September 17th, 2007, Beatrice had already died from
a massive heart attack while waiting to be seen by a doctor.

Sadly, Beatrice is not the only one who has suffered   3
from the hands of overwhelmed, sometimes inconsistent,
and sometimes incompetent emergency
room staff members. Similar scenes occur   Lisa states her thesis
in hospitals across the country. According   and backs it up with
to experts on the frontline, such as Dr. Brent   an expert's opinion;
Eastman, Chief Medical Advisor at Scripps   source's credibility,
Health Hospital in San Diego, America's   she names his title
emergency rooms are in a crisis that could   and affiliation.
jeopardize everyone in this room and all their loved ones.

Today, we'll uncover the catastrophic   Lisa's preview
conditions existing in America's emer-   statement indicates
gency rooms, discover what is causing these   a problem-cause-
conditions, and look at how to restore our   solution pattern.
faith in a system that has—to quote from an
editorial in the June 21st, 2006, edition of the *New York
Times*—"reached a breaking point."

To begin, emergency rooms are des-   Lisa introduces
perately overcrowded. According to a   the first problem
landmark series of three reports on the   plaguing the ER
breakdown of our emergency room sys-   system.
tem conducted by the Institute of Medicine, the need
for emergency rooms has increased by 26 percent since

1993; during the same period, 425 emergency departments closed their doors. The average emergency room wait is now almost four hours, according to a report broadcast on *Good Morning America* on September 18th, 2006, but patients could be asked to wait up to forty-eight hours before they are allowed into an inpatient bed.

Citing recent statistics from a credible source about the ER system emphasizes the gravity of the situation.

The United States emergency care system is also seriously understaffed, especially with regard to specialists. As reported in the *New York Times* editorial, emergency rooms find it very difficult to get specialists to take emergency room and trauma center calls. Specialists such as neurosurgeons shy away from emergency room procedures because of the lack of compensation associated with treating so many uninsured patients, as well as the risk of seeing their malpractice premiums rise.

Lisa introduces the second problem—understaffing.

Not only are emergency rooms understaffed; existing staff often are unprepared for disasters. An investigation in the July 6th, 2006, edition of the *Columbus Dispatch* found that EMTs received only one hour of training for major disaster preparation. What's even scarier, says Maria Perotin in the June 15th, 2006, edition of the *Fort Worth Star Telegram*, with one major disaster—if a terrorist's bomb exploded or an epidemic broke out—our emergency care service could fall apart completely.

7

The third problem with our current system is not surprising. There is simply not enough money to adequately fund our emergency rooms.

Lisa introduces the third problem plaguing the ER system.

The *New York Times* reports that emergency rooms are notorious money losers. Most emergency rooms operate in the red even while being asked to operate securely and safely. Additionally, as reported in the June 15th, 2006, edition of the *Pittsburgh Tribune Review*, because of the lack of money, there are now 200,000 fewer hospital beds in the United States than there were in 1993, even as the need for them has increased tremendously.

9

She briefly summarizes the nature of the problem before transitioning to the causes.

So, our emergency rooms are broke, overcrowded, and understaffed. Don't you feel secure?

10

We can pinpoint three specific causes for the emergency room crisis. These include the highly fragmented emergency

Lisa now turns to the causes of the crisis.

medical care system, the uninsured patients, and the lack
of money.

Fragmentation occurs on all levels because there are no   12
standardized procedures and no clear chain of command.
On the regional level, emergency vehicles fail to communicate effectively with ER and trauma care centers, causing
poorly managed patient flow. On the national level, there
are no standardized procedures for the training and certi-
fication of emergency room personnel.

To complicate matters even more, there is no lead   13
agency to control emergency room and trauma care
centers.

So, as you can see, this lack of organization, from poorly managed patient flow to
the absences of standardized training and
certifying personnel, causes chaos and confusion in what should be a streamlined and
secure service industry.

An internal
summary of the
first cause of the
problem.

Consider the second cause of the crisis.

Transitioning into
the second cause.

Uninsured patients cause about as
much chaos in the emergency room as does fragmentation. According to the July 6th, 2006, *Columbus Dispatch*,
through no fault of their own, there are now 46 million
uninsured in the United States. This of course leads to
more unpaid ER bills, which leads to more financial problems for the emergency rooms.

But please understand, I am not blaming the patients   17
who simply cannot afford or are not offered health insurance. They are merely the effect of a larger cause: a society
that doesn't place a premium on affordable health care. A
lack of affordable health care only perpetuates the cycle
in which no affordable health care means no insurance,
which in turn leads to unpaid ER bills.

The vast numbers of uninsured leads
us to the third and final cause of the emergency room breakdown. Emergency rooms
are plagued by insufficient reimbursements
from insurers and insufficient funding by the government.

Lisa transitions
from the second to
the third cause of
the crisis.

Lack of money is a major cause of the shortage of capac-   19
ity and staffing stability in the emergency rooms. Maria
Perotin of the *Fort Worth Star Telegram* reports that emergency rooms received only 4 percent of the $3.38 billion that
was allotted to them by the Homeland Security Department
in 2002 and 2003 for emergency medical preparation. As
government budgets continue to be slashed, the quality of
our health care will continue to deteriorate.

So, how can we renovate a cycle that seems beyond control? Well, we can look to solutions on a national level and then on a personal level.

The first step to defeating the chaos in the emergency 21 rooms is to create a coordinated, regionalized system with national standards and a lead agency. Everyone—from 911, to ambulances, to emergency care services—needs to coordinate their operations effectively and efficiently in order to ensure each patient a safe and secure emergency room visit. Additionally, the Institute of Medicine suggests that a lead agency be started in the Department of Health and Human Services in order to control emergency room and trauma care centers.

On a personal level, the National Association of Emer- 22 gency Physicians asks us to be responsible before going to the emergency room. Before going to the emergency room, ask yourself, do I really need to go the emergency room, or can my primary care physician take care of my needs? Urge your community leaders to lessen the impact of the uninsured on emergency rooms by following the lead of the people of Columbus, Ohio, who, according to the July 6th, 2006 edition, of the *Columbus Dispatch*, are building affordable primary care clinics in some of the poor neighborhoods.

Today we have uncovered some of the catastrophic conditions existing in America's emergency rooms. Armed with a greater understanding of what is causing these issues—overcrowding, lack of specialization and training, and funding—we can now look to the future and focus our energy on solving this national crisis.

Unfortunately, while it is too late for Beatrice Vance, 24 authorities did rule that her death was a homicide because she was not given an EKG within 10 minutes of admission to the emergency room. This paves the way for criminal prosecution of the Vista Medical Center and puts emergency rooms across the country on notice that they too could be found liable should they be found similarly negligent.

Perhaps this terrible tragedy will turn out to be the 25 wake-up call that the United States has needed in order to restore safety and stability to our emergency care system.

Works Cited

Amen, Rob. "Emergency Rooms Turn Away More Patients."
Pittsburgh Tribune Review, June 16, 2006.

Campo-Flores, Arian. "How to Stop the Bleeding." *Newsweek*, May
8, 2007. www.newsweek.com/id/34803.

"Code Blue." Editorial. *Columbus Dispatch*, July 6, 2006, 18A.
www.dispatch.com.

Committee on the Future of Emergency Care in the United
States Health System. *Emergency Medical Services*: *At the
Crossroads*. Bethesda, MD: National Academies Press, 2007.

"Emergency in the Emergency Rooms." Opinion. *New York
Times*, June 21, 2006. www.nytimes.com/2006/06/21/
opinion/21Wed4.html?ex=1189137600&en=fdd466fef8f1534c
&ei=5070.

"Illinois Woman's ER Wait Death Ruled a Homicide." *Good Morning
America*, September 17, 2006. Accessed September 26, 2007.
abcnews.go.com/GMA/Health/story?id=2454685&page=1.

"Inexcusable Death." *ABC Nightly News*, September 18, 2006.
Accessed September 26, 2007. abcnews.go.com/Video/
playerIndex?id=2457808.

National Association of EMS Physicians. Summary of "Future
of Emergency Care: Hospital-Based Emergency Care at the
Breaking Point" Recommendations. Accessed September 26,
2007. www.naemsp.org.

Perotin, Maria M. "Serious Condition." *Fort Worth Star Telegram*,
June 15, 2006, C1.

SAMPLE PERSUASIVE SPEECH
(MONROE'S MOTIVATED SEQUENCE)

In this speech, Stephanie Poplin argues that by volunteering we can enrich our lives (a claim of value). Stephanie
organizes the speech using Monroe's five-step motivated
sequence pattern. She begins with the *attention step*,
making the speech relevant to listeners. She next points
to audience members' innate thirst for fulfillment in life

(the *need step*) and suggests that volunteering can satisfy or solve this need (the *satisfaction step*). Next, Stephanie offers vivid examples of how listeners will feel when they volunteer (the *visualization step*). She concludes by directly asking the audience to get involved (the *action step*).

The Importance of Community Engagement and Volunteerism

STEPHANIE POPLIN
University of Oklahoma

"Great social forces are the mere accumulation of indi-   1
vidual actions." Think about that—"*Great social forces
are the mere accumulation of individual actions.*" This was
said by noted economist and antipoverty
activity Jeffrey Sachs in a March 2005 *Time*
magazine essay about helping the world's
poor. And it's true, right? Every great volunteer organization and every great social
movement, from the Red Cross to the
Peace Corps to the Civil Rights Movement,
achieved what it did through individual actions, yet all
those actions were history changing.

> Stephanie establishes the attention step by stating that listeners have the power to make profound changes in the world.

I'm Stephanie Poplin, and I would like to speak to you   2
today about why it is imperative that you give yourself
the opportunity to live a more successful and meaningful life. One way of achieving this is by contributing—by
putting yourself into the community that surrounds you.
I'm referring to community service and civic engagement.
Today, I will talk to you about what you can personally
gain from your involvement and participation in your
community.

Volunteering may seem like it requires too
much time and energy. In truth, it's a require-
ment for happiness. Marian Wright Edelman,
founder of the Children's Defense Fund,
made this observation: "We make a living by
what we get, we make a life by what we give."
Echoing this, Helen Keller, who was both
blind and deaf, yet devoted her life to others,
said, "The unselfish effort to bring cheer to
others will be the beginning of a happier life for ourselves."

> Stephanie introduces the *need* step by claiming that volunteering is a "requirement for happiness."

> Stephanie quotes two credible sources to illustrate her point.

Now, traditionally, when you hear the words *commu-*   4
nity service and *volunteer*, what do you think of? Some
of us become confused by "community service," since it

can refer to both an alternative to jail time and to an altruistic act of giving to the community. Here I am speaking about the latter. And what about the term *volunteer*? Here, we think of someone who wants to do good—someone who wants to improve the lives of those who are less fortunate. And while this remains true, attitudes towards volunteering are changing. Volunteers are realizing that in addition to satisfying altruistic goals, community service offers some major personal benefits.

Clarifying potentially unclear terms is important, regardless of speech type.

In today's job market, for example, it's becoming evident that college graduates need more than just paper qualifications. We'll need to be able to stand out from the crowd, to be resourceful, to be initiators, to be team players, and to possess a get-up-and-go attitude. These are now the desired skills of employers, and volunteering can provide all of this.

She establishes the need step by appealing to her listeners' core concerns and self-actualization needs.

Research bears this out. Student Volunteering UK conducted large-scale research into the benefits of volunteering. Results show that volunteering can enhance employability and develop and strengthen new and different job skills. In our own country, the Corporation for National and Community Service has found that volunteering makes us better problem solvers, a key trait employers look for. I think we'd all agree this is a necessity for us, especially given the stages our lives are in right now.

Demonstrating how volunteering can solve our innate need for fulfillment, Stephanie transitions into the satisfaction step.

Stephanie uses sources that her college audience is likely to find credible.

Virtually every paid job can be mirrored by a volunteering opportunity, according to both the Corporation for National and Community Service and Student Volunteering UK. Taking part in community service is a new and pioneering form of work experience. Not only is it seen as work experience, but employers view job applicants who have volunteered as having greater initiative and commitment than applicants without volunteer experience.

7

Research from Student Volunteering UK and the Corporation for National and Community Service also lists outcomes, other than résumé building, that students felt they had gained through their participation in volunteering. Here's some of what they found:

Stephanie demonstrates the visualization steps, which reinforces outcomes associated with the solution (volunteering).

- Volunteering built confidence.
- It helped them decide on a career path.

- Making a difference gave them a feeling of exhilaration.
- Their service opened up unexpected opportunities and challenges.

Volunteering also benefits physical and emotional 9 health. The Corporation for National and Community Service did a review of recent research on the health benefits of volunteering. It found that volunteering builds social support networks and enhances a sense of achievement and meaning, which in turn leads to lowered rates of depression and even lowered mortality rates.

Just as volunteering can help individuals become happier and healthier, it helps strengthen communities. *Community building* is an incredibly important social outcome of volunteering. According to the Corporation for National and Community Service, volunteers are absolutely crucial to creating and sustaining healthy communities.

Fortunately, since the tragedy of 9/11 now nearly a 11 decade ago, as well as the election of President Barack Obama and his call to national service, there has been a surge in student volunteers. Volunteering has increased so much since 2001 that today's student volunteers are sometimes called the "9/11 generation" by leaders of charitable organizations. The Corporation reports, for example, that each year since 2001, 3.3 million college students—over 30 percent of the college population—gave their time, up from 27 percent before 9/11. Tutoring and mentoring are the most popular volunteer activities, with 44 percent of students spending at least 12 hours a week on these activities. Students who take service learning courses and who work part time volunteer more often than those who don't have jobs.

Knowing that people tend to adopt a behavior if they know that people like themselves have done so, Stephanie mentions examples of student volunteers.

I have experienced the benefits of community service firsthand through my involvement in Habitat for Humanity. Habitat for Humanity is an international organization fueled by hundreds of thousands of volunteers who join with future homeowners to build simple and affordable houses.

Still in the visualization step, Stephanie offers personal testimony to demonstrate how volunteering can make a real impact.

It wasn't until my first experience building a home, 13 here in Norman, that I realized the impact this organization has on its volunteers and the families involved. I've always had a bedroom of my own to escape to, and I've always had a kitchen to make breakfast in the morning, but there are two little boys who now have this for the first time, thanks to the University of Oklahoma's chapter of Habitat for Humanity. I have always taken my home for granted, but now I can be a part of giving these little boys a home of their own.

Sometimes big changes follow from small events, such as my sheetrocking an empty space that will eventually become a living room that these little boys and their mom and dad can enjoy together.

> These words link back to the speech's central idea to promote thematic unity.

Someone once told me, "You don't find yourself; you create yourself." As college students, we have every opportunity in the world to create a life that is successful and meaningful. Use your good fortune, and choose to create a life that is service-oriented. Walk over to OU's Volunteer Programs office on West California, or go to their Web page. You'll find great ways to combine volunteering with earning your degree. You can also go to *Step Up*'s community volunteer network—just Google "Step Up!"—to find volunteer opportunities in your area. Visit the *Habitat for Humanity* Web site and click on "Local Affiliates" to find the branch nearest you. These are just a few ways to find volunteer opportunities. Many others exist, from countless nonprofits, to houses of worship, to local, state, and federal government programs.

> 15

> Here Stephanie transitions to the fifth and final step, the *action step*.

> To encourage action, Stephanie offers contact information for volunteer organizations.

We have seen how you can personally benefit from contributing to your community. Whether you want to make new friends, improve your job prospects, test a potential career, or build confidence, help build communities, beat depression, and even live longer, volunteering can be the answer. People who have spent time volunteering report they get back in personal fulfillment and satisfaction more than they ever expend in inconvenience and effort.

> Stephanie signals the conclusion.

> Stephanie briefly reiterates the main points.

We all have the power to make an impact one way or another. After all, "Great social forces are the mere accumulation of individual actions."

> Stephanie concludes by repeating the quote from the introduction, bringing the speech full circle.

Works Cited

Corporation for National and Community Service. *College Students Helping America*. October 2006. www.nationalservice.gov/pdf/06_1016_RPD_college_ full.pdf.

Motivational Quotes Web site. Quotes on Volunteering Page.
www.motivationalquotes.com/pages/volunteer-quotes.html.

Sachs, Jeffrey D. "The End of Poverty." *Time,* March 6, 2005.

Student Volunteering UK. *The Art of Crazy Paving: Volunteering for Enhanced Employability.* Accessed January 8, 2008. www.studentvolunteering.org.uk/.

25   Speaking on Special Occasions

A **special occasion speech** is one that is prepared for a specific occasion and for a purpose dictated by that occasion. Special occasion speeches can be either informative or persuasive or, often, a mix of both. However, neither of these functions is the main goal; the underlying function of a special occasion speech is to entertain, celebrate, commemorate, inspire, or set a social agenda:

- In speeches that *entertain,* listeners expect a lighthearted, amusing speech; they may also expect the speaker to offer a certain degree of insight into the topic at hand.
- In speeches that *celebrate* (a person, a place, or an event), listeners look to the speaker to praise the subject of the celebration; they also anticipate a degree of ceremony in accordance with the norms of the occasion.
- In speeches that *commemorate* an event or a person (at dedications of memorials or at gatherings held in someone's honor), listeners expect the speaker to offer remembrance and tribute.
- In speeches that *inspire* (including inaugural addresses, keynote speeches, and commencement speeches), listeners expect to be motivated by examples of achievement and heroism.
- In speeches that *set social agendas* (such as occur at gatherings of cause-oriented organizations, fund-raisers, campaign banquets, conferences, and conventions), listeners expect the articulation and reinforcement of the goals and values of the group.

Special occasion speeches include speeches of introduction, speeches of acceptance, speeches of presentation, roasts and toasts, eulogies and other speeches of tribute, after-dinner speeches, and speeches of inspiration.

Speeches of Introduction

The object of a **speech of introduction** is to prepare or "warm up" the audience for the main speaker—to heighten audience interest and build the speaker's credibility. A good speech of introduction balances four elements: the speaker's background, the subject of the speaker's message, the occasion, and the audience.

- *Describe the speaker's background and qualifications.* Relate the speaker's achievements, offices held, and other facts to demonstrate why the speaker is relevant to the occasion. Mention the speaker's accomplishments, but not so many that the audience glazes over.

- *Briefly preview the speaker's topic.* Give the audience a sense of why the subject is of interest, bearing in mind that it is not the introducer's job to evaluate the speech. The rule is: Get in and out quickly with a few well-chosen remarks.

- *Invite the audience to welcome the speaker.* This can be done simply by saying something like "Please welcome Cesar Cruz."

- *Be brief.* Speak just long enough to accomplish the goals of preparation and motivation. One well-known speaker recommends a two-minute maximum.[1]

✓ **CHECKLIST: Preparing a Speech of Introduction**

✓ Identify the speaker correctly. Assign him or her the proper title, such as "vice president for public relations" or "professor emeritus."

✓ Practice a difficult-to-pronounce name several times before introducing the speaker.

✓ Contact the speaker ahead of time to verify any facts about him or her that you plan to cite.

✓ Consider devices that will capture the audience's attention, such as quotes, short anecdotes, or startling statements.

> ### QUICK TIP
>
> **Respond to the Introduction**
> *Whenever you are introduced by another speaker, acknowledge and thank him or her for the introduction. Common methods of responding include "I appreciate those kind words" and "Thank you for making me feel welcome...." Accept praise with humility and perhaps even with humor: "Your description was so gracious that I did not realize you were speaking about me...."*

Speeches of Acceptance

A **speech of acceptance** is made in response to receiving an award. Its purpose is to express gratitude for the honor bestowed on the speaker. The speech should reflect that gratitude.

- *Prepare in advance.* If you know or even suspect that you are to receive an award, decide before the event what you will say.

- *Express what the award means to you.* Convey to the audience the value you place on the award. Express yourself genuinely and with humility.

- *Express gratitude.* Thank by name each of the relevant persons or organizations involved in giving you the award. Acknowledge any team players or others who helped you attain the achievement for which you are being honored.

Upon winning an Academy Award in 2011 for his role in the film *The King's Speech*, actor Colin Firth expressed elation at receiving the award with humility and humor:

> I'm afraid I have to warn you that I'm experiencing stirrings somewhere in the upper abdominals which are threatening to form themselves into dance moves. Joyous as they may be for me, it would be extremely problematic if they make it to my legs before I get offstage.[2]

Speeches of Presentation

The goal of the **speech of presentation** is twofold: to communicate the meaning of the award and to explain why the recipient is receiving it.

- *Convey the meaning of the award.* Describe what the award is for and what it represents. Mention the sponsors and describe the link between the sponsors' goals and values and the award.

- *Explain why the recipient is receiving the award.* Describe the recipient's achievements and special attributes that qualify him or her as deserving of the award.

Roasts and Toasts

A **roast** is a humorous tribute to a person, one in which a series of speakers jokingly poke fun at him or her. A **toast** is a brief tribute to a person or an event being celebrated. Both roasts and toasts call for short speeches whose goal is to celebrate an individual and his or her achievements.

- *Prepare.* Impromptu though they might appear, the best roasts and toasts reflect time spent drafting and rehearsing. As you practice, time the speech.
- *Highlight remarkable traits of the person being honored.* Restrict your remarks to one or two of the person's most unusual or recognizable attributes. Convey the qualities that have made him or her worthy of celebrating.
- *Be positive and be brief.* Even if the speech is poking fun at someone, as in a roast, keep the tone positive. Remember, your overall purpose is to pay tribute to the honoree. Also, be considerate of the other speakers by refraining from taking up too much time. This is particularly important for toasts, which are expected to be very brief.

At the 2010 annual White House Correspondents' Dinner, President Barack Obama used self-deprecating humor to poke fun at himself:

> It's been quite a year since I've spoken here last. Lots of ups, lots of downs, except for my approval ratings, which have just gone down. But that's politics, it doesn't bother me. Besides, I happen to know that my approval ratings are still very high in the country of my birth.[3]

Eulogies and Other Tributes

The word **eulogy** derives from the Greek word meaning "to praise." Those delivering eulogies, usually close friends or family members of the deceased, are charged with celebrating and commemorating the life of someone while consoling those who have been left behind.

- *Balance delivery and emotions.* The audience looks to the speaker for guidance in dealing with the loss and for a sense of closure, so stay in control. If you do feel that you are about to break down, pause, take a breath, and focus on your next thought.

- *Refer to the family of the deceased.* Families suffer the greatest loss, and a funeral is primarily for their benefit. Show respect for the family, and mention each family member by name.

- *Be positive but realistic.* Emphasize the deceased's positive qualities while avoiding excessive praise.

QUICK TIP

Commemorate Life—Not Death

A eulogy should pay tribute to the deceased person as an individual and remind the audience that he or she is still alive, in a sense, in our memories. Rather than focus on the circumstances of death, focus on the life of the person. Talk about the person's contributions and achievements, and demonstrate the person's character. Consider telling an anecdote that illustrates the type of person you are eulogizing. Even humorous anecdotes may be appropriate if they effectively humanize the deceased.

After-Dinner Speeches

Its name notwithstanding, the contemporary **after-dinner speech** is just as likely to occur before, during, or after a lunch seminar or other type of business, professional, or civic meeting as it is to follow a formal dinner. In general, an after-dinner speech is expected to be lighthearted and entertaining. At the same time, listeners expect to gain insight into the topic at hand and/or to hear an outline of priorities and goals for the group.

- *Recognize the occasion.* Connect the speech with the occasion. Delivering a speech that is unrelated to the event may leave the impression that the speech is **canned**—one that the speaker uses again and again in different settings.

- *Keep remarks sufficiently low-key to accompany the diges-tion of a meal.* Even when charged with addressing a seri-ous topic, keep the tone somewhat low-key.

QUICK TIP

Be Yourself When Using Humor
The most convincing speakers are the ones who are naturally believable. Trying to become funnier—or more serious—than you normally are can lead to an inauthentic delivery. If you are naturally very funny, use that skill. If you have more of a dry sense of humor, plan jokes that reflect that kind of humor.

Speeches of Inspiration

A **speech of inspiration** seeks to uplift members of the audi-ence and to help them see things in a positive light. Sermons, commencement addresses, "pep talks," and nomination speeches are all inspirational in nature. Effective speeches of inspiration touch on deep feelings in the audience. Through emotional force, they urge us toward purer motives and harder effort and remind us of a common good.

- *Appeal to audience members' emotions.* Three means of evoking emotion are *touching upon shared values, vivid description,* and *storytelling* (see Chapter 24). Techniques of language such as repetition, alliteration, and parallel-ism can also help transport the audience from the mun-dane to a loftier level (see Chapter 16).

- *Use real-life stories.* Few things move us as much as real-life examples and stories, such as that of an ordinary per-son whose struggles result in triumph over adversity and the realization of a dream.

- *Be dynamic.* If it fits your personality, use a dynamic speaking style to inspire through delivery. Combining an energetic style with a powerful message can be one of the most successful strategies for inspirational speaking.

- *Make your goal clear.* Inspirational speeches run the risk of being vague, leaving the audience unsure what the message was. Whatever you are trying to motivate your listeners to do, let them know.

- *Consider a distinctive organizing device.* Many successful inspirational speakers use devices such as *acronyms* or steps to help the audience to remember the message. For example, a football coach speaking at a practice session might organize an inspirational speech around the word *WIN*. His main points might be "Work," "Intensity," and "No excuses," forming the acronym *WIN*.

- *Close with a dramatic ending.* Use a dramatic ending to inspire your audience to feel or act. Recall from Chapter 15 the various methods of concluding a speech, including quotations, stories, rhetorical questions, and a call to action.

QUICK TIP

Tailor Your Message to the Audience and Occasion
Always plan your special occasion speech with audience expectations firmly in mind. People listening to a eulogy, for example, will be very sensitive to what they perceive to be inappropriate humor or lack of respect. Those attending a dedication ceremony for a war memorial will expect the speaker to offer words of inspiration. When a speaker violates audience expectations in situations like these, audience reaction will usually be pronounced.

SAMPLE SPECIAL OCCASION SPEECH

This commencement speech by J. K. Rowling, author of the Harry Potter books, does what any good speech of inspiration must do: It focuses on uplifting audience members and arousing their better instincts. Rowling achieves this by sharing her hard-won life lessons with the graduates. Rhetorically, Rowling uses rhythmic language, emotional appeals, and a dynamic style of delivery, all key components of speeches of inspiration.

2008 Harvard University Commencement Address

J. K. ROWLING

President Faust, members of the Harvard Corporation and the Board of Overseers, members of the faculty, proud parents, and, above all, graduates.

The first thing I would like to say is "thank you." Not only has Harvard given me an extraordinary honor, but the weeks

When delivering a special occasion speech, it is especially important to acknowledge members of the audience, as Rowling does here.

of fear and nausea I have endured at the thought of giving this commencement address have made me lose weight. A win-win situation! Now all I have to do is take deep breaths, squint at the red banners and convince myself that I am at the world's largest Gryffindor reunion....

> Rowling's use of humor draws the audience in.

...I have wracked my mind and heart for what I 3
ought to say to you today. I have asked myself what I wish I had known at my own graduation, and what important lessons I have learned in the 21 years that have expired between that day and this.

I have come up with two answers....I have decided to talk to you about the benefits of failure. And as you stand on the threshold of what is sometimes called "real life," I want to extol the crucial importance of imagination.

These may seem quixotic or paradoxical choices, but please bear with me.

> Because inspirational speeches run the risk of being vague, it is important to tell audience members what your message will be about, as Rowling does here.

Looking back at the 21-year-old that I was at gradua- 6
tion is a slightly uncomfortable experience for the 42-year-old that she has become. Half my lifetime ago, I was striking an uneasy balance between the ambition I had for myself, and what those closest to me expected of me.

> Recalling how she felt as a 21-year-old establishes a common bond with listeners, encouraging identification with Rowling and receptivity to her message.

I was convinced that the only thing I wanted to do, ever, was to write novels. However, my parents, both of whom came from impoverished backgrounds and neither of whom had been to college, took the view that my overactive imagination was an amusing personal quirk that would never pay a mortgage, or secure a pension. I know that the irony strikes with the force of a cartoon anvil, now.

So they hoped that I would take a vocational degree; 8
I wanted to study English Literature. A compromise was reached that in retrospect satisfied nobody, and I went up to study Modern Languages. Hardly had my parents' car rounded the corner at the end of the road than I ditched German and scuttled off down the Classics corridor.

> Many audience members will likely identify with the struggle between the lure of creativity and the pull of practicality.

... Of all the subjects on this planet, I think they would 9
have been hard put to name one less useful than Greek

mythology when it came to securing the keys to an executive bathroom.

... I cannot criticize my parents for hoping that I would 10
never experience poverty. They had been poor themselves,
and I have since been poor, and I quite agree with them
that it is not an ennobling experience. Poverty entails fear,
and stress, and sometimes depression; it means a thousand
petty humiliations and hardships....

What I feared most for myself at your age was not pov- 11
erty, but failure....

Ultimately, we all have to decide for ourselves what 12
constitutes failure, but the world is quite eager to give you
a set of criteria if you let it. So I think it fair to say that by
any conventional measure, a mere seven years after my
graduation day, I had failed on an epic scale. An exception-
ally short-lived marriage had imploded, and I was jobless,
a lone parent, and as poor as it is possible to be in modern
Britain, without being homeless. The fears
that my parents had had for me, and that I
had had for myself, had both come to pass,
and by every usual standard, I was the big-
gest failure I knew.

> Everyone can identify with fears of failure.

Now, I am not going to stand here and tell you that 13
failure is fun. That period of my life was a dark one, and
I had no idea that there was going to be what the press
has since represented as a kind of fairy tale resolution. I
had no idea then how far the tunnel extended, and for
a long time, any light at the end of it was a hope rather
than a reality.

So why do I talk about the benefits of
failure? Simply because failure meant a
stripping away of the inessential. I stopped
pretending to myself that I was anything other than what
I was, and began to direct all my energy into finishing the
only work that mattered to me. Had I really succeeded at
anything else, I might never have found the determination
to succeed in the one arena I believed I truly belonged. I
was set free, because my greatest fear had been realized,
and I was still alive, and I still had a daughter whom I
adored, and I had an old typewriter and a big idea. And
so rock bottom became the solid foundation on which I
rebuilt my life....

> An effective use of a rhetorical question.

Failure gave me an inner security that I had never 15
attained by passing examinations. Failure taught me
things about myself that I could have learned no other

way. I discovered that I had a strong will, and more discipline than I had suspected; I also found out that I had friends whose value was truly above the price of rubies.... So given a Time Turner, I would tell my 21-year-old self that personal happiness lies in knowing that life is not a checklist

> Repeating the word "failure" several times in succession—a rhetorical device called anaphora—creates rhythm and thereby implants ideas in listeners' minds.

of acquisition or achievement. Your qualifications, your CV, are not your life, though you will meet many people of my age and older who confuse the two. Life is difficult, and complicated, and beyond anyone's total control, and the humility to know that will enable you to survive its vicissitudes.

Now you might think that I chose my second theme, the importance of imagination, because of the part it played in rebuild-

> Rowling clearly states her second theme.

ing my life, but that is not wholly so. Though I personally will defend the value of bedtime stories to my last gasp, I have learned to value imagination in a much broader sense. Imagination is not only the uniquely human capacity to envision that which is not, and therefore the fount of all invention and innovation. In its arguably most transformative and revelatory capacity, it is the power that enables us to empathize with humans whose experiences we have never shared.

One of the greatest formative experiences of my life 18 preceded Harry Potter, though it informed much of what I subsequently wrote in those books. This revelation came in the form of one of my earliest day jobs... at the African research department at Amnesty International's headquarters in London.

There in my little office I read hastily scribbled letters 19 smuggled out of totalitarian regimes by men and women who were risking imprisonment to inform the outside world of what was happening to them. I saw photographs of those who had disappeared without trace.... I read the testimony of torture victims and saw pictures of their injuries....

> Relating real-life stories is a very effective way to inspire audience members.

Every day, I saw more evidence about the evils human- 20 kind will inflict on their fellow humans, to gain or maintain power. I began to have nightmares, literal nightmares, about some of the things I saw, heard, and read.

And yet I also learned more about human goodness 21 at Amnesty International than I had ever known before.

Amnesty mobilizes thousands of people who have   22
never been tortured or imprisoned for their beliefs to
act on behalf of those who have. The power of human
empathy, leading to collective action, saves
lives, and frees prisoners. Ordinary people,   Effective speeches
whose personal well-being and security are   of inspiration make
                                                  frequent use of
assured, join together in huge numbers   emotional appeals.
to save people they do not know, and will   Here Rowling
never meet. My small participation in that   appeals to the
                                                  human impulse to
process was one of the most humbling and   fight against evil.
inspiring experiences of my life.

Unlike any other creature on this planet, humans can   23
learn and understand, without having experienced. They
can think themselves into other people's places.

Of course, this is a power, like my brand of fictional   24
magic, that is morally neutral. One might use such an ability to manipulate, or control, just as much as to understand or sympathize.

And many prefer not to exercise their imaginations at   25
all. They choose to remain comfortably within the bounds
of their own experience, never troubling to wonder how
it would feel to have been born other than they are. They
can refuse to hear screams or to peer inside cages; they can
close their minds and hearts to any suffering that does not
touch them personally; they can refuse to know....

Those who choose not to empathize enable real mon-   26
sters. For without ever committing an act of outright evil
ourselves, we collude with it, through our own apathy.

One of the many things I learned at the end of that   27
Classics corridor down which I ventured at the age of 18,
in search of something I could not then
define, was this, written by the Greek author   Rowling shares
Plutarch: What we achieve inwardly will   a profound and
                                                 timeless lesson.
change outer reality.

That is an astonishing statement and yet proven a thou-   28
sand times every day of our lives. It expresses, in part, our
inescapable connection with the outside world, the fact
that we touch other people's lives simply by existing.

But how much more are you, Harvard graduates of   29
2008, likely to touch other people's lives? Your intelligence, your capacity for hard work, the education you have
earned and received, give you unique status, and unique
responsibilities. Even your nationality sets you apart. The
great majority of you belong to the world's only remaining
superpower. The way you vote, the way you live, the way

you protest, the pressure you bring to bear on your government, has an impact way beyond your borders. That is your privilege, and your burden.

If you choose to use your status and influence to raise your voice on behalf of those who have no voice; if you choose to identify not only with the powerful, but with the powerless; if you retain the ability to imagine yourself into the lives of those who do not have your advantages, then it will not only be your proud families who celebrate your existence, but thousands and millions of people whose reality you have helped change....

> Rowling begins successive sentences with the same phrase ("If you choose…"), creating a rhythm that sustains attention.

I am nearly finished. I have one last hope for you, which is something that I already had at 21. The friends with whom I sat on graduation day have been my friends for life. They are my children's godparents, the people to whom I've been able to turn in times of trouble, people who have been kind enough not to sue me when I took their names for Death Eaters....

> Rowling very directly signals the conclusion of her speech.

So today, I wish you nothing better than similar friendships. And tomorrow, I hope that even if you remember not a single word of mine, you remember those of Seneca, another of those old Romans I met when I fled down the Classics corridor, in retreat from career ladders, in search of ancient wisdom:

As is a tale, so is life: not how long it is, but how good it is, is what matters.

> A final classical quotation encapsulates Rowling's theme of taking risks in pursuit of a meaningful life and leaves the audience with a powerful message.

I wish you all very good lives. Thank you very much.

Part 8
Online, Group, and Business Contexts

26. Preparing Online Presentations 232
27. Communicating in Groups 238
28. Presenting in Teams 243
29. Business and Professional Presentations 247

As virtual communications technologies gain in sophistication and travel costs rise in the "bricks-and-mortar" world of traditional public speaking, the demand for people skilled in speaking to remote audiences will continue to grow. Whether addressing classmates, co-workers, or customers, you'll want to feel confident in your ability to prepare and deliver presentations for distribution online.

Apply Your Knowledge of Face-to-Face Speaking

Online presentations require the same basic elements of planning and delivery as **face-to-face (FtF) presentations**. As in traditional public speaking, an online speaker will select among the three general speech purposes of informing, persuading, or marking an event. Both kinds of speaking call for careful audience analysis, credible supporting materials, and a natural style of delivery. And whether presenting electronically or in-person, a speaker must continually engage the audience; when separated physically, this focus becomes all the more critical.

Understand the Unique Demands of Virtual Delivery

While much is similar, important differences exist between online and FtF speaking, in both the means of delivery and nature of the audience. As you plan your presentations, apply the traditional techniques of public speaking you already know while making the necessary adjustments to transmit your message effectively in the virtual world.

Review the Equipment

Unlike FtF speeches, online presentations require at least some familiarity with electronic connectivity tools. Well before the actual delivery time, review any equipment you'll be using, and rehearse your presentation several times with it. Preparation may not always avert technical failure, but it will almost always speed recovery time.

Following are tools used to produce and display online presentations:

- Broadband Internet connection; Web site or Intranet connection for distribution to audience

- Hardware for recording audio and video (Webcam/video camera/microphone)
- Software for recording and editing audio and video (e.g., Adobe Audition)
- Video capture software (e.g., ScreenFlow, Camtasia)
- Web-based presentation software (e.g., Prezi, SlideRocket)
- Podcasting software (e.g., Propaganda, Audacity)
- Popular commercial Web sites (e.g., YouTube, Vimeo)
- Online conferencing tools (e.g., Glance, GoToMeeting, Yugma Skype)

Focus on Vocal Variety

In an online presentation, the audience cannot interact with your physical presence, making your voice an even more critical conduit of communication. In place of body movement, *vocal variety*—alternations in volume, pitch, speaking rate, pauses, and pronunciation and articulation—must hold audience interest. Especially important to eliminate are vocal fillers such as "umm" and "aww." In place of these, use strategic pauses to help audience members process information. Enthusiasm and naturalness are key (see Chapter 18).

QUICK TIP

Sounding Enthusiastic Online

Staring into a computer screen rather than listeners' eyes makes it difficult to infuse your voice with the enthusiasm and naturalness that eye contact encourages. To circumvent this problem, seasoned online presenters suggest delivering your first presentations with someone else in the room, talking to that person rather than to the screen. Alternatively, experiment with addressing your remarks to a picture, photograph, or even your own reflection in a mirror.[1]

Provide Superior Visual Aids

The audience might not see you in person, but with presentation aids you can still provide them with a compelling visual experience. Consider how you can illustrate your talking points in eye-catching text form or with photos, animations, and video clips (see Chapters 20–22).

Plan for the Delivery Mode

Online presentations can be "streamed" in real time, or recorded for distribution later whenever an audience wants to access them. Understanding the advantages and limitations of both delivery modes can help you plan more effectively.

Real-Time Presentations

Real-time presentations connect presenter and audience live, in **synchronous communication**. Interactivity is a chief advantage of this type of presentation: Speaker and audience can respond to one another even though they are not in the same location. As in traditional speaking situations, audience feedback allows you to adapt topic coverage according to real-time audience input and questions, for example, or adjust technical issues as they occur.

A chief limitation of real-time presentations is scheduling them around conflicting time zones. The more geographically dispersed the audience, the greater the logistical challenge. As such, many speakers reserve real-time presentations for occasions when they are in nearby time zones of the audience.

Recorded Presentations

In a **recorded presentation**, transmission and reception occur at different times, in **asynchronous communication**. Viewers can access the presentation at their convenience, such as listening to a podcast at night.

Lack of direct interaction with the audience poses challenges, however. Without immediate feedback from the audience to enliven the presentation, you must work harder to produce something polished and engaging.

Online Presentation Platforms

Online presentation platforms include videos, pod/vodcasts, Webinars, and graphical presentations, any of which may be streamed in real time or recorded for later delivery.

Video

Many people get their message out by presenting it visually via video: from individuals using a personal Flip camera or Web cam, to professional companies sending out messages using high definition digital video cameras. With video capture software, such as CamVerce and Debut, you can seamlessly incorporate video clips into an online presentation.

You can also use video capture software, dedicated screencasting software, to create screencasts. A **screencast** captures whatever is displayed on your computer screen, from text to slides to streaming video. Screencasts can be streamed in real-time or recorded for playback or export to a hosting Web site. The screencast format is especially useful for training purposes. For example, a presentation relying on screen captures can be used to demonstrate how to create a screencast using QuickTime Player on the Mac.

Podcasts and Vodcasts

A **podcast** is a digital audio recording of a speech or presentation captured and stored in a form that is accessible via the Web. A **vodcast** (also called *vidcast* and *video podcasting*) is a podcast containing video clips.

News sites, government information repositories such as the Library of Congress (www.loc.gov/podcasts/), and academic institutions offer countless examples of podcasts and vodcasts (see Figure 26.1). Commercial recording outlets such as iTunes also provide a wide selection of pod- and vodcasts.

Recording, storing, and delivering a speech via podcast requires a microphone attached to a computer; simple, cost-free digital audio recording software (e.g., Audacity); and a Web site to host the podcast and provide your audience

FIGURE 26.1 Podcast Offerings from Tunxis Community College

with access to it. Using PowerPoint, you can use the "Record Narration" feature in the slide creation function to produce a podcast-like presentation file; the file can be used and distributed as you would any PowerPoint file, even via e-mail.

✓ CHECKLIST: Creating a Podcast

Most current models of desktop, laptop, and tablet computers include the basic equipment and software needed to create a podcast. The only other pieces you may need are an external microphone and audio recording software such as Audacity (http://audacity.sourceforge.net/). Then try these steps:

✓ Plan what you want to say.

✓ Seat yourself in an upright, direct position facing your computer, with the microphone no more than eight inches from your mouth.

✓ Make sure that your external microphone is plugged into your computer, or that your built-in microphone is operational.

✓ Open your audio recording software. Be familiar with how to start, pause, and stop a recording.

✓ Activate the recording software and begin speaking into the microphone. You're now making your presentation.

✓ At the conclusion of your presentation, stop the recording.

✓ Save the new recording as an audio file, such as .mp3.

✓ Close your audio recording software and disengage the microphone.

✓ Go to the new audio file saved to your computer, and open and play it. Now you are listening to your recorded presentation.

✓ Transfer the saved file to a Web site, blog, or podcast hosting site.

Webinars

Webinars are real-time seminars, meetings, training sessions, or other presentations that connect presenters and audiences from their computers or mobile devices, regardless of where they are in the world.[2] Webinars typically include video capture and screencasting, as well as interactive functions such as chat and polling.

As in any speech or presentation, planning a Webinar starts with considering the audience's needs and wants. Many Webinars are team presentations, so use the guidelines on p. 245 during the planning stages.[3]

1. Start with a title that indicates what the Webinar will do for the audience (e.g., "How the New Healthcare Regulations Will Affect You").

2. Time each aspect of the Webinar and distribute the following information to each presenter:

   Introduction of speaker(s) and purpose

   Length and order of each speaker's remarks

   Length of question-and-answer session, if separate

3. Rehearse the Webinar (remotely if necessary).

4. Check meeting room for noise and visual distractions; check equipment.

5. Have printouts on hand and create backup plans in case of technical problems

---

QUICK TIP

Put a Face to the Speaker(s)
To encourage a feeling of connection between yourself and the audience during a Webinar, consider displaying a photographic headshot, captioned by your name and title. A second slide might announce start and finish times; a third, a list of speech objectives.[4] During the presentation, you can alternate displays of text and graphic slides with views of your photograph (and/or other presenters) or, in some cases, side-by-side with the aids.

Online Presentation Planning Checklist

Keeping in mind both the traditional guidelines for preparing and presenting a speech as well as those unique qualities of online presentations, here are some additional tips to follow.[5]

- *Be well organized.* Offer a clear statement of purpose and preview of main points. Proceed with a solid structure that the audience can easily follow. Conclude by restating your purpose, reviewing the main points, and encouraging the audience to watch or listen for more.

- *Have reasonable expectations.* Fit the amount of content to the allotted time. Don't pack too much into too little time.

- *Design powerful presentation aids.* For video and Webcasts, plan for meaningful graphics and images that properly convey your ideas.

- *Keep your audience engaged.* In real-time presentations, encourage audience interaction by incorporating chat, instant messaging, or polling features. In recorded presentations, offer an e-mail address, Weblog comment, URL, or Twitter address where audience members can submit comments and questions. Use these tools to acquire feedback from your audience, much the way you would use eye contact in a face-to-face speech or presentation.

- *Prepare a contingency plan in case of technology glitches.* For example, have a backup computer running simultaneously with the one used to deliver the presentation. Provide a list of FAQs or a Web page with instructions for audience members to manage technology problems.

- *Maintain ethical standards.* Use the same degree of decorum as you would in a FtF speech, bearing in mind that online presentations have the potential to go viral.

- *Get in plenty of practice time.* Rehearse, record, and listen to yourself as many times as needed.

27 Communicating in Groups

Most of us will spend a substantial portion of our educational and professional lives participating in **small groups** or teams (usually between three and twenty people); and many of the experiences we have as speakers—in the classroom, workforce, and in virtual groups online—occur in a group setting. Groups often report on the results they've achieved, and some groups form solely for the purpose of coordinating oral presentations (see Chapter 28). Thus, understanding how to work cooperatively within a group setting is a critical skill.

Focus on Goals

How well or poorly you meet the objectives of the group is largely a function of how closely you keep sight of the group's goals and avoid behaviors that detract from these goals. Setting an **agenda** can help participants stay on track by identifying items to be accomplished during a meeting; often it will specify time limits for each item.

Plan on Assuming Dual Roles

In a group, you will generally assume dual roles: a task role and a maintenance role. **Task roles** are the hands-on roles that directly relate to the group's accomplishment of its objectives. Examples include "recording secretary" (takes notes) and "moderator" (facilitates discussion). Members also adopt various **maintenance roles** that help facilitate effective group interaction, such as "the harmonizer" (smoothes out tension) and "the gatekeeper" (keeps the discussion moving and gets everyone's input).[1] Online maintenance roles include the "moderator" or "master" (coordinates and sometimes screens members' comments) and the "elder" (long-standing and respected group member).[2]

Sometimes, group members focus on individual needs irrelevant to the task at hand. **Anti-group roles** such as "floor hogger" (not allowing others to speak), "blocker" (being overly negative about group ideas; raising issues that have been settled), and "recognition seeker" (calling attention to oneself rather than to group tasks) do not further the group's goals and should be avoided.

QUICK TIP

Handling Trolls Online

Groups who meet online may encounter members who adopt the anti-group role of "troll"—someone who intentionally inserts irrelevant and inflammatory comments into online discussions in order to stir up controversy. Experts advise refraining from responding to such a person's abusive comments, noting that "feeding the troll" will only encourage further provocation.[3]

Center Disagreements around Issues

Whenever people come together to consider an important issue, conflict is inevitable. But conflict doesn't have to be destructive. In fact, the best decisions are usually those that emerge from productive conflict.[4] In *productive conflict,* group members clarify questions, challenge ideas, present counterexamples, consider worst-case scenarios, and reformulate proposals. Productive conflict centers disagreements around issues rather than personalities. In *person-based conflict,* members argue with one another instead of about the issues, wasting time and impairing motivation; *issues-based conflict* allows members to test and debate ideas and potential solutions. It requires each member to ask tough questions, press for clarification, and present alternative views.[5]

Resist Groupthink

For groups to be truly effective, members need to form a *collective mind,* that is, engage in communication that is critical, careful, consistent, and conscientious.[6] At the same time, they must avoid **groupthink**, the tendency to accept information and ideas without subjecting them to critical analysis.[7] Groups prone to groupthink typically exhibit these behaviors:

- Participants reach a consensus and avoid conflict in order not to hurt others' feelings, but without genuinely agreeing.
- Members who do not agree with the majority feel pressured to conform.
- Disagreement, tough questions, and counterproposals are discouraged.
- More effort is spent justifying the decision than testing it.

QUICK TIP

Optimize Decision Making in Groups

*Research suggests that groups can reach the best decisions by adopting two methods of argument: **devil's advocacy** (arguing for the sake of raising issues or concerns about the idea under discussion) and **dialectical inquiry** (devil's advocacy that goes a step further by proposing a countersolution to the idea).[8] Both approaches help expose underlying assumptions that may be preventing participants from making the best decision. As you lead a group, consider how you can encourage both methods of argument.*

Adopt an Effective Leadership Style

When called upon to lead a group, bear in mind the four broad styles of leadership, and select the *participative model*:

- *Autocratic* (leaders make decisions and announce them to the group)
- *Consultative* (leaders make decisions after discussing them with the group)
- *Delegative* (leaders ask the group to make the decision)
- *Participative* (leaders make decisions with the group)[9]

Research suggests that often the most effective leader is participative—that is, one who facilitates a group's activities and interaction in ways that lead to a desired outcome.

Set Goals

As a leader, aim to be a catalyst in setting and reaching goals in collaboration with other group members. It is the leader's responsibility to ensure that each group member can clearly identify the group's purpose(s) and goal(s).

Encourage Active Participation

Groups tend to adopt solutions that receive the largest number of favorable comments, whether these comments emanate from one individual or many. If only one or two members participate, it is their input that sets the agenda, whether or not their solution is optimal.[10] When you lead a group, take these steps to encourage group participation:

- *Directly ask members to contribute.* Sometimes one person, or a few people, dominate the discussion. Encourage others to contribute by redirecting the discussion in their direction ("Patrice, we haven't heard from you yet" or "Juan, what do you think about this?").
- *Set a positive tone.* Some people are reluctant to express their views because they fear ridicule or attack. Minimize such fears by setting a positive tone, stressing fairness, and encouraging politeness and active listening.
- *Make use of devil's advocacy and dialectical inquiry* (see Quick Tip on p. 240). Raise pertinent issues or concerns, and entertain solutions other than the one under consideration.

Use Reflective Thinking

To reach a decision or solution that all participants understand and are committed to, guide participants through the six-step process of reflective thinking shown in Figure 27.1, which is based on the work of educator John Dewey.[11]

Step 1   Identify the Problem
• What is being decided upon?
Group leader summarizes problem, ensures that all group members understand problem, and gains agreement from all members.

↓

Step 2   Conduct Research and Analysis
• What information is needed to solve the problem?
Conduct research to gather relevant information.
Ensure that all members have relevant information.

↓

Step 3   Establish Guidelines and Criteria
• Establish criteria by which proposed solutions will be judged.
Reach criteria through consensus and record criteria.

↓

Step 4   Generate Solutions
• Conduct brainstorming session.
Don't debate ideas; simply gather and record all ideas.

↓

Step 5   Select the Best Solution
• Weigh the relative merits of each idea against criteria. Select one alternative that can best fulfill criteria.
If more than one solution survives, select solution that best meets criteria.
Consider merging two solutions if both meet criteria.
If no solution survives, return to problem identification step.

↓

Step 6   Evaluate Solution
• Does the solution have any weaknesses or disadvantages?
• Does the solution resemble the criteria that were developed?
• What other criteria would have been helpful in arriving at a better solution?

FIGURE 27.1 Making Decisions in Groups: John Dewey's Six-Step Process of Reflective Thinking

28 Presenting in Teams

Team presentations are oral presentations prepared and delivered by a group of three or more individuals. Regularly assigned in the classroom and frequently delivered in the workplace, successful team presentations require close cooperation and planning.

Working in Teams

Preparing and delivering a successful team presentation depends on effective communication among members. Use the guidelines in Chapter 27 on group communication to set goals, assign roles and tasks, and manage conflict.

Analyze the Audience and Set Goals

Even if the topic is assigned and the audience consists solely of the instructor and classmates (perhaps virtually), consider the audience's interests and needs with respect to the topic and how you can meet them. Then, just as you would during group work, establish goals for the presentation that all can agree upon.

Assign Roles and Tasks

First, designate a *team leader* to help guide coordination among members, beginning with the selection of roles and tasks. Next, assign members to various aspects of the research, perhaps selecting different members to present the introduction, body of the presentation, and conclusion, or other responsibilities. Set firm time limits for each portion of the presentation.

QUICK TIP

Team Cohesion Pays Off
When dividing tasks among the team, make certain that each member stays up to speed regarding the others' responsibilities and progress. Knowing how all the parts will come together is crucial to conveying a sense of cohesion to the audience.[1]

Establish Transitions between Speakers

Work out transitions between speakers ahead of time—for example, whether one team member will introduce every speaker or whether each speaker will introduce the next speaker upon the close of his or her presentation. The quality of the presentation will depend in great part on smooth transitions between speakers.

Consider the Presenters' Strengths

Audiences become distracted by marked disparities in style, such as hearing a captivating speaker followed by an extremely dull one. If you are concerned about an uneven delivery, consider choosing the person with the strongest presentation style and credibility level for the opening. Put the more cautious presenters in the middle of the presentation. Select another strong speaker to conclude the presentation.[2]

Coordinate the Presentation Aids

To ensure design consistency, consider assigning one person the job of coordinating templates for slides, video, and/or audio. The team can also assign a single individual the task of presenting the aids as the other team members speak. If this is done, be sure to position the person presenting the aids unobtrusively so as not to distract the audience from the speaker.

QUICK TIP

Be Mindful of Your Nonverbal Behavior
During a team presentation, the audience's eyes will fall on everyone involved, not just the person speaking. Thus any signs of disinterest or boredom by a team member will be easily noticed. Give your full attention to the other speakers on the team, and project an attitude of interest toward audience members.

Rehearse the Presentation Several Times

Together with the whole group, members should practice their portions of the presentation, with any presentation aids they will use, in the order they will be given in the final form. Rehearse several times, until the presentation proceeds smoothly, using the techniques for rehearsal described in Chapter 19.

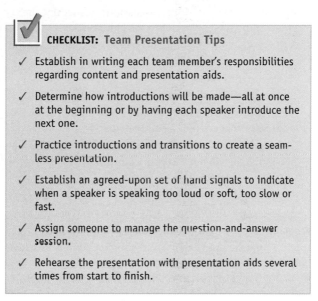

CHECKLIST: Team Presentation Tips

✓ Establish in writing each team member's responsibilities regarding content and presentation aids.

✓ Determine how introductions will be made—all at once at the beginning or by having each speaker introduce the next one.

✓ Practice introductions and transitions to create a seamless presentation.

✓ Establish an agreed-upon set of hand signals to indicate when a speaker is speaking too loud or soft, too slow or fast.

✓ Assign someone to manage the question-and-answer session.

✓ Rehearse the presentation with presentation aids several times from start to finish.

Presenting in Panels, Symposia, and Forums

Panels, symposia, and forums are group discussions in which multiple speakers share their expertise with an audience; forums are convened specifically to discuss issues of public interest. Members of panels, symposia, and forums often may not meet beforehand to coordinate their remarks.

Panel Discussions

In a **panel discussion**, a group of people (at least three, and generally not more than nine) discusses a topic in the presence of an audience. Panel discussions do not feature formally prepared speeches. Instead, they require the presence of a skilled chairperson or **moderator** to direct the discussion, who begins by describing the purpose of the panel and introducing panel members. The moderator then launches the discussion by directing a question to one or more of the participants. At the conclusion of the panel, the moderator summarizes the discussion and directs questions from the audience.

When preparing remarks for a panel discussion, or when preparing to serve as a moderator, consider the following:

- What is the agenda for the discussion? (Generally, the moderator will deliver this to the panelists.)
- Who is your audience, and what do they know about the topic? What do they need to know about it?
- What are the ground rules? (Generally, the moderator will prepare a list and distribute it to each participant.)
- What aspects of the topic will the other participants address? What are their areas of expertise?
- How much time is allotted for the question-and-answer session? You will need to plan accordingly.

Symposia

A **symposium** is a formal meeting at which various speakers deliver short speeches on different aspects of the same topic. Symposia are organized to provide audiences with a detailed look at a topic by providing multiple perspectives on it. Sometimes the symposium concludes with a question-and-answer period; at other times, it is followed by a panel discussion among symposium participants.

When preparing a presentation for a symposium, consider the following:

- What aspects of the topic will the other participants address?
- In what order will the speakers address the audience?
- What are your time constraints?
- Who is your audience?
- Will you engage in questions and answers with the other speakers, or just with the audience?

Forums

A **forum** is an assembly for the discussion of issues of public interest. Forums are often convened to help policymakers and voters alike deliberate about key policy issues. Forums can take place in a physical space, such as a town hall, or online, in moderated Web chats and other forms of virtual forums.

Forums may feature a panel or a symposium, followed by an extensive question-and-answer period with the audience. One well-known forum is the **town hall meeting**, in which citizens deliberate on issues of importance to the community. City and state governments sponsor town hall meetings to gather citizen input about issues that affect them, using this input to formulate policy.

When participating in public forums (not as a featured speaker, but as a member of the audience), consider the following:

- Organize your thoughts as much as possible in advance by jotting down your question or comment on a piece of paper. Use the guidelines for impromptu speaking described in Chapter 17.

- Do not duplicate someone else's questions or comments unless it adds to the discussion.

- Use no more time than necessary to make your points.

- If appropriate, include a call to action at the conclusion of your comments.

29 Business and Professional Presentations

In many business and professional positions, delivering presentations is part of the job. Whether the task is informing managers of a project's progress or pitching a service to customers, the skilled speaker will get noticed and, often, promoted.

Rather than being a formal public speech, **presentational speaking**—reports delivered by individuals or teams addressing people in the workplace (or in the classroom; see p. 255)—has much in common with formal public speaking, yet important differences exist:[1]

- *Degree of formality.* Presentational speaking is *less formal* than public speaking; on a continuum, it would lie midway between public speaking at one end and conversational speaking at the other.

- *Audience factors.* Public-speaking audiences tend to be self-selected or voluntary participants, and they regard the speech as a onetime event. Attendees of oral presentations are more likely to be part of a "captive" audience, as in the workplace or classroom, and may be required to attend frequent presentations. Due to the ongoing relationship among the participants, the attendees also share more information with one another than those who attend a public speech and thus can be considered more homogeneous.

- *Speaker expertise.* Listeners generally assume that a public speaker has more expertise or firsthand knowledge than they do on a topic. Presentational speakers, by contrast, are more properly thought of as "first among equals."

Apart from these differences, the rules of public speaking described in this *Pocket Guide* apply equally to both oral presentations and public speeches.

QUICK TIP

Speak Ethically at Work

As in public speeches, the ethical standards of trustworthiness, respect, responsibility, and fairness (see Chapter 4) must infuse any workplace presentation. Such presentations should also comply with legal standards and adhere to internal rules and regulations.[2]

Five of the most common of these presentations in the workplace are the *sales presentation*, *proposal*, *staff report*, *progress report*, and *crisis-response presentation*. The *case study*, described at the end of this chapter, is unique to the classroom environment.

Sales Presentations

A **sales presentation,** also called a **sales pitch,** attempts to lead a potential buyer to purchase a service or a product. Sales pitches are persuasive in nature.

Audience

The target audience for a sales presentation depends on who has the authority to make the purchase under consideration. Some sales presentations are invited by the potential buyer; others are "cold sales" in which the presenter/ seller approaches a first-time potential buyer with a product or a service. In some cases the audience might be an intermediary—a firm's office manager, for example, who then makes a recommendation to the firm's director.

Successful sales pitches clearly show how the product or service meets the needs of the potential buyer and demonstrates how it surpasses other options available.

Organization

Plan on organizing a sales presentation as you would a persuasive speech, selecting among the comparative advantage, problem-solution/problem-cause-solution, or motivated sequence patterns (see Chapter 24). The *comparative advantage pattern* works well when the buyer must choose between competing products and seeks reassurance that the product being presented is indeed superior. The *problem-solution* or *problem-cause-solution pattern* is especially effective when selling to a buyer who needs a product to solve a problem.

Sometimes called the *basic sales technique*, the *motivated sequence*, with its focus on audience needs, offers an excellent means of appealing to buyer psychology. To use it to organize a sales presentation, do the following:

1. Draw the potential buyer's attention to the product.
2. Isolate and clarify the buyer's need for the product.
3. Describe how the product will satisfy the buyer's need.
4. Invite the buyer to purchase the product.

QUICK TIP

Adapt the Motivated Sequence to the Selling Situation
When making a sales pitch following the motivated sequence, the extent to which you focus on each step depends on the nature of the selling situation. In cold-call sales situations, consider spending more time discovering the potential buyer's needs. For invited sales presentations, spend more time detailing the characteristics of the product and showing how it will satisfy the buyer's needs.

Proposals

Organizations must constantly make decisions based on whether to modify or adopt a product, procedure, or policy, such as upgrading a telephone system or implementing a new employee-grievance procedure. Called a **proposal,** this type of presentation may be strictly informative, as when a facilities manager provides information to his or her superiors. Often, proposals are persuasive in nature, with the presenter arguing in favor of one course of action over another.

Audience

The audience for a proposal can vary from a single individual to a large group; the individual or individuals have primary or sole decision-making responsibility. Because many proposals seek to persuade listeners, careful adaptation to the audience is critical to an effective presentation.

Organization

A proposal can be quite lengthy and formally organized or relatively brief and loosely structured. Organize lengthy proposals as follows:

1. Introduce the issue.
2. State the problem.
3. Describe the method by which the problem was investigated.
4. Describe the facts learned.
5. Offer explanations and an interpretation of the findings.
6. Offer recommendations.

Organize brief proposals as follows:

1. State your recommendations.
2. Offer a brief overview of the problem.
3. Review the facts on which the recommendations are based.

Staff Reports

A **staff report** informs managers and other employees of new developments that affect them and their work, or reports on the completion of a project or task.

Audience

The audience for a staff report is usually a group, but it can be an individual. The recipients of a staff report then use the information to implement new policy, to coordinate other plans, or to make other reports to other groups.

Organization

Formal staff reports are typically organized as follows:

1. State the problem or question under consideration (sometimes called a "charge" to a committee or a subcommittee).
2. Provide a description of procedures and facts used to address the issue.
3. Discuss and analyze the facts that are most pertinent to the issue.
4. Provide a concluding statement.
5. Offer recommendations.

Progress Reports

A **progress report** is similar to a staff report, with the exception that the audience can include people *outside* the organization as well as within it. A progress report updates clients or principals on developments in an ongoing project. On long-term projects, progress reports may be given at designated intervals or at the time of specific task completions. On short-term projects, reports can occur daily.

Audience

The audience for a progress report might be supervisors, clients, or customers; developers and investors; company officers; media representatives; or same-level co-workers. Progress reports are commonplace in staff meetings in which subcommittees report on their designated tasks. Audience questions are common at the end of progress reports (see Appendix B on handling question-and-answer sessions).

Organization

Different audiences may want different kinds of reports, so establish expectations with your intended audience, then modify the following accordingly:

1. Briefly review progress made up to the time of the previous report.
2. Describe new developments since the previous report.
3. Describe the personnel involved and their activities.
4. Detail the time spent on tasks.

5. Explain supplies used and costs incurred.

6. Explain any problems and their resolution.

7. Provide an estimate of tasks to be completed for the next reporting period.

Crisis-Response Presentations

Crisis-response presentations (also called "crisis communication") are meant to reassure an organization's various audiences (its "publics") and restore its credibility in the face of an array of threats, such as contaminated products, layoffs, chemical spills, or bankruptcy. These are often conveyed via media such as television and radio.

Audience

Crisis-response presentations may target one, several, or multiple audiences. A personnel manager may address a group of disgruntled engineers unhappy over a new policy. Seeking to allay fears of ruin and shore up stockholder confidence, the CEO of an embattled corporation may target anxious employees and shareholders alike.

Organization

A variety of strategies exists for organizing a crisis-response presentation, ranging from simple denial to admitting responsibility for a crisis and asking forgiveness.[3] Familiarity with a range of image restoration strategies will allow the speaker to select those techniques that best apply to the situation at hand.[4] In essence, the crisis-response presentation is based on persuasion and argument. Sound reasoning and evidence are essential to its effectiveness. Depending on the issue and audience(s) involved, use one or another of the organizational patterns described in Chapter 24, especially problem-solution and refutation.

In the Classroom: Case Study Presentations

A **case study** is a detailed analysis of a real (or realistic) business situation. Instructors often require business students to report orally on case studies, either alone or in teams. Students are typically expected to consider the case study carefully and then report on the following items:

1. Description/overview of the major issues involved in the case

2. Statement of the major problems and issues involved

3. Identification of any relevant alternatives to the case
4. Presentation of the best solutions to the case, with a brief explanation of the logic behind them
5. Recommendations for implementing the solutions, along with acknowledgment of any impediments

---

QUICK TIP

Build Career Skills

Approach your business presentation assignments as a way to build critically important career skills. Many prospective employers will ask about such classroom experience, and you will deliver similar presentations throughout your business career. Entry-level business and professional employees with superior oral presentation skills tend to get promoted sooner than their co-workers.

Part 9
Speaking across the Curriculum

30. Presentations Assigned across
    the Curriculum 255
31. Science and Mathematics Courses 261
32. Technical Courses 265
33. Social Science Courses 267
34. Arts and Humanities Courses 270
35. Education Courses 272
36. Nursing and Allied Health Courses 274

No matter which major you select, oral presentations will be part of your academic career. Rather than being formal public speeches, classroom presentations are another type of *presentational speaking*; see p. 247 for a review.

Chapter 31–36 describe various course-specific presentations, from the *scientific talk* to the *design review*. This chapter contains guidelines for presentation formats frequently assigned in various courses across the curriculum, including the *review of an academic article*, the *debate,* the *poster presentation*, and the *service learning presentation*. Some of these assignments may require an online component; for more information about speaking online, see Chapter 26.

The Review of Academic Articles

A commonly assigned speaking task in many courses is the **review of academic articles**. A biology instructor might ask you to review a study on cell regulation, for example, or a psychology teacher might require that you talk about a study on fetal alcohol syndrome. Typically, when you are assigned to review an academic article, your instructor will expect you to do the following:

- Identify the author's thesis or hypothesis.
- Explain the methods by which the author arrived at his or her conclusions.
- Explain the author's findings.
- Identify the author's theoretical perspective, if applicable.
- Evaluate the study's validity, if applicable.
- Describe the author's sources, and evaluate their credibility.
- Show how the findings of the study might be applied to other circumstances, and make suggestions about ways in which the study might lead to further research.[1]

The Team Presentation

Team presentations are oral presentations prepared and delivered by a group of three or more individuals. Regularly used in the classroom, successful team presentations require cooperation and planning. (See Chapter 28 for detailed guidelines on how to prepare and deliver team presentations.)

The Debate

Debates are a popular presentation format in many college courses, calling upon skills in persuasion (especially the reasoned use of evidence), in delivery, and in the ability to think quickly and critically. Much like a political debate, in an *academic debate* two individuals or groups consider or argue an issue from opposing viewpoints. Generally there will be a winner and a loser, lending this form of speaking a competitive edge.

Take a Side

Opposing sides in a debate are taken by speakers in one of two formats. In the **individual debate format**, one person takes a side against another person. In the **team debate format**, multiple people (usually two) take sides against another team, with each person on the team assuming a speaking role.

The *affirmative* side in the debate supports the topic with a *resolution*—a declarative statement asking for change or consideration of a controversial issue. "Resolved, that the United States government should punish flag burners" is a resolution that the affirmative side must support and defend. The affirmative side tries to convince the audience (or judges) to address, support, or agree with the topic under consideration. The *negative* side in the debate attempts to defeat the resolution by dissuading the audience from accepting the affirmative side's arguments.

Advance Strong Arguments

Whether you take the affirmative or negative side, your primary responsibility is to advance strong arguments in support of your position. Arguments usually consist of the following three parts (see also Chapter 24):

- *Claim:* A claim makes an assertion or a declaration about an issue: "Females are discriminated against in the workplace." Depending on your debate topic, your claim may be one of fact, value, or policy.
- *Evidence:* Evidence is the support offered for the claim: "According to a recent report by the U.S. Department of Labor, women make 28 percent less than men in

comparable jobs and are promoted 34 percent less frequently."

- *Reasoning:* Reasoning (e.g., warrants; see p. 195) is a logical link or explanation of why the evidence supports the claim: "Females make less money and get promoted less frequently than males."

QUICK TIP

Flowing the Debate

In formal debates (in which judges take notes and keep track of arguments), debaters must attack and defend each argument. "Dropping" or ignoring an argument can seriously compromise the credibility of the debater and her or his side. To ensure that you respond to each of your opponent's arguments, try using a simple technique adopted by formal debaters called "flowing the debate" (see Figure 30.1). Write down each of your opponent's arguments, and then draw a line or arrow to indicate that you (or another team member) have refuted it.

Debates are characterized by *refutation*, in which each side attacks the arguments of the other. Refutation can be made against an opponent's claim, evidence, reasoning, or some combination of these elements. In the previous argument, an opponent might refute the evidence by arguing, "The report used by my opponent is three years old, and a new study indicates that we are making substantial progress in equalizing the pay among males and females; thus we are reducing discrimination in the workplace."

Refutation also involves rebuilding arguments that have been refuted or attacked by the opponent. This is done by adding new evidence or attacking the opponent's reasoning or evidence.

Affirmative	Negative	Affirmative	Negative	Affirmative	Negative
Nonviolent prisoners should be paroled more often.	Nonviolent prisoners can become violent when they are paroled.	Studies show nonviolent prisoners commit fewer crimes upon their release.	Those studies are outdated and involve only a few states.	My studies are recent and include big states like New York and California.	The studies from New York and California were flawed due to poor statistics.

FIGURE 30.1 Flowchart of the Arguments for the Resolution "Resolved, That Nonviolent Prisoners Should Be Paroled More Often"

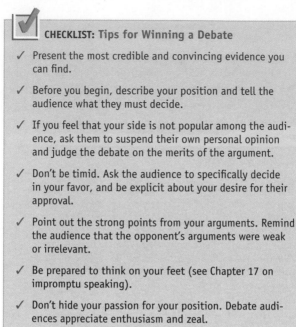

CHECKLIST: Tips for Winning a Debate

✓ Present the most credible and convincing evidence you can find.

✓ Before you begin, describe your position and tell the audience what they must decide.

✓ If you feel that your side is not popular among the audience, ask them to suspend their own personal opinion and judge the debate on the merits of the argument.

✓ Don't be timid. Ask the audience to specifically decide in your favor, and be explicit about your desire for their approval.

✓ Point out the strong points from your arguments. Remind the audience that the opponent's arguments were weak or irrelevant.

✓ Be prepared to think on your feet (see Chapter 17 on impromptu speaking).

✓ Don't hide your passion for your position. Debate audiences appreciate enthusiasm and zeal.

The Poster Presentation

A **poster presentation** includes information about a study, an issue, or a concept displayed concisely and visually on a large (roughly 4 feet high by 6 feet wide) poster. Usually, poster presentations follow the structure of a scientific journal article, which includes an abstract, an introduction, a description of methods, a results section, a conclusion, and references (if applicable); see p. 261. Presenters display their key findings on posters, arranged so session participants can examine them freely; on hand are copies of the written report, with full details of the study.

A good poster presenter considers his or her audience, understanding that with so much competing information, the poster must be concise, visually appealing, and restricted to the most important points of the study. Different disciplines (e.g., geology vs. sociology) require unique poster formats, so be sure that you follow the guidelines specific to the discipline.

When preparing the poster:

• Select a concise and informative title; make it 84-point type or larger.

• Include an abstract (a brief summary of the study) describing the essence of the report and how it relates to other research in the field. Offer compelling and "must know" points to hook viewers and summarize information for those who will only read the abstract.

- Ensure a logical and easy-to-follow flow from one part of the poster to another.
- Ruthlessly edit text to a minimum, using clear graphics wherever possible.
- Select a muted color for the poster itself, such as gray, beige, light blue, or white and use a contrasting, clear font color (usually black).
- Make sure your font size is large enough to be read comfortably from at least three feet away.
- Design figures and diagrams to be viewed from a distance, and label each one.
- Include a concise summary of each figure in a legend below each one.
- Be prepared to provide brief descriptions of your poster and to answer questions; keep your explanations short.

The Service Learning Presentation

In a **service learning presentation**, students learn about and help address a need or problem in a community agency or nonprofit organization, such as may exist in a mental-health facility, an economic development agency, or antipoverty organization. Typically, presentations about participation in a service learning project include the following information:

1. Description of the service task.
   a. What organization, group, or agency did your project serve?
   b. What is the problem or issue and how did you address it?
2. Description of what the service task taught you about those you served.
   a. How were they affected by the problem or issue?
   b. How did your solution help them? What differences did you observe?
3. Explanation of how the service task and outcome related to your service learning course.
   a. What course concepts, principles, or theory relate to your service project, and how?
   b. What observations give you evidence that the principles apply to your project?

4. Application of what was learned to future understanding and practice.

   a. How was your understanding of the course subject improved or expanded?

   b. How was your interest in or motivation for working in this capacity affected by the project?

   c. What do you most want to tell others about the experience and how it could affect them?

Preparing for On-the-Job Audiences

Instructors may ask that you tailor your oral presentations to a mock (practice) on-the-job audience, with your classmates serving as stand-ins. The types of audiences you will likely address on-the-job include the **expert or insider audience**, **colleagues within the field**, the **lay audience**, and the **mixed audience**:

TYPES OF AUDIENCES IN THE WORKING WORLD	
TYPE OF AUDIENCE	**CHARACTERISTICS**
Expert or insider audience	People who have intimate knowledge of the topic, issue, product, or idea being discussed (e.g., an investment analyst presents a financial plan to a group of portfolio managers).
Colleagues within the field	People who share the speaker's knowledge of the general field under question (e.g., psychology or computer science), but who may not be familiar with the specific topic under discussion (e.g., short-term memory or voice recognition systems, respectively).
Lay audience	People who have no specialized knowledge of the field related to the speaker's topic or of the topic itself (e.g., a physical education teacher discusses the proper diet and exercise regimen with a group of teenagers).
Mixed audience	An audience composed of a combination of people—some with expert knowledge of the field and topic and others with no specialized knowledge. This is perhaps the most difficult audience to satisfy (e.g., an attending surgeon describes experimental cancer treatment to a hospital board comprising medical professionals, financial supporters, and administrative personnel).

The primary purpose of most science and math presentations is to inform listeners of the results of original or replicated research. Instructors want to know the processes by which you arrived at your experimental results. For example, your biology instructor may assign an oral report on the extent to which you were able to replicate an experiment on cell mitosis. A math instructor may ask you to apply a concept to an experiment or issue facing the field. In a geology course, you might describe how glacial striations in bedrock can help determine the direction of a glacier's movement.

QUICK TIP

What Do Science-Related Courses Include?

Known for their focus on exacting processes, science-related disciplines *include the physical sciences (e.g., chemistry and physics), the natural sciences (e.g., biology and medicine), and the earth sciences (e.g., geology, meteorology, and oceanography). Fields related to mathematics include accounting, statistics, and applied math.*

Research ("Scientific Talk") Presentation

In the **research presentation** (also called the "scientific talk" or **oral scientific presentation**), you describe original research you have done, either alone or as part of a team. The research presentation usually follows the standard model used in scientific investigation and includes the following elements:

1. *An introduction* describing the research question and the scope and objective of the study.

2. *A description of methods* used to investigate the research question, including where it took place and the conditions under which it was carried out.

3. *The results of the study* summarizing key results and highlighting insights to the questions/hypotheses investigated; this is the "body" of the presentation.

4. *A conclusion* (also called "Discussion"), in which the speaker interprets the data or results and discusses their

significance. As in any speech, the conclusion should link back to the introduction, reiterating the research question and highlighting the key findings.

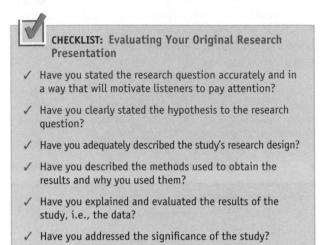

CHECKLIST: Evaluating Your Original Research Presentation

✓ Have you stated the research question accurately and in a way that will motivate listeners to pay attention?

✓ Have you clearly stated the hypothesis to the research question?

✓ Have you adequately described the study's research design?

✓ Have you described the methods used to obtain the results and why you used them?

✓ Have you explained and evaluated the results of the study, i.e., the data?

✓ Have you addressed the significance of the study?

Methods/Procedure Presentation

The **methods/procedure presentation** describes how an experimental or a mathematical process works and under what conditions it can be used. This is generally a ten- to fifteen-minute individual presentation. In a theoretical math class, for example, your assignment might be to describe an approach to solving a problem, such as the Baum Welch algorithm, including examples of how this approach has been used, either inappropriately or appropriately. This type of presentation generally does the following:

1. Identifies the conditions under which the process should be used

2. Offers a detailed description of the process (at times including a demonstration)

3. Discusses the benefits and shortcomings of the process

Research Overview Presentation

The **research overview presentation** provides background for a research question that will form the basis of an impending experiment or investigation. Instructors often ask students to organize research overviews with the following sections:

1. Overview of research that is relevant to the question at hand
2. Discussion of key studies that are central to the question
3. Analysis of the strengths and weaknesses of research in light of the current hypothesis or question

The format for the research overview may be an individual presentation or a panel discussion in which group members explore specific lines of research that contribute to a general hypothesis (see p. 245 on panel discussions).

Field Study Presentation

A **field study presentation** describes research conducted in naturalistic surroundings; for example, an environmental studies major might describe animal behavior in an oil spill. Field study presentations may be assigned as individual, team, or poster-session presentations. Whatever the discipline and nature of the observations, field study presentations address the following:

1. Overview and scope of the field research
2. Description of the site
3. Methods used in the research (e.g., participant observation, type of sample collection, measurement techniques)
4. Interpretation/analysis of the data
5. Future directions for the research

QUICK TIP

Make the Introduction Motivating

As in any kind of oral presentation, if you lose the audience in the introduction phase of a scientific presentation, chances are slim that you'll regain their attention. Instead of simply stating the hypothesis, tell the audience why you believe the research is important and why solving the problem is relevant. Revealing enthusiasm for the research will spark the audience's interest in the research.

Preparing Effective Presentations in Science and Mathematics

Science and mathematics instructors, and employers and colleagues on the job, will expect your presentations to be grounded in the scientific method. Credible presentations must clearly illustrate the nature of the research question, ideally in a way that audience members will find compelling and relevant, describe the methods used in gathering and analyzing data, and explain the results.

Clearly executed presentation aids often are critical to scientific and mathematical presentations, and instructors generally require them. Aids can range from data tables and graphs to equations drawn on a chalkboard.

Typically, instructors will expect you to do the following:

- *Use observation, proofs, and experiments as support for your points.*

- *Be selective in your focus on details,* highlighting critical information but not overwhelming listeners with details they can learn about by referring to the written paper and the cited sources.

- *Use analogies to build on prior knowledge and demonstrate underlying causes* (see Chapter 23 on guidelines on explaining difficult concepts).

- *Use graphics to illustrate important concepts.*

Scientific and mathematical presentations need not be dry and merely factual. Experimentation is a process of discovery, and the fits and starts that often accompany their completion can make for compelling anecdotes during your talk.

CHECKLIST: Tips for Preparing Successful Scientific Presentations

✓ Create an informative title that describes the research.

✓ Place your presentation in the context of a major scientific principle.

✓ Focus on a single issue and adjust it to the interests of your audience.

✓ Identify the underlying question you will address, divide it into subquestions, and answer each question.

✓ Follow a logical line of thought.

✓ Explain scientific concepts unambiguously, with a minimum of jargon.

✓ Use analogies to increase understanding.

✓ End with a clearly formulated conclusion related to your chosen scientific principle.[1]

Oral presentations in technical courses often focus on the design of a product or system, whether it is a set of plans for a building, a prototype robot, or an innovative computer circuit design. Of the various types of presentations assigned in technical courses, the *design review* is perhaps the most common. Other types of presentations include *requests for funding* and *progress reports* (see Chapter 29, pp. 251–252, for progress reports).

QUICK TIP

What Are the Technical Disciplines?

Technical disciplines include the range of engineering fields (mechanical, electrical, chemical, civil, aeronautical, nuclear, among others), computer science–oriented fields (computer hardware and software), and design-oriented fields (industrial design, architecture, graphic design).

Engineering Design Review

The **engineering design review** explains the problem-solving steps in devising a product or system in response to an identified need. Virtually all capstone engineering courses require that students prepare design reviews, which are generally informative in nature, although their purpose may include convincing the audience that the design decisions are sound. (In varying formats, design reviews are also assigned in basic science and mathematics courses.) Design reviews may incorporate a **prototype** (model) demonstration and are usually delivered as team presentations or in poster sessions. Design reviews typically include the following:

1. Identification of problem to be solved/need to be met and overview of objectives

2. Description of design concept and specifications

3. Discussion of why the proposed design will solve the problem

4. Discussion of any experimental testing that has been completed on the design

5. Discussion of future plans and unresolved problems

6. Discussion of schedule, budget, and marketing issues

Architecture Design Review

The **architecture design review** combines two functions: It enables the audience to visualize the design, and it sells it. A narrative approach, in which you tell the "story" of the design, combined with a *spatial organizational pattern,* in which you arrange main points in order of physical proximity of the design (see Chapter 13), can help you do this. At a minimum, architecture design reviews typically cover:

1. Background on the site
2. Discussion of the design concept
3. Description and interpretation of the design

Request for Funding

In the **request for funding presentation**, a team member or the entire team provides evidence that a project, a proposal, or a design idea is worth funding. Requests for funding, which are persuasive in nature, cover the following ground:

1. Overview of customer specifications and needs
2. Analysis of the market and its needs
3. Overview of the design idea or project and how it meets those needs
4. Projected costs for the project
5. Specific reasons why the project should be funded

Preparing Effective Technical Presentations

Technical presentations sell ideas, provide hard data, use concrete imagery, rely on visual aids, and are results oriented: [1]

- *Sell your ideas.* The technical presenter must persuade clients, managers, or classmates that a design, an idea, or a product is a good one. As one instructor notes, "You can never assume that your product or design will just sell—*you* have to do that." [2]
- *Provide hard data.* Good technical presentations are detailed and specific and use numbers as evidence. Instead of offering general, sweeping statements, provide hard data and clearly stated experimental results.
- *Use ample presentation aids.* Use diagrams, prototypes, and drawings, including design specifications, computer

simulations, physical models, and spreadsheets. Construct aids early in the process, and practice the presentation with them.

- *Use concrete imagery* to help listeners visualize how your design will appear in use or its intended site.

- *Gear the information to the appropriate level.* Typically, people who attend technical presentations possess a range of technical knowledge, from little or none to an expert understanding of the topic at hand.

- *Strive to work interdependently with other team members.*

QUICK TIP

Prepare Technical Presentations Carefully
Professionals working in technical fields observe three major obstacles to designing and delivering a successful technical presentation: (1) too much information crammed into aids, (2) insufficient preparation with fellow team members, and (3) failure to select an appropriate organization and structure for the presentation.[3] Bearing these pitfalls in mind during preparation will set you on a winning path.

---

33 Social Science Courses

Students in the social sciences (including psychology, sociology, political science, and communication) learn to evaluate and conduct *qualitative research* (in which the emphasis is on observing, describing, and interpreting behavior) as well as *quantitative research* (in which the emphasis is on statistical measurement).[1] Often the focus of inquiry is explaining or predicting human behavior or social forces, answering questions such as "What?," "How?," and "Why?"[2]

Oral presentations in social science courses frequently include the *review-of-the-literature presentation, theoretical research presentation,* and *policy recommendation report* (see this chapter). Other commonly assigned presentations are the *poster presentation* (see p. 258), *scientific research presentation* (see p. 261), *methods/procedure presentation* (see p. 262), *field study presentation* (see p. 263), *evidence-based practice presentation* (see p. 274), and *case study presentation* (see p. 275).

Review of the Literature

Frequently, instructors ask students to review the body of research related to a given topic or issue and offer conclusions about the topic based on this research. A communications student, for example, might review the literature on gender bias in the hiring of journalists. In addition to describing the available research, the student would offer conclusions uncovered by the research and suggest directions for future research. A **review-of-the-literature presentation** typically includes the following:

1. Statement of the topic under review
2. Description of the available research, including specific points of agreement and disagreement among sources
3. Evaluation of the usefulness of the research
4. Conclusions that can be drawn from the research
5. Suggested directions for future study

Debate Controversial Topics

Students taking social science courses often prepare for *debates* on controversial issues (see p. 256 for guidelines on preparing for a debate). Sometimes an assignment involves advocating a position that you do not support. Whatever side of an issue you address, you will need to prepare a well-composed argument with strong supporting evidence.

Apply Theories to a Research Question

Instructors often ask students in the social sciences to critically examine theories relevant to research questions such as "Why do some college students abuse alcohol?" or "What leads to infant neglect?" A **theoretical research presentation** typically addresses the following:

1. Introduction of the research question
2. Discussion of relevant theories of how and why it occurs, as described by the research
3. Evaluation of the research and suggestions for future research

Narrow Your Topic
Since most of your social scientific research and literature review presentations will be relatively brief, make sure to sufficiently narrow your topic or research question and scale your findings to fit the time allotted. To ensure that you report the research accurately, maintain a working bibliography of your sources.

Evaluate Policies and Programs

In addition to explaining social phenomena, social scientists often measure the effectiveness of programs developed to address these issues. Instructors may ask you to evaluate a program or policy, perhaps one you observed in a service learning assignment. Typically, the **program evaluation presentation** includes the following:

1. Explanation of the program's mission
2. Description of the program's accomplishments
3. Discussion of how the accomplishments were measured, including any problems in evaluation
4. Conclusions regarding how well or poorly the program has met its stated objectives

Recommend Policies

As well as evaluating programs and policies, you may be asked to recommend a course of action on an issue or a problem. A **policy recommendation report** typically includes the following:

1. Definition and brief discussion of the problem
2. Recommendations to solve the problem or address the issue
3. Application of forecasting methods to show likely results of the recommended policy
4. Plan for implementation of the recommendations
5. Discussion of future needs or parameters to monitor and evaluate the recommendations

Preparing Effective Presentations in the Social Sciences

Good social scientific presentations explain the research question clearly, refer to current research, and use timely data.

- *Illustrate the research question.* Pay special attention to illustrating clearly the nature of the research question and the means by which the results were achieved.

- *Refer to current research.* Credible social scientific presentations refer to recent findings in the field. Instructors are more likely to accept experimental evidence if it is replicable over time and is supported by current research.

- *Use timely data.* Instructors expect student presentations to include timely data and examples. A report on poverty rates for a sociology course must provide up-to-date data, because poverty rates change yearly.

34   Arts and Humanities Courses

Speaking assignments in arts and humanities courses (including English, history, religion, philosophy, foreign languages, art history, theater, and music) often require that you interpret the meaning of a particular idea, event, person, story, or artifact. Your art history professor, for example, may ask you to identify the various artistic and historical influences on a sculpture or a painting, or an instructor of literature may ask you to explain the theme of a novel or a poem. Some presentations may be performative in nature, with students expressing artistic content.

Rather than focusing on quantitative research, presentations in the arts and humanities rely on your analysis and interpretation of the topic at hand. These interpretations are nonetheless grounded in the conventions of the field and build on research within it.

Informative Talks of Description and Analysis

Often in the arts and humanities, students prepare informative presentations (see Chapter 23) in which they explain the relevance of a historical or a contemporary person or event; a genre or school of philosophical thought; or a piece of literature, music, or art. For example, an art history professor may require students to discuss the artist Bernini's contribution to St. Peter's Cathedral in Rome. Presentation aids are often a key part of such presentations; here, audiences would expect to see relevant reproductions and photographs.

Presentations That Compare and Contrast

Another common assignment in the arts and humanities is to compare and contrast events, stories, people, or artifacts in order to highlight similarities or differences. For example, you might compare two works of literature from different time periods or two historical figures or works of art. These presentations may be informative or persuasive. Presentations that compare and contrast include the following elements:

1. *Thesis statement* outlining the connection between the events, stories, people, or artifacts

2. *Discussion of main points,* including several examples that highlight similarities and differences

3. *Concluding evaluative statement* about the comparison (e.g., if the presentation is persuasive, why one piece of literature was more effective than another; if informative, a restatement of similarities and differences)

Debates

Often, students will engage in debates on opposing ideas, historical figures, or philosophical positions. In a history class, for example, students might argue whether women in sixteenth-century Western Europe experienced a Renaissance. The speaker must present a brief assertion (two to three minutes) about the topic; the opposing speaker then responds with a position. Whatever side of an issue you address, prepare a well-composed argument with strong supporting evidence.

QUICK TIP

Be Prepared to Lead a Discussion

Many students taking arts and humanities courses must research a question and then lead a classroom discussion on it. For example, a student of English may lead a discussion on Anton Chekhov's play The Cherry Orchard. *The speaker would be expected to provide a synopsis of the plot, theme, and characters and offer an analysis of the play's meaning. For directions on leading a discussion, see p. 273.*

Preparing Effective Arts and Humanities Presentations

Good presentations in the arts and humanities help the audience to think of the topic in a new way by providing an original interpretation of it. A presentation on the historical significance of Reconstruction after the Civil War of 1861–1865, for example, will be more effective if you offer a new way of viewing the topic rather than reiterating what other people have said or what is already generally accepted knowledge. A debate on two philosophical ideas will be most effective when you assert issues and arguments that are different from those that the audience has thought of before. Because many speaking events in the arts and humanities call for interpretation, the more original the interpretation (while remaining logical and supported by evidence), the more compelling the presentation will be for the audience.

35 Education Courses

In education courses (including subfields such as curriculum and instruction, physical education, secondary and elementary education, and education administration), the most common speaking assignments focus on teaching and related instructional tasks, such as giving a lecture or demonstrating an activity. In a mathematics education course, you may give a mini-lecture on a particular geometric theorem. In a learning-styles course, you may tailor an activity to a variety of different learners.

Delivering a Lecture

A **lecture** is an informational speech for an audience of student learners. Standard lectures range from thirty minutes to one hour in length; a *mini-lecture presentation*, designed to give students an opportunity to synthesize information in a shorter form, generally lasts about fifteen to twenty minutes. Typically, lectures include the following:

1. A clear introduction of the topic (see Chapter 15)
2. Statement of the central idea of the lecture
3. Statement of the connection to previous topics covered
4. Discussion of the main points

5. Summary of the lecture and preview of the next assigned topic

6. Question-and-answer period

QUICK TIP

Be an Active Lecturer
Good lecturers actively engage students in the learning process, pausing to pose questions about the topic, allowing time for discussion, and incorporating short activities into the mix.[1] Rather than delivering a monologue, focus on engaging student participation.

Facilitating a Group Activity

In the **group activity presentation**, the speaker describes an activity to be completed following a lecture. Typically this short presentation includes the following:

1. A brief review of the main idea of the lecture
2. An explanation of the goal of the activity
3. Directions on carrying out the activity
4. A preview of what students will gain from the activity and what the discussion following it will cover

Facilitating a Classroom Discussion

In the **classroom discussion presentation**, the speaker leads a discussion following a lecture, offering brief remarks and then guiding the discussion as it proceeds.

1. Begin by outlining critical points to be covered.
2. Prepare several general guiding questions to launch the discussion.
3. Prepare relevant questions and examples for use during the discussion.

Preparing Effective Education Presentations

Good presentations in education are marked by clear organization, integration of the material into the broader course content, two-way communication, and student-friendly supporting material.

- *Organize material logically.* Presentations in education must be tightly organized so that the audience can easily access information. The simpler the organizational structure, the better (see Chapters 12 and 24). Use organizing devices such as preview statements, internal summaries, and transitions to help listeners follow ideas in a lecture, for example.

- *Integrate discussion to overall course content.* Describe how the lecture for the day relates to the previous day's lecture. In a discussion or group activity, make clear connections between students' comments and other topics that have been raised or will be raised later in the course.

- *Tailor examples and evidence to the audience.* Use familiar examples and evidence that the audience can grasp easily. Don't support an idea with a statistical proof, for example, unless students are trained in statistics. Using familiar examples will enhance learning (see section on analogies in Chapter 23); try to choose examples that are close to the students' experiences.

36 Nursing and Allied Health Courses

Speaking assignments in nursing and allied health courses—physical therapy, occupational therapy, radiology, pharmacy, and other areas of health care—range from the *service learning presentation, poster presentation,* and *review of academic articles* (see Chapter 30 for detailed guidelines) to the *evidence-based practice presentation, clinical case study, quality improvement proposal, case conference,* and *shift report* (see the following sections). Students are assigned a mix of individual and team presentations.

Evidence-Based Practice Presentation

The **evidence-based practice (EBP) presentation** reviews the scientific literature on a clinical problem, critically evaluates the findings, and suggests best practices for standards of care. To fulfill these criteria, EBP presentations do the following:

- Define the research problem (e.g., the clinical issue).
- Critically review the scientific literature on a practice related to the clinical issue, describing method/design, sample size, and reliability.

- Discuss the strength of the evidence and indicate whether or not the practice should be adopted into clinical practice.[1]

Clinical Case Study Presentation

A **clinical case study** is a detailed analysis of a person or group with a particular disease or condition. Clinical case studies inform medical teams or other audiences about the following:

- Overview of patient information (presentation and background)
- Description of pre-treatment workup, including results
- Review of treatment options/plan of care
- Outcome of treatment plan
- Surveillance plan (follow-up patient care based on evidence-based practice)

Quality Improvement Proposal

In the **quality improvement proposal**, the speaker recommends the adoption of a new (or modified) health practice or policy, such as introducing an improved treatment regimen at a burn center. This report (sometimes assigned as part of a capstone course) addresses the following:

- Review of existing practice
- Description of proposed quality improvement
- Review of the scientific literature on the proposed practice
- Plan of action for implementation

Treatment Plan Reports

The ability to communicate information about patients or clients is important for all health care providers. Either individually or as part of a health care team, people in the helping professions often report patients' conditions and outline plans of treatment to other health care providers. One form of treatment plan report, called the **case conference**, includes the following:

- Description of patient status
- Explanation of the disease process
- Steps in the treatment regimen

- Goals for patient and family
- Plans for patient's care at home
- Review of financial needs
- Assessment of resources available

The **shift report** is a concise overview of the patient's status and needs, delivered to the oncoming caregiver. It includes the following information:

- Patient name, location, and reason for care
- Current physical status
- Day on clinical pathway for particular diagnosis
- Pertinent psychosocial data, including plans for discharge and involvement of caregivers
- Care needs (physical, hygiene, activity, medication, nutritional)

Preparing Effective Presentations in Nursing and Allied Health Courses

Good presentations in health-related courses communicate scientific knowledge while reviewing the patient's clinical status and potential treatment options. The presenter will support any assertions and recommendations with relevant scientific literature supporting evidence-based clinical practice. Instructors will expect you to do the following:

- Use evidence-based guidelines.
- Demonstrate a solid grasp of the relevant scientific data.
- Organize the presentation in order of severity of patient problems.
- Present the patient as well as the illness.
- Include only essential facts, but be prepared to answer any questions about all aspects of the patient and care.[2]

Appendices

A. Citation Guidelines 278

B. Question-and-Answer Sessions 292

C. Preparing for Mediated
    Communication 294

D. Tips for Non-Native Speakers
    of English 296

Instructors will often require that you include a bibliography of sources with your speech (see Chapters 4 and 9). You can document sources by following documentation systems such as *Chicago,* APA, MLA, CSE, and IEEE.

Chicago Documentation

Two widely used systems of documentation are outlined in *The Chicago Manual of Style,* Sixteenth Edition (2010). The first, typically used by public speakers in a variety of disciplines, provides for bibliographic citations in endnotes or footnotes. This method is illustrated below. The second form employs an author-date system: Sources are cited in the text with full bibliographic information given in a concluding list of references. For information about the author-date system—and more general information about *Chicago*-style documentation—consult the *Chicago Manual,* Chapters 14 and 15.

1. BOOK BY A SINGLE AUTHOR   Give the author's full name followed by a comma. Then italicize the book's title. In parentheses, give the city of publication followed by a colon, the publisher's name followed by a comma, and publication date. Place a comma after the closing parenthesis; then give page numbers from which your paraphrase or quotation is taken.

    1. Eric Alterman, *What Liberal Media? The Truth about Bias and the News* (New York: Basic Books, 2003), 180–85.

2. BOOK BY MULTIPLE AUTHORS

    2. Bill Kovach and Tom Rosenstiel, *The Elements of Journalism: What Newspeople Should Know and the Public Should Expect,* rev. ed. (New York: Three Rivers Press, 2007), 57–58.

3. EDITED WORK AND WORK WITHIN AN EDITED COLLECTION

    3. Joseph B. Atkins, ed., *The Mission: Journalism, Ethics, and the World* (Ames: Iowa State University Press, 2002), 150–57.

    3. Jonathan Dube, "Writing News Online," in *Shop Talk and War Stories: American Journalists Examine Their Profession,* ed. Jan Winburn (Boston: Bedford/St. Martin's, 2003), 202.

4. ENCYCLOPEDIA OR DICTIONARY   After the title of the work, add "s.v." (Latin *sub verbo,* "under the word") and the term you looked up. If the citation is from an online reference work, add the URL (Internet address) and the publication date or date of last revision; if neither is available, use your access date.

4. *Encyclopedia Britannica Online*, s.v. "Yellow Journalism," accessed October 17, 2007, http://www.britannica.com/eb/article-9077903/yellow-journalism.

5. ARTICLE IN A MAGAZINE

5. John Leo, "With Bias toward All," *U.S. News & World Report,* March 18, 2002, 8.

6. ARTICLE IN A JOURNAL   Give the author's full name, the title of the article in quotation marks, the title of the journal in italics, the volume and issue numbers, the year of publication in parentheses followed by a colon, and the pages used. If the journal article was found online, list the URL or use the DOI (digital object identifier) instead of the URL if one is available. It is not necessary to include page numbers for articles accessed online.

6. Tom Goldstein, "Wanted: More Outspoken Views; Coverage of the Press Is Up, but Criticism Is Down," *Columbia Journalism Review* 40, no. 4 (2001): 144–45.

6. Bree Nordenson, "Vanity Fire," *Columbia Journalism Review* 45, no. 5 (2007), http://www.cjr.org/profile/vanity_fire.php.

7. ARTICLE IN A NEWSPAPER

7. Felicity Barringer, "Sports Reporting: Rules on Rumors," *New York Times,* February 18, 2002, sec. C.

8. WEB SITE   Give the name of the author (if not available, use the name of the site sponsor); the title of the page, in quotation marks, followed by a comma; the title of the Web site (if the site is an online publication, place the title in italics); the sponsor of the site, if different from the name of the site or name of the author; the date of publication or modification (if no date is provided, or if your instructor requests it, include the date accessed, preceded by the word "accessed"; and the URL.

8. FAIR (Fairness & Accuracy in Reporting), "Challenging Hate Radio: A Guide for Activists," accessed February 9, 2012, http://www.fair.org/index.php?page=112.

9. E-MAIL MESSAGE

9. Grace Talusan, e-mail message to author, March 20, 2011.

10. ELECTRONIC MAILING LIST

10. Ola Seifert to Society of Professional Journalists mailing list, August 23, 2002, http://f05n16.cac.psu.edu.

11. BLOG POST

11. Brian Stetler, "Study: Some Viewers Were Misinformed by TV News," *Media Decoder* (blog), *New York Times,* December 17, 2010, http://mediadecoder.blogs.nytimes.com.

12. ARTICLE IN AN ELECTRONIC DATABASE
Provide the DOI (if available), or the name of the database and the document number.

12. Mark J. Miller, "Tough Calls: Deciding When a Suicide Is Newsworthy and What Details to Include Are among Journalism's More Sensitive Decisions," *American Journalism Review* 24, no. 10 (2002): 43, Expanded Academic ASAP (A95153129).

13. GOVERNMENT DOCUMENT

13. U.S. Congress, *Electronic Freedom of Information Amendments of 1996* (Washington, D.C.: GPO, 1996), 22.

14. PERSONAL COMMUNICATION

14. Soo Jin Oh, letter to author, August 13, 2005.

15. INTERVIEW

15. Walter Cronkite, interview by Daniel Schorr, *Frontline,* PBS, April 2, 1996.

16. VIDEO RECORDING

16. *All the President's Men,* directed by Alan J. Pakula (1976; Burbank, CA: Warner Home Video, 1998), VHS.

17. SOUND RECORDING

17. Noam Chomsky, *The Emerging Framework of World Power,* read by the author (AK Press, 2003), compact disc.

17. Antonio Vivaldi, *The Four Seasons,* Boston Symphony Orchestra, conducted by Seiji Ozawa, Telarc 80070, compact disc.

APA Documentation

Most disciplines in the social sciences—psychology, anthropology, sociology, political science, education, and economics—use the author-date system of documentation established by the American Psychological Association (APA). This citation style highlights dates of publication because the currency of published material is of primary importance in these fields.

In the author-date system, use an author or organization's name in a signal phrase or parenthetical reference within the main text to cite a source.

For example, you could cite Example 1 on this page with the author's name in a signal phrase as follows:

Nakazawa (2009) states that stress hormones like cortisol can dramatically alter how immune cells work.

Or with a parenthetical reference as follows:

Stress hormones such as cortisol travel to the immune system and can dramatically alter how immune cells work (Nakazawa, 2009).

Each in-text citation refers to an alphabetical references list that you must create.

For more information about APA format, see the *Publication Manual of the American Psychological Association,* Sixth Edition (2010). The manual advises users to omit retrieval dates for content that is unlikely to change, such as published journal articles, and to omit the database from which material is retrieved as long as an identifier such as a URL (Internet address) or DOI (digital object identifier) is included.

The numbered entries that follow introduce and explain some conventions of this citation style using examples related to the topic of stress management. Note that in the titles of books and articles only the first word of the title and subtitle and proper nouns are capitalized.

1. **BOOK BY A SINGLE AUTHOR**   Begin with the author's last name and initials, followed by the date of publication in parentheses. Next, italicize the book's title, and end with the place of publication, including city and state or country, and the publisher.

Nakazawa, D. J. (2009). *The autoimmune epidemic.* New York, NY: Simon & Schuster.

2. BOOK BY MULTIPLE AUTHORS OR EDITORS

Williams, S., & Cooper, L. (2002). *Managing workplace stress: A best practice blueprint*. New York, NY: Wiley.

3. ARTICLE IN A REFERENCE WORK If an online edition of the reference work is cited, give the retrieval date and the URL. Omit end punctuation after the URL.

Beins, B. C. (2010). Barnum effect. In I. B. Weiner & W. E. Craighead (Eds.), *The Corsini encyclopedia of psychology* (4th ed., Vol. 4, pp. 203–204). Hoboken, NJ: Wiley.

Biofeedback. (2007). In *Encyclopaedia Britannica online*. Retrieved from http://www.britannica.com/EBchecked/topic/65856/biofeedback

4. GOVERNMENT DOCUMENT

U.S. Department of Health and Human Services. (1997). *Violence in the workplace: Guidelines for understanding and response*. Washington, DC: Government Printing Office.

5. JOURNAL ARTICLE Begin with the author's last name and initials followed by the date of publication in parentheses. Next, list the title of the article and italicize the title of the journal in which it is printed. Then give the volume number, italicized, and the issue number in parentheses if the journal is paginated by issue. End with the inclusive page numbers of the article. For an article found online, if a DOI number is given, add "doi:" and the number after the publication information. Otherwise, add "Retrieved from" and the URL of the journal home page. Omit the end period after a DOI or URL.

Dollard, M. F., & Metzer, J. C. (1999). Psychological research, practice, and production: The occupational stress problem. *International Journal of Stress Management, 6*(4), 241–253.

Christian, M. S., Bradley, J. C., Wallace, J. C., & Burke, M. J. (2009, September). Workplace safety: A meta-analysis of the roles of person and situation factors. *Journal of Applied Psychology, 94*, 1103–1127. doi:10.1037/a0016172

6. MAGAZINE ARTICLE

Cobb, K. (2002, July 20). Sleepy heads: Low fuel may drive brain's need to sleep. *Science News, 162*, 38.

7. NEWSPAPER ARTICLE

Zimmerman, E. (2010, December 19). Learning to tame your
office anxiety. *The New York Times,* p. BU8.

Zimmerman, E. (2010, December 19). Learning to tame your
office anxiety. *The New York Times.* Retrieved from http://
www.nytimes.com

8. UNSIGNED NEWSPAPER ARTICLE

Stress less: It's time to wrap it up. (2002, December 18). *Houston
Chronicle,* p. A1.

9. DOCUMENT FROM A WEB SITE List the author, the date of publication (use "n.d." if there is no date), the title of the document, italicized, the words "Retrieved from" and the URL for the document. If there is no author, begin the entry with the document title. Do not include a retrieval date unless the content is likely to change. Omit punctuation at the end of the URL.

Centers for Disease Control and Prevention. (1999). *Stress . . .
at work* (NIOSH Publication No. 99 101). Retrieved from
http://www.cdc.gov/niosh/docs/99-101

10. PERSONAL WEB SITE Simply note the site in your speech:

Dr. Wesley Sime's stress management page is an excellent
resource (http://www.unl.edu/stress/mgmt/).

11. ELECTRONIC MAILING LIST, NEWSGROUP, ONLINE FORUM, OR DISCUSSION GROUP MESSAGE

Lippin, R. (2008, November 2). Re: The relation between
work-related psychosocial factors and the development of
depression [Electronic mailing list message]. Retrieved from
Occupational & Environmental Medicine Mailing List, http://
lists.unc.edu/read/archive?id=4872034

Dimitrakov, J. (2001, February 21). Re: Immune effects of
psychological stress [Online discussion group message].
Retrieved from http://groups.google.com/groups?q=stress
&start=40&hl=en&lr=&ie=UTF-8&selm=3A9ABDE4%
40MailAndNews.com&rnum=44

12. BLOG POST

Lippin, R. (2007, July 31). US corporate EAP programs: Oversight,
Orwellian or Soviet psychiatry redux? [Web log post].

Retrieved from http://medicalcrises.blogspot.com/2007/07/
us-corporate-eap-programs-oversight.html

13. E-MAIL MESSAGE   Simply note the message in your speech:
An e-mail message from the staff of AltaVista clarifies this point
(D. Emanuel, personal communication, May 12, 2005).

14. MATERIAL FROM AN ONLINE DATABASE

Waring, T. (2002). Stress management: A balanced life is good
        for business. *Law Society Journal, 40,* 66–68. Retrieved from
        http://www.lawsociety.com.au

**15. ABSTRACT FROM AN INFORMATION SERVICE OR ONLINE DATA-
BASE**   Begin the entry with the publication information as
for a print article. End the entry with "Abstract retrieved"
followed by the URL of the database or the name of the database and any identifying number.

Viswesvaran, C., Sanchez, J., & Fisher, J. (1999). The role
        of social support in the process of work stress: A meta-
        analysis. *Journal of Vocational Behavior, 54,* 314–334.
        Abstract retrieved from ERIC database. (EJ581024)

16. PERSONAL INTERVIEW   Simply note the interview in your
speech:
During her interview, Senator Cole revealed her enthusiasm for
        the new state-funded stress management center (M. Cole,
        personal communication, October 7, 2005).

MLA Documentation

Created by the Modern Language Association, MLA documentation style is fully outlined in the *MLA Handbook for
Writers of Research Papers,* Seventh Edition (2009). Disciplines that use MLA style include English literature, the
humanities, and various foreign languages.

In MLA format, you document materials from other
sources with in-text citations that incorporate signal phrases
and parenthetical references.

For example, you could cite Example 1 below with the
author's name in a signal phrase as follows:

Berg notes that "'Chicano' is the term made popular by the
Mexican American civil rights movement in the 1960s and
1970s" (6).

Or with a parenthetical reference as follows:

The term "Chicano" was "made popular by the Mexican American civil rights movement in the 1960s and 1970s" (Berg 6).

Each in-text citation refers to an alphabetical works-cited list that you must create.

The sample citations given here all relate to a single topic: film appreciation and criticism.

1. BOOK BY A SINGLE AUTHOR   Citations for most books are arranged as follows: (1) the author's name, last name first; (2) the title and subtitle, italicized; and (3) the city of publication, an abbreviated form of the publisher's name, and the date. Each of these three pieces of information is followed by a period and one space. End the citation with the medium of publication (Print) and a period.

Berg, Charles Ramírez. *Latino Images in Film: Stereotypes,*
    Subversion, and Resistance. Austin: U of Texas P, 2002. Print.

2. BOOK BY MULTIPLE AUTHORS OR EDITORS   Give the first author's name, last name first; then list the name(s) of the other author(s) in regular order with a comma between authors and the word *and* before the last one. The final name in a list of editors is followed by a comma and "ed." or "eds."

Grieveson, Lee, and Haidee Wasson, eds. *Inventing Film Studies.*
    Durham: Duke UP, 2008. Print.

3. ARTICLE IN A REFERENCE WORK   If the citation is to an online version of the work, give the author, article title, and name of the Web site. Then add the publisher or sponsor of the site, the date of publication or last update, the medium (Web), and the date you accessed the work (day, month, year). End with a period.

Katz, Ephraim. "Film Noir." *The Film Encyclopedia.* 6th ed. 2008.
    Print.

"Auteur Theory." *Encyclopaedia Britannica Online.* Encyclopaedia
    Britannica, 2007. Web. 22 Oct. 2007.

4. GOVERNMENT DOCUMENT

United States. Cong. House. Committee on the Judiciary. *National*
    Film Preservation Act of 1996. 104th Cong., 2nd sess. H.
    Rept. 104–558. Washington: GPO, 1996. Print.

United States. Cong. House. Committee on House Administration.
*Library of Congress Sound Recording and Film Preservation
Programs Reauthorization Act of 2008.* 110th Cong., 2nd
sess. H. Rept. 110–683. *GPOAccess, Congressional Reports.*
Web. 15 Jan. 2012.

5. MAGAZINE ARTICLE   If you are citing the article from an online edition of the magazine, after the title of the article, add
the name of the Web site in italics, followed by a period. Then
add the publisher or sponsor of the site, the date of publication, the medium (Web), and the date you accessed the article.

Ansen, David. "Shock and Yawn." *Newsweek* 26 Oct. 2009: 48.
Print.

Horn, Robert. "From Bangkok to Cannes, Thai Political Tensions
Remain." *Time.* Time, 24 May 2010. Web. 3 Nov. 2010.

6. JOURNAL ARTICLE   If an article is accessed online through
a database service, after the publication information, add the
name of the database in italics, followed by a period. Then
give the medium (Web) and your date of access. End with a
period.

Skrebels, Paul. "*All Night Long*: Jazzing around with Othello."
Literature/Film Quarterly 36.2 (2008): 147–56. Print.

Holcomb, Mark. "A Classic Revisited: *To Kill a Mockingbird*." *Film
Quarterly* 55.4 (2002): 34–40. *Academic OneFile.* Web.
22 Oct. 2011.

7. NEWSPAPER ARTICLE   If you are citing a newspaper article
found online, after the title of the article, give the name of
the newspaper's Web site followed by a period. Then specify
the publisher or sponsor of the site, the date of publication,
the medium consulted (Web), and the date you accessed the
article.

Peers, Martin. "HBO Could Draw True Blood Online." *Wall Street
Journal* 23 Oct. 2010: B16+. Print.

Dargis, Manohla. "Unblinking Eye, Visual Diary: Warhol's Films."
New York Times. New York Times, 21 Oct. 2007. Web.
30 Oct. 2007.

8. NEWSPAPER EDITORIAL

"Avatars Don't Smoke." Editorial. *New York Times* 8 Jan. 2010:
A26. Print.

9. ONLINE SCHOLARLY PROJECT OR REFERENCE DATABASE

"Origins of American Animation." *American Memory*. Lib. of Cong.
31 Mar. 1999. Web. 26 June 2011.

10. PERSONAL OR COMMERCIAL WEB SITE

Last, Kimberly. *007*. Kimberly Last, n.d. Web. 18 Oct. 2007.

"American Beauty." *Crazy for Cinema*. N.p., n.d. Web.
24 Oct. 2011.

11. POSTING OR COMMENT ON A BLOG Give the author's name;
the title of the post or comment in quotation marks (if there
is no title, use the description "blog post" or "blog comment"); the title of the blog, italicized, the sponsor of the
blog (if there is none, use "N.p."); the date of the most recent
update; the medium (Web); and the date of access.

Scola, Nancy. "And the White House Tweets Back." *techPresident*.
Personal Democracy Forum, 5 May 2009. Web. 5 May 2009.

12. ARTICLE IN AN ONLINE PERIODICAL

Williams, Mary Elizabeth. "The NC-17 Rating's Perverse
Failure." *Salon*. Salon Media Group, 8 Dec. 2010. Web.
11 Jan. 2012.

13. POSTING TO A DISCUSSION GROUP

Granger, Susan. "Review of *The Cider House Rules*." *Rotten
Tomatoes*. IGN Entertainment, 30 Mar. 2000. Web.
2 Oct. 2011.

14. E-MAIL MESSAGE

Boothe, Jeanna. "Re: Top 100 Movies." Message to the author.
16 Feb. 2012. E-mail.

15. SINGLE-ISSUE CD-ROM, DISKETTE, OR MAGNETIC TAPE

"Pulp Fiction." *Blockbuster Movie Trivia*. 3rd ed. New York:
Random, 1998. CD-ROM.

16. WORK OF ART OR PHOTOGRAPH

Christenberry, William. *Coleman's Café*. 1971. Ektacolor Brownie
    Print. Hunter Museum of Art, Chattanooga.

17. INTERVIEW

Sanderson, Andrew. Telephone interview. 12 June 2011.

CSE Documentation

The CSE (Council of Science Editors) style is most frequently used in the fields of biology and environmental
science. The current CSE style guide is *Scientific Style and
Format: The CSE Manual for Authors, Editors, and Publishers,* Seventh Edition (2006). Publishers and instructors
who require the CSE style do so in three possible formats: a
citation-sequence superscript format, a name-year format,
or a citation-name format, which combines aspects of the
other two systems.

- Citation-sequence superscript format: Use superscript
  numbers for in-text references. In the references list,
  number and arrange the references in the sequence in
  which they are first cited in the speech.

- Name-year format: Use the name and year, in parentheses, for the in-text reference. In the references list, give
  the references, unnumbered, in alphabetical order.

- Citation-name format: Use superscript numbers for
  in-text references. In the references list, arrange the
  references in alphabetical order and number the list
  sequentially.

In the following examples, all of which refer to environmental issues, you will see that the citation-sequence format
calls for listing the date after the publisher's name in references for books and after the name of the periodical in references for articles. The name-year format calls for listing the
date immediately after the author's name in any kind of reference. Notice also the absence of a comma after the author's
last name, the absence of a period after an initial, and the
absence of italics in titles of books or journals.

1. BOOK BY ONE AUTHOR   Be sure to list the total number of
pages in the book.

Citation-Sequence and Citation-Name

[1] Houghton JT. Global warming: the complete briefing. 4th ed. Cambridge (UK): Cambridge University Press; 2009. 456 p.

Name-Year

Houghton JT. 2009. Global warming: the complete briefing. 4th ed. Cambridge (UK): Cambridge University Press. 456 p.

2. BOOK BY TWO OR MORE AUTHORS

Citation-Sequence and Citation-Name

[2] Harf JE, Lombardi MO. Taking sides: clashing views on global issues. 6th ed. New York: McGraw-Hill; 2010. 432 p.

Name-Year

Harf JE, Lombardi MO. 2010. Taking sides: clashing views on global issues. 6th ed. New York: McGraw-Hill. 432 p.

3. JOURNAL ARTICLE   If citing a journal on the Internet, add the medium, date cited, and the URL. Also give the DOI code if available. Omit end punctuation after a URL or DOI.

Citation-Sequence and Citation-Name

[3] Brussard PF, Tull JC. Conservation biology and four types of advocacy. Conserv Biol. 2007; 21(1):21–24.

[3] Brussard PF, Tull JC. Conservation biology and four types of advocacy. Conserv Biol. [Internet]. 2007 [cited 2010 Oct 22]; 21(1):21–24. Available from: http://www.blackwell-synergy.com/toc/cbi/21/1 doi:10.1111/j.1523-1739.2006.00640.x

Name-Year

Brussard PF, Tull JC. 2007. Conservation biology and four types of advocacy. Conserv Biol. 21(1):21–24.

Brussard PF, Tull JC. 2007. Conservation biology and four types of advocacy. Conserv Biol [Internet]. [cited 2010 Oct 22]; 21(1):21–24. Available from: http://www.blackwell -synergy.com/toc/cbi/21/1 doi:10.1111/j.1523-1739.2006.00640.x

4. MAGAZINE ARTICLE

Citation-Sequence and Citation-Name

[4] Sheppard K. Bad breakup: why BP doesn't have to tell the EPA—
     or the public—what's in its toxic dispersants. Mother Jones.
     2010 Sep-Oct:41.

Name-Year

Sheppard K. 2010 Sep-Oct. Bad breakup: why BP doesn't have to
     tell the EPA—or the public—what's in its toxic dispersants.
     Mother Jones. 41.

5. NEWSPAPER ARTICLE

Citation-Sequence and Citation-Name

[5] Zeller T Jr. Negotiators at climate talks face deep set of fault
     lines. New York Times. 2009 Dec 6; Sect. WK:3 (col. 1).

Name-Year

Zeller T Jr. 2009 Dec 6. Negotiators at climate talks face deep set
     of fault lines. New York Times. Sect. WK:3 (col. 1).

6. WEB SITE   For material found on a Web site, give the author's name (if any) and the title of the material, followed by "Internet" in brackets. Add the place of publication, the publisher, date of publication, followed by the date of citation in brackets. Add "Available from:" and the URL.

Citation-Sequence and Citation-Name

[6] Coastal Programs: The Barnegat Bay Estuary Program [Internet].
     Trenton (NJ): Department of Environmental Protection,
     Division of Watershed Management. c1996-2004 [updated
     2010 Feb 18; cited 2011 Oct 23]. Available from: http://
     www.nj.gov/dep/watershedmgt/bbep.htm

Name-Year

Coastal Programs: The Barnegat Bay Estuary Program [Internet].
     c1996-2004. Trenton (NJ): Department of Environmental
     Protection, Division of Watershed Management. [updated

2010 Feb 18; cited 2011 Oct 23]. Available from: http://
www.nj.gov/dep/watershedmgt/bbep.htm

7. E-MAIL MESSAGE CSE recommends mentioning personal
communications in text, but not listing them in the list of
references. An explanation of the material should go in the
"Notes."

... (2012 e-mail from Maura O'Brien to me; unreferenced, see
   "Notes").

8. E-MAIL DISCUSSION LIST OR NEWSGROUP MESSAGE

[8] Affleck-Asch W. Lawncare methods causing heavy damage
    to environment [discussion list on the Internet].
    2004 Aug 17, 2:30 pm [cited 2011 Dec 2]. [about 10
    paragraphs]. Available from: http://www.mail-archive.com/
    ecofem%40csf.colorado.edu

IEEE Documentation

The Institute of Electrical and Electronics Engineers
(IEEE) style requires that references appear at the end
of the text, not in alphabetical order but in the order in
which the references are cited in the text or speech. A
bracketed reference number beginning with *B* precedes
each entry. For more information on IEEE documentation, check the *IEEE Standards Style Manual* online at
https://development.standards.ieee.org/myproject/Public/
mytools/draft/styleman.pdf.

1. BOOK

[B1] Thomas, R. E., Albert, R. J., and Toussaint G. J., *The
     Analysis and Design of Linear Circuits*, 6th ed. Hoboken, NJ:
     Wiley, 2009, p. 652.

2. PERIODICAL

[B2] Melfi, M., Evon, S., and McElveen R., "Induction versus
     permanent magnet motors," *IEEE Industry Applications
     Magazine*, vol. 15, no. 6, pp. 28–35, Nov./Dec. 2009. doi:
     10.1109/MIAS.2009.934443

3. WEB PAGE

[B3] National Academy of Engineering, "Lasers and fiber optics timeline," *Greatest Engineering Achievements of the 20th Century*, 2010.*

*Available at www.greatachievements.org.

B	Question-and-Answer Sessions

Deftly fielding questions is a final critical component of making a speech or a presentation. As the last step in preparing your speech, anticipate and prepare for questions the audience is likely to pose to you. Write these questions down, and practice answering them. Spend time preparing an answer to the most difficult question that you are likely to face. The confidence you will gain from smoothly handling a difficult question should spill over to other questions.[1]

Protocol during the Session

As a matter of courtesy, call on audience members in the order in which they raise their hands. Consider the following guidelines:

- *Repeat or paraphrase the question* ("The question is 'Did the mayor really vote against …'"). This will ensure that you've heard it correctly, that others in the audience know what you are responding to, and that you have time to reflect upon and formulate an answer. Note that there are a few exceptions to repeating the question, especially when the question is hostile. One expert suggests that you should always repeat the question when speaking to a large group; when you're in a small group or a training seminar, however, doing so isn't necessary.[2]

- *Initially make eye contact with the questioner; then move your gaze to other audience members.* This makes all audience members feel as though you are responding not only to the questioner but to them as well.

- *Remember your listening skills.* Give questioners your full attention, and don't interrupt them.

- *Don't be afraid to pause while formulating an answer.* Many speakers feel they must feed the audience instantaneous responses; this belief sometimes causes them to say things that they later regret. This is especially the case in media interviews (see Appendix C). Pauses that seem long to you may not appear lengthy to listeners.

- *Keep answers concise.* The question-and-answer session is not the time to launch into a lengthy treatise on your favorite aspect of a topic.

Handling Hostile and Otherwise Troubling Questions

When handling hostile questions, do not get defensive. Doing so will damage your credibility and only encourage the other person. Maintain an attitude of respect, and stay cool and in control. Attempt to defuse the hostile questioner with respect and goodwill. Similarly, never give the impression that you think a question is stupid or irrelevant, even if it clearly is.

- *Do not repeat or paraphrase a hostile question.* This only lends the question more credibility than it is worth. Instead, try to rephrase it more positively [3] (e.g., in response to the question "Didn't your department botch the handling of product X?" you might respond, "The question was 'Why did product X experience a difficult market entry?' To that I would say that ...").

- *If someone asks you a seemingly stupid question, do not point that out.* Instead, respond graciously.[4]

Ending the Session

Never end a question-and-answer session abruptly. As time runs out, alert the audience that you will take one or two more questions and then must end. The session represents one final opportunity to reinforce your message, so take the opportunity to do so. As you summarize your message, thank your listeners for their time. Leave an air of goodwill behind you.

Preparing for Mediated Communication

The underlying principles described throughout this guide will stand you in good stead as you prepare to communicate online, as discussed in Chapter 26, or on television or radio. These speaking situations do present some unique challenges, however.

Speaking on Television

On television, you are at the mercy of reporters and producers who will edit your remarks to fit their time frame. Therefore, before your televised appearance, find out as much as you can about the speech situation—for example, how long you will be on camera and whether the show will be aired live or taped. You may need to convey your message in *sound bite* form—succinct statements that summarize your key points in twenty seconds or less.

Eye Contact, Body Movements, and Voice

Knowing where to direct your gaze is critical in televised appearances, as is controlling body movement and voice. The following are some guidelines:

- Don't play to the camera. In a one-on-one interview, focus on the interviewer. Do not look up or down or tilt your head sideways; these movements will make you look uncertain or evasive.[1]

- If there is an audience, treat the camera as just another audience member, glancing at it only as often as you would at any other individual during your remarks.

- If there is only you and the camera, direct your gaze at it as you speak.

- Keep your posture erect.

- Exaggerate your gestures slightly.

- Project your voice, and avoid speaking in a monotone.

Dress and Makeup

To compensate for the glare of studio lights and distortions caused by the camera, give careful consideration to dress and grooming:

- Choose dark rather than light-colored clothing. Dark colors such as blue, gray, green, and brown photograph better than lighter shades.
- Avoid stark white, because it produces glare.
- Avoid plaids, dots, and other busy patterns because they tend to jump around on the screen.
- Avoid glittering jewelry, including tie bars.
- Wear a little more makeup than usual because bright studio lights tend to make you look washed out.

Speaking on Radio: The Media Interview

The following are guidelines for preparing for media interviews on the radio. These same guidelines can be applied to the television interview.

- Know the audience and the focus of the program. What subjects does the broadcast cover? How long will the interview be? Will it be in real-time or recorded?
- Brush up on background information, and have your facts ready. Assume that the audience knows little or nothing about the subject matter.
- Use the interviewer's name during the interview.
- Prepare a speaking outline on notecards for the interview. Remember that the microphone will pick up the sound of papers being shuffled.
- Remember that taped interviews may be edited. Make key points in short sentences, and repeat them using different words.[2] Think in terms of sound bites.
- Anticipate questions that might arise, and decide how you will answer them.
- Use transition points to acknowledge the interviewer's questions and to bridge your key message points, such as "I am not familiar with that, but what I can tell you is …"; "You raise an interesting question, but I think the more important matter is …"[3]
- Avoid the phrase "No comment." It will only exaggerate a point you are trying to minimize. Instead, say "I am not at liberty to comment/discuss…"

In addition to the normal fear of being at center stage, non-native speakers of English face the burden of worrying about delivering a speech in a non-native language. If English is your first language, remind yourself of how difficult it would be for you to deliver a speech in another language. As you listen to a non-native speaker, place yourself in his or her shoes. If necessary, politely ask questions for clarification.

If you are a non-native speaker of English, think about public speaking as an opportunity to learn more about the English language and how to use it. As you listen to your classmates' speeches, for example, you will gain exposure to spoken English. Practicing your speech will give you time to work on any accent features you want to improve.[1] Research shows that thinking positively about preparing speeches actually *reduces anxiety* and helps you prepare a better speech. So tell yourself that by studying public speaking you will find many good opportunities to improve your English and become a better communicator of English. In addition, by spending time writing and outlining your speech, you will gain confidence in your written language skills. Here are a few tips to get you started:

- *Take your time and speak slowly.* This will give your listeners time to get used to your voice and to focus on your message.

- *Identify English words that you have trouble saying.* Practice saying these words five times. Pause. Then say the words again five times. Progress slowly until the word becomes easier to pronounce.

- *Avoid using language that you don't really have to use, such as jargon* (see Chapter 16). Learn to use a thesaurus to find synonyms—words that mean the same thing—that are simpler and easier to pronounce.

- *Offer words from your native language to emphasize your points.* This will help the audience to better appreciate your native language and accent. For example, the Spanish word *corazón* has a lyrical quality that makes it sound much better than its English counterpart, "heart." Capitalize on the beauty of your native tongue.

Learn by Listening

Listening is the key to learning a language. Using textbooks to study usage and grammar is important, but it is through spoken language—hearing it and speaking it—that we gain fluency.

Listening to the speeches of colleagues or classmates, as well as those broadcast by television channels such as C-Span, can help you hone the skills you need to become a better speaker. Nearly all college libraries own many DVDs and other recorded materials made specifically for ESL (English as a second language) speakers such as yourself, and the reference librarian will be happy to locate them for you. The Internet also offers many helpful listening resources. Among the many sites you can find is the *Talking Merriam Webster English Dictionary* (at www.webster.com/). This online dictionary allows you to hear the correct pronunciations of words.

Broaden Your Listeners' Perspectives

Consider sharing a personal experience with the audience. Stories from other lands and other ways of life often fascinate listeners. Unique cultural traditions, eyewitness accounts of newsworthy events, or tales passed down orally from one generation to the next are just some of the possibilities. Depending on the goal of your speech, you can use your experiences as supporting material for a related topic or as the topic itself.

One freshman public-speaking student from Poland related what life for her was like after the fall of communism in 1989. She described how goods she had never seen before suddenly flooded the country. A wondrous array of fruit and meat left the most vivid impression on the then 11-year-old; both had been nearly impossible to find under the old regime. Her audience was fascinated with her first-hand account of historical events, and the speaker found that sharing her unique experiences boosted her confidence.

Record Yourself Practicing

Most experts recommend that you prepare for delivering your first speech (as well as for subsequent speeches) by practicing with a video or an audio recorder.[2] Non-native speakers may wish to pay added attention to pronunciation and articulation as they play back the recorded speech. *Pronunciation* is the correct formation of word sounds. *Articulation* is the clarity or forcefulness with which the sounds are made, regardless of whether they are pronounced correctly. It is important to pay attention to and work on both areas.

Because languages vary in the specific sounds they use and the way these sounds are produced by the vocal cords, each of us will speak a non-native language a bit differently than do native speakers. That is, we speak with some sort of accent. This should not concern you in and of itself. What is important is identifying which specific features of your pronunciation, if any, seriously interfere with your ability to make yourself understandable. Listening to your speech on a video or an audio recording, perhaps in the presence of a native speaker, will allow you to identify trouble spots. Once you have identified which words you tend to mispronounce, you can work to correct the problem. If possible, try to arrange an appointment with an instructor to help you identify key linguistic issues in your speech practice recording. If instructors are unavailable, try asking a fellow student.

Use Vocal Variety

Non-native speakers may be accustomed to patterns of vocal variety—volume, pitch, rate, and pauses—that are different from a native English speaker. The pronunciation of English depends on learning how to combine a series of about forty basic sounds (fifteen vowels and twenty-five consonants) that together serve to distinguish English words from one another. Correct pronunciation also requires that the speaker learn proper word stress, rhythm, and intonation or pitch.[3] As you practice your speeches, pay particular attention to these facets of delivery. Seek feedback from others,

---

QUICK TIP

Check for Correct Articulation

As you listen to your recording, watch also for your articulation of words. ESL students whose first languages don't differentiate between the /sh/ sound and its close cousin /ch/, for example, may say "share" when they mean "chair" or "shoes" when they mean "choose."[4] It is important therefore that you also check to make sure that you are using the correct meaning of the words you have selected for your speech.

including your teacher, making sure that your goal of shared meaning can be met when you do deliver your speech.

Counteract Problems in Being Understood

Virtually everyone who learns to speak another language will speak that language with an accent. What steps can you take when your accent will make your oral presentation difficult for the audience to understand?

In the long term, interacting with native speakers in everyday life will help enormously. With immersion, non-native speakers can begin to stop translating things word for word and start thinking in English. Using a video or an audio recorder and practicing your speech in front of others are also very important.

But what if your experience with English is limited and you must nonetheless give an oral presentation? Robert Anholt, a scientist and the author of *Dazzle 'Em with Style: The Art of Oral Scientific Presentation*, suggests the following:

- Practice the presentation often, preferably with a friend who is a native English speaker.
- Learn the presentation almost by heart.
- Create strong presentation aids that will convey most of the story by themselves, even if your voice is hard to understand.[5]

Glossary

abstract language Language that is general or nonspecific.

active listening Listening that is focused and purposeful.

ad hominem fallacy A logical fallacy that targets the person instead of the issue at hand in an attempt to discredit an opponent's argument. See also *logical fallacy*.

after-dinner speech A speech that is likely to occur before, after, or during a formal dinner; a breakfast or lunch seminar; or other type of business, professional, or civic meeting.

agenda A document identifying the items to be accomplished during a meeting.

agora In ancient Greece, a public square or marketplace. See also *forum* and *public forum*.

alliteration The repetition of the same sounds, usually initial consonants, in two or more neighboring words or syllables.

almanac A reference work that contains facts and statistics in many categories or on a given topic, including those that are related to historical, social, political, and religious subjects.

analogy An extended metaphor or simile that compares an unfamiliar concept or process with a more familiar one in order to help the listener understand the one that is unfamiliar. See also *imagery*.

anaphora A rhetorical device in which the speaker repeats a word or phrase at the beginning of successive phrases, clauses, or sentences.

anecdote A brief story of an interesting, humorous, or real-life incident that links back to the speaker's theme.

anti-group roles Disruptive roles such as "floor hogger" and "blocker" that detract from a group's roles and so should be avoided.

antithesis A rhetorical device in which two ideas are set off in balanced (parallel) opposition to each other.

anxiety stop-time A technique for dealing with pre-performance anxiety by allowing anxiety to present itself for a few minutes and then declaring time for confidence to step in to help complete practicing a speech.

appeal to tradition A logical fallacy suggesting that something is true because traditionally it has been true. See also *logical fallacy*.

architecture design review A type of oral presentation that enables the audience to visualize an architectural design.

argument A stated position, with support, for or against an idea or issue; contains the core elements of claim, evidence, and warrants.

articulation The clarity or forcefulness with which sounds are made, regardless of whether they are pronounced correctly.

asynchronous communication Communication in which interaction between speaker and receiver does not occur simultaneously. See also *recorded presentation*.

atlas A collection of maps, text, and accompanying charts and tables.

attitudes Our general evaluations of people, ideas, objects, or events.

audience analysis The process of gathering and analyzing demographic and psychological information about audience members.

audience-centered Focused on the needs, attitudes, and values of the audience.

average Information calculated on the basis of typical characteristics.

bandwagoning A logical fallacy that uses (unsubstantiated) general opinion as its (false) basis. See also *logical fallacy*.

begging the question A logical fallacy in which what is stated cannot help but be true, even though no evidence has been presented. See also *logical fallacy*.

beliefs The ways in which people perceive reality or determine the very existence or validity of something.

biased language Any language that relies on unfounded assumptions, negative descriptions, or stereotypes of a given group's age, class, gender, disability, geographic, ethnic, racial, or religious characteristics.

blog Short for "Weblog," an online personal journal.

body (of speech) The part of the speech in which the speaker develops the main points intended to fulfill the speech's purpose.

body language The bodily activity of the speaker and the meaning the audience assigns to this activity.

brainstorming A problem-solving technique that involves the spontaneous generation of ideas; includes making lists, using word association, and mapping topics.

brief example A single illustration of an idea, item, or event being described.

call to action A challenge to audience members to act in response to a speech; placed at the conclusion of a persuasive speech.

canned speech A speech used repeatedly and without sufficient adaptation to the rhetorical speech situation.

canons of rhetoric A classical approach to speechmaking in which the speaker divides the process into five parts: invention, arrangement, style, memory, and delivery.

captive audience An audience required to attend.

case conference An oral report prepared by health care professionals evaluating a patient's condition and outlining a treatment plan.

case study A detailed illustration of a real or hypothetical business situation.

causal (cause-effect) pattern of arrangement A pattern of organizing speech points in order of causes and then in order of effects, or vice versa.

causal reasoning Offering a cause-and-effect relationship as proof of a claim.

central processing A mode of processing a persuasive message that involves thinking critically about the contents of the message and the strength and quality of the speaker's arguments.

channel The medium through which the speaker sends a message, such as sound waves, air waves, and so forth.

chart A method of representing data and their relationship to other data in a meaningful form. Several different types of charts are helpful for speakers: flow charts, organization charts, and tabular charts (tables).

cherry-picking Selectively presenting only those facts and statistics that buttress one's point of view while ignoring competing data.

chronological pattern of arrangement A pattern of organizing speech points in a natural sequential order; used when describing a series of events in time or when the topic develops in line with a set pattern of actions or tasks.

claim The declaration of a state of affairs in which a speaker attempts to prove something by providing evidence and reasoning.

claim of fact An argument that focuses on whether something is or is not true or whether something will or will not happen.

claim of policy An argument that recommends that a specific course of action be taken, or approved, by an audience.

claim of value An argument that addresses issues of judgment.

classroom discussion presentation A type of oral presentation in which the speaker presents a brief overview of the topic under discussion and introduces a series of questions to guide students through the topic.

cliché An overused phrase such as "burning the midnight oil" or "works like a dog."

clinical case study A presentation that provides medical personnel with a detailed analysis of a person or group with a particular disease or condition and reviews plans for treatment.

closed-ended question A question designed to elicit a small range of specific answers supplied by the interviewer.

co-culture A community of people whose perceptions and beliefs differ significantly from those of other groups within the larger culture.

code-switching The selective use of dialect within a speech.

colleagues within the field audience An audience of persons who share the speaker's knowledge of the general field under question but who may not be familiar with the specific topic under discussion.

colloquial expression An informal expression characterized by regional variations of speech. See also *idiom*.

common knowledge Information that is likely to be known by many people and is therefore in the public domain; the source of such information need not be cited in a speech.

comparative advantage pattern of arrangement A pattern of organizing speech points so that the speaker's viewpoint or proposal is shown to be superior to one or more alternative viewpoints or proposals.

conclusion (of speech) The part of the speech in which the speaker reiterates the speech theme, summarizes main points, and leaves the audience with something about which to think or act.

concrete language Nouns and verbs that convey specific (as opposed to abstract) meaning.

connotative meaning The individual associations that different people bring to bear on a word.

context Anything that influences the speaker, the audience, or the occasion, and affects the message of the speech.

conversation stoppers Speech that discredits, demeans, or belittles.

coordinate points Ideas that are given the same weight in an outline and are aligned with one another; thus Main Point II is coordinate with Main Point I.

coordination and subordination The logical placement of ideas in an outline relative to their importance to one another. Ideas that are coordinate are given equal weight. An idea that is subordinate to another is given relatively less weight.

copyright A legal protection afforded original creators of literary or artistic works.

Creative Commons An organization that allows creators of works to decide how they want other people to use their copyrighted works.

crisis-response presentation A type of oral presentation in which the speaker seeks to reassure an organization's various audiences ("publics") and restore its credibility in the face of potentially reputation-damaging situations.

decoding The process of interpreting a message.

deductive reasoning Reasoning from a general condition to a specific instance. See *inductive reasoning*.

deep Web The large portion of the Web that general search engines cannot access because the information is licensed and/or fee-based.

defamatory speech Speech that potentially harms an individual's reputation at work or in the community and is thus subject to legal action. See also *reckless disregard for the truth*.

defensive listening A poor listening behavior in which the listener reacts defensively to a speaker's message.

definition by example Defining something by providing an example of it.

definition by negation Defining something by explaining what it is not.

definition by synonym Defining something by comparing it with another term that has an equivalent meaning. For example: "A friend is a comrade, or a buddy."

definition by word origin (etymology) Defining something by providing an account of a word's history.

delivery The vocal and nonverbal behavior that a speaker uses in a public speech; one of the five canons of rhetoric.

delivery cues Brief reminder notes or prompts placed in the speaking outline that can refer to transitions, timing, speaking rate and volume, presentation aids, quotations, statistics, and difficult-to-pronounce or remember names or words.

demographics Statistical characteristics of a given population. Characteristics typically considered in the analysis of audience members include age, gender, ethnic or cultural background, socioeconomic status (including income, occupation, and education), and religious and political affiliation.

denotative meaning The literal or dictionary definition of a word.

devil's advocacy Arguing for the sake of raising issues or concerns about the idea under discussion.

diagram A schematic drawing that explains how something works or how it is constructed or operated; useful in simplifying and clarifying complicated procedures, explanations, and operations.

dialect A distinctive way of speaking associated with a particular region or social group.

dialectical inquiry Devil's advocacy that goes a step further by proposing a countersolution to an idea.

dialogic communication Sharing ideas through dialogue.

dignity The feeling that one is worthy, honored, or respected as a person.

direct quotation Statement made verbatim—word for word—by someone else. Direct quotations should always be acknowledged in a speech.

disinformation The deliberate falsification of information.

DLP (digital light processing) projector A projector designed for computer images that is equipped with an illumination, or light source, in its own case, thereby eliminating the need for an overhead projector.

domain The suffix at the end of a Web address that describes the nature of the Web site: business/commercial (.com), educational (.edu), government (.gov), military (.mil), network (.net), or nonprofit organization (.org).

dyadic communication Communication between two people, as in a conversation.

either-or fallacy A logical fallacy stated in terms of two alternatives only, even though there are additional alternatives.

encoding The process of organizing a message, choosing words and sentence structure, and verbalizing the message.

encyclopedia A reference work that summarizes knowledge found in original form elsewhere and provides an overview of subjects.

engineering design review An oral presentation that provides information on the results of an engineering design project.

ethos The Greek word for "character." According to the ancient Greek rhetorician Aristotle, audiences listen to and trust speakers if they exhibit competence (as demonstrated by the speaker's grasp of the subject matter) and good moral character.

eulogy A speech whose purpose is to celebrate and commemorate the life of someone while consoling those who are left behind; typically delivered by close friends and family members.

evidence Supporting material that provides grounds for belief.

evidence-based practice (EBP) presentation A presentation that reviews the scientific literature on a clinical problem, critically evaluates the findings, and suggests best practices for standards of care.

example (as form of support) An illustration whose purpose is to aid understanding by making ideas, items, or events more concrete and by clarifying and amplifying meaning.

expert or insider audience An audience of persons with an intimate knowledge of the topic, issue, product, or idea being discussed.

expert testimony Any findings, eyewitness accounts, or opinions by professionals who are trained to evaluate or report on a given topic; a form of supporting material.

explanatory research presentation A type of oral presentation focusing on studies that attempt to analyze and explain a phenomenon; frequently delivered in social scientific fields.

extended example Multifaceted illustration of the idea, item, or event being described, thereby getting the point across and reiterating it effectively.

face-to-face (FtF) speaking A presentation delivered in the physical presence of others; an "offline" presentation.

fact book See *almanac*.

facts Documented occurrences, including actual events, dates, times, places, and people involved.

fairness An ethical ground rule; making a genuine effort to see all sides of an issue; being open-minded.

fair use doctrine Legal guidelines permitting the limited use of copyrighted works without permission for the purposes of scholarship, criticism, comment, news reporting, teaching, and research.

faulty analogy An inaccurate or misleading comparison suggesting that because two things are similar in some ways, they are necessarily similar in others.

feedback Audience response to a message, which can be conveyed both verbally and nonverbally through gestures. Feedback from the audience often indicates whether a speaker's message has been understood.

feedback loop The ongoing adjustment in response between speaker and listeners.

field study presentation A type of oral presentation typically delivered in the context of science-related disciplines in which the speaker provides (1) an overview of the field research, (2) the methods used in the research, (3) an analysis of the results of the research, and (4) a time line indicating how the research results will be used going forward.

figures of speech Expressions, such as metaphors, similes, analogies, and hyperbole, in which words are used in a nonliteral fashion.

First Amendment The amendment to the U.S. Constitution that guarantees freedom of speech. ("Congress shall make no law abridging the freedom of speech.")

fixed-alternative question A closed-ended question that contains a limited choice of answers, such as "Yes," "No," or "Sometimes."

flip chart A large (27–34 inch) pad of paper on which a speaker can illustrate speech points.

flowchart A diagram that shows step-by-step the progression through a procedure, relationship, or process.

font A set of type of one size and face.

forum In ancient Rome, a public space in which people gathered to deliberate about the issues of the day. See also *agora* and *public forum.*

frequency A count of the number of times something occurs.

full-sentence transition A signal to listeners, in the form of a declarative sentence, that the speaker is turning to another topic.

gender Social or psychological sense of self as male or female.

general speech purpose A statement of the broad speech purpose that answers the question, "Why am I speaking on this topic for this particular audience and occasion?" Usually the general speech purpose is to inform, to persuade, or to celebrate or commemorate a special occasion. See also *specific speech purpose.*

graph A graphical representation of numerical data. Graphs neatly illustrate relationships among components or units and demonstrate trends. Four major types of graphs are line graphs, bar graphs, pie graphs, and pictograms.

group activity presentation An oral presentation that introduces students to an activity and provides them with clear directions for its completion.

groupthink The tendency of a group to accept information and ideas without subjecting them to critical analysis.

handout Printed material that conveys information that is either impractical to give to the audience in another manner or intended to be kept by audience members after a presentation.

hasty generalization A logical fallacy in which an isolated instance is used to make an unwarranted general conclusion. See also *logical fallacy.*

hate speech Any offensive communication—verbal or nonverbal—directed against people's race, ethnicity, religion, gender, disability, or other characteristics. Racist, sexist, or ageist slurs, gay bashing, and cross burnings are all forms of hate speech.

hierarchy of needs A classic model of human action developed by Abraham Maslow built on the principle that people are motivated to act on the basis of their needs.

hypothetical example An illustration of something that could happen in the future if certain events were to occur.

identification A feeling of commonality with another. Effective speakers attempt to foster a sense of identification between themselves and audience members.

idiom Language specific to a certain region or group of people. See also *colloquial expression.*

imagery Colorful and concrete words that appeal to the senses. See also *analogy, metaphor,* and *simile.*

indentation In an outline, the plotting of speech points to indicate their weight relative to one another; subordinate points are placed underneath and to the right of higher-order points.

individual debate format A debate in which one person takes a side against another.

inductive reasoning Reasoning from specific instances to a general condition. See *deductive reasoning.*

information Data set in a context for relevance.

informative speaking Speech providing new information, new insights, or new ways of thinking about a topic. The general purpose of informative speaking is to increase the audience's understanding and awareness of a topic.

integrity The quality of being incorruptible; the unwillingness to compromise for the sake of personal expediency.

internal preview An extended transition that alerts audience members to ensuing speech content.

internal summary An extended transition that draws together important ideas before proceeding to another speech point.

intonation The rising and falling of voice pitch across phrases and sentences.

introduction (of speech) The first part of a speech, in which the speaker establishes the speech purpose and its relevance to the audience and previews the topic and the main points.

invective Abusive speech.

jargon Specialized terminology developed within a given endeavor or field of study.

key-word outline The briefest form of outline; uses the smallest possible units of understanding associated with a specific point to outline the main and supporting points.

keywords Words and phrases that describe the main concepts of topics. Internet search engines index information by keywords tagged within documents.

lavaliere microphone A microphone that attaches to a lapel or a collar.

lay audience An audience of persons lacking specialized knowledge of the general field related to the speaker's topic and of the topic itself.

lay testimony Firsthand findings, accounts, or opinions from nonexperts such as eyewitnesses.

lazy speech A poor speech habit in which the speaker fails to properly articulate words.

LCD (liquid crystal display) panel A device connected to a computer used to project slides stored in the computer.

learning styles Preferred ways of processing information; one learning theory model suggests visual, aural, read/write, and kinesthetic modes of learning.

lecture An informational speech to an audience of student learners.

library portal An entry point to a large collection of research and reference information that has been selected and reviewed by librarians.

listening The conscious act of receiving, comprehending, interpreting, and responding to messages.

listening distraction Anything that competes for a listener's attention. The source of the distraction may be internal or external.

logical fallacy A statement that is based on an invalid or deceptive line of reasoning. See also *ad hominem argument, appeal to tradition, bandwagoning, begging the question, either-or fallacy, hasty generalization, non sequitur, red herring fallacy,* and *slippery slope.*

logos The Greek rhetorician Aristotle used this term to refer to persuasive appeals to reason and logic.

main points Statements that express the key ideas and major themes of a speech. Their function is to make claims in support of the thesis statement.

maintenance roles In a small group, roles that help facilitate effective group interaction, such as the "harmonizer" and the "gatekeeper." See *task roles.*

malapropism The inadvertent use of a word or phrase in place of one that sounds like it.

mass communication Communication that occurs between a speaker and a large audience of unknown people. The receivers of the message are not present with the speaker or are part of such an immense crowd that there can be little or no interaction between speaker and listener. Television, radio news broadcasts, and mass rallies are examples of mass communication.

mean The sum of the scores divided by the number of scores; the arithmetic (or computed) average.

median A type of average that represents the center-most score in a distribution; the point above and below which 50 percent of the scores fall.

message The content of the communication process—thoughts and ideas put into meaningful expressions. A message can be expressed both verbally (through the sentences and points of a speech) and nonverbally (through eye contact and gestures).

metaphor A figure of speech used to make implicit comparisons without the use of "like" or "as" (e.g., "Love is a rose"). See also *imagery*.

methods/procedure presentation An oral presentation describing and sometimes demonstrating an experimental or mathematical process, including the conditions under which it can be applied; frequently delivered in scientific and mathematics related fields.

mind mapping See *topic mapping*.

misinformation Information that is false.

mixed audience An audience composed of a combination of persons—some with expert knowledge of the field and topic and others with no specialized knowledge.

mixed metaphor A comparison that juxtaposes two unlike, often clichéd, expressions, such as "He went off the deep end like a bull in a china shop."

mode A type of average that represents the most frequently occurring score(s) in a distribution.

model A three-dimensional, scale-size representation of an object such as a building.

moderator A person who presides over a discussion or meeting.

motivated sequence pattern of arrangement An organizational pattern for a persuasive speech based on a five-step process developed by Alan Monroe that begins with arousing attention and ends with calling for action.

multimedia A single production that combines several media (stills, sound, video, text, and data).

mumbling Slurring words together at low volume and pitch so they are barely audible.

narrative A story based on personal experiences or imaginary incidents. See also *story*.

narrative organizational pattern A pattern of organizing speech points so that the speech unfolds as a story, with characters, plot, and setting. In practice, this pattern often is combined with other organizational patterns.

noise Anything that interferes with the communication process between a speaker and an audience so that the message cannot be understood; source may be external (in the environment) or internal (psychological factors).

non sequitur ("does not follow") A logical fallacy in which the conclusion is not connected to the reasoning. See also *logical fallacy*.

nonverbal communication The meaning of a speaker's words conveyed by voice, body language, and appearance.

nonverbal immediacy Acts that create the perception of psychological closeness between the speaker and audience members.

one-sided message In persuasive speaking, a message that does not mention opposing claims. See *two-sided message*.

online presentation A presentation delivered over any distance via the Internet; can include both real-time and recorded presentations.

open-ended question A survey or interview question designed to allow respondents to elaborate as much as they want.

operational definition Defining something by describing what it does. For example: A computer is something that processes information.

oral citation A means of crediting the source of speech material derived from other people's works or ideas.

oral scientific presentation A type of oral presentation following the model used in scientific investigations, including an introduction, description of methods, results, and conclusion; commonly found in the disciplines of science and mathematics. See also *research overview presentation*.

oratory In classical terms, the art of public speaking.

overhead transparency An image on a transparent background that can be viewed by projection.

paid inclusion The practice of paying a fee to a search engine company for inclusion in its index of possible results, without a guarantee of ranking.

paid placement The practice of paying a fee to a search engine company to guarantee a higher ranking within its search results.

pandering Identifying with values not one's own in order to win approval from an audience.

panel discussion A type of oral presentation in which a group of persons (at least three, and generally not more than nine) discusses a topic in the presence of an audience and under the direction of a moderator.

parable A story illustrating a moral or religious lesson.

parallel form The statement of equivalent speech points in similar grammatical form and style.

parallelism The arrangement of words, phrases, or sentences in similar grammatical and stylistic form. Parallel structure can help the speaker emphasize important ideas in the speech.

paraphrase A restatement of someone else's statements or written work that alters the form or phrasing but not the substance of that person's ideas.

pathos The Greek rhetorician Aristotle used this term for appeals to emotion. Such appeals can get the audience's attention and stimulate a desire to act but must be used ethically.

pauses Strategic elements of a speech used to enhance meaning by providing a type of punctuation, emphasizing a point, drawing attention to a key thought, or just allowing listeners a moment to contemplate what is being said.

percentage The quantified portion of a whole.

performance anxiety A feeling of anxiety that occurs the moment one begins to perform.

periodical A regularly published magazine or journal.

peripheral processing A mode of processing a persuasive message that does not consider the quality of the speaker's message, but is influenced by such noncontent issues as the speaker's appearance or reputation, certain slogans or one-liners, and obvious attempts to manipulate emotions. Peripheral processing of messages occurs when people lack the motivation or the ability to pay close attention to the issues.

persuasive speaking Speech whose goal is to influence the attitudes, beliefs, values, or acts of others.

phrase outline A delivery outline that uses a partial construction of the sentence form of each point, instead of using complete sentences that present the precise wording for each point.

pitch The range of sounds from high to low (or vice versa) determined by the number of vibrations per unit of time; the more vibrations per unit (also called *frequency*), the higher the pitch, and vice versa.

plagiarism The act of using other people's ideas or words without acknowledging the source.

podcast A digital audio recording of a presentation captured and stored in a form accessible via the Internet.

policy recommendation report An oral presentation that offers recommendations for solving a problem or addressing an issue.

poster A large (36" x 50"), bold, two-dimensional design incorporating words, shapes, and, if desired, color, placed on an opaque backing; used to convey a brief message or point forcefully and attractively.

poster session A format for the visual presentation of posters, arranged on freestanding boards, containing a display summarizing a study or an issue for viewing by participants at professional conferences. The speaker prepares brief remarks and remains on hand to answer questions as needed.

preparation anxiety A feeling of anxiety that arises when a speaker begins to prepare for a speech, at which point he or she might feel overwhelmed at the amount of time and planning required.

pre-performance anxiety A feeling of anxiety experienced when a speaker begins to rehearse a speech.

pre-preparation anxiety A feeling of anxiety experienced when a speaker learns he or she must give a speech.

presentation aids Objects, models, pictures, graphs, charts, video, audio, or multimedia used to illustrate speech points.

presentational speaking A type of oral presentation in which individuals or groups deliver reports addressing colleagues, clients, or customers within a business or professional environment.

previews Transitions that tell the audience what to expect next.

preview statement Statement included in the introduction of a speech in which the speaker identifies the main speech points.

primary source Original or firsthand research, such as interviews and surveys conducted by the speaker. See also *secondary source*.

problem-cause-solution pattern of arrangement A pattern of organizing speech points so that they demonstrate (1) the nature of the problem, (2) reasons for the problem, and (3) proposed solution(s).

problem-solution pattern of arrangement A pattern of organizing speech points so that they demonstrate the nature and significance of a problem first, and then provide justification for a proposed solution.

program evaluation presentation A report on a program's mission with a description of its accomplishments and how they were measured, and conclusions on how well or poorly the program has met its stated objectives.

progress report A report that updates clients or principals on developments in an ongoing project.

pronunciation The correct formation of word sounds.

prop Any live or inanimate object used by a speaker as a presentation aid.

propaganda Information represented in such a way as to provoke a desired response.

proposal presentation A type of business or professional presentation in which the speaker provides information needed for decisions related to modifying or adopting a product, procedure, or policy.

prototype A model of a design.

public discourse Open conversation or discussion in a public forum.

public domain Bodies of work, including publications and processes, available for public use without permission; not protected by *copyright* or patent.

public forum Any space (physical or virtual) in which people gather to voice their ideas about public issues.

public speaking A type of communication in which a speaker delivers a message with a specific purpose to an audience of people who are present during the delivery of the speech. Public speaking always includes a speaker who has a reason for speaking, an audience that gives the speaker its attention, and a message that is meant to accomplish a purpose.

public-speaking anxiety Fear or anxiety associated with a speaker's actual or anticipated communication to an audience.

quality improvement proposal A report that recommends the adoption of a new (or modified) health practice or policy.

questionnaire A written survey designed to gather information from a pool of respondents.

real-time presentation A presentation broadcast at the time of delivery via the Internet; real-time presentations connect the presenter and the audience live and at the same time. See also *synchronous communication*.

reasoning Establishing a logical explanation of a claim by linking it to evidence. See also *warrant*.

reasoning by analogy Comparing two similar cases to imply that what is true in one case is true in the other.

receiver The recipient of a source's message; may be an individual or a group of people.

reckless disregard for the truth A quality of defamatory speech that is legally liable. See also *defamatory speech*.

recorded presentation A presentation in which speaker and audience are separated by time and space and the presentation is stored and played back from a digital medium. See also *asynchronous communication*.

red herring fallacy A fallacy of reasoning in which the speaker relies on irrelevant information to support an argument.

refutation pattern of arrangement A pattern of organizing speech points in which each main point addresses and then refutes (disproves) an opposing claim to a speaker's position.

request for funding presentation A type of oral presentation providing evidence that a project, proposal, or design idea is worth funding; frequently delivered in technical fields such as engineering, computer science, and architecture.

research overview presentation A presentation that provides background for a research question that will form the basis of an impending experiment or investigation. See also *oral scientific presentation.*

research presentation An oral presentation describing original research undertaken by the speaker, either alone or as part of a team; it is frequently delivered in the fields of science and social science.

respect To feel or show deferential regard. For the ethical speaker, respect ranges from addressing audience members as unique human beings to refraining from rudeness and other forms of personal attack.

responsibility A charge, trust, or duty for which one is accountable.

restate-forecast transition A type of transition in which the speaker restates the point just covered and previews the point to be covered next.

review of academic articles A type of oral presentation in which the speaker reports on one or more articles or studies published in an academic journal.

review of the literature presentation A type of oral presentation in which the speaker reviews the body of research related to a given topic or issue and offers conclusions about the topic based on this research; frequently delivered in social scientific fields.

rhetoric A term with multiple meanings, all of which relate to aspects of human communication and encompass the art of public speaking.

rhetorical device A technique of language to achieve a desired effect.

rhetorical question A question that does not invite actual responses but is used to make the listener or the audience anticipate answers from the speaker.

rhetorical situation The circumstances that call for a public response.

roast A humorous tribute to a person; one in which a series of speakers jokingly poke fun at the individual being honored.

roman numeral outline An outline format in which main points are enumerated with roman numerals (I, II, III); supporting points with capital letters (A, B, C); third-level points with Arabic numerals (1, 2, 3); and fourth-level points with lowercase letters (a, b, c).

rules of engagement Standards of conduct for communicating with others in the public arena.

sales presentation (sales pitch) A type of oral presentation that attempts to lead a potential buyer to purchase a service or product described by the presenter.

sans serif typeface   A typeface that is blocklike and linear and is designed without tiny strokes or flourishes at the top and bottom of each letter.

scale question   A closed-ended question that measures the respondent's level of agreement or disagreement with specific issues.

scanning   A technique for creating eye contact with audiences; the speaker moves his or her gaze across an audience from one listener to another and from one section to another, pausing to gaze briefly at each individual.

screencast   An online presentation that relies on software that captures whatever is displayed on a computer, from text to slides to streaming video.

secondary source   Information gathered by others; can include published facts and statistics, texts, documents, and any other information not originally collected and generated by the researcher. See also *primary source.*

selective perception   A psychological principle that posits that listeners pay attention selectively to certain messages and ignore others.

sentence outline   An outline in which each main and supporting point is stated in sentence form and in precisely the way the speaker wants to express the idea; generally used for working outlines.

serif typeface   A typeface that includes small flourishes, or strokes, at the top and bottom of each letter.

service learning presentation   A presentation based on experience and knowledge gained by students actively participating in addressing a need or problem in a community or organization.

shared meaning   The mutual understanding of a message between speaker and audience.

shift report   Oral report by a health care worker that concisely relays patient status and needs to incoming caregivers.

signposts   Conjunctions or phrases (such as "next," "in the first case," etc.) that indicate *transitions* between supporting points.

simile   A figure of speech used to compare one thing with another by using the words "like" or "as" (e.g., "He works like a dog"). See also *imagery.*

six-by-six rule   Rule of design that suggests using no more than six words per line and six lines or bullet points per slide or other visual aid.

slippery slope   A logical fallacy in which one instance of an event is offered as leading to a series of events or actions. See also *logical fallacy.*

small group   A collection of between three and twenty people.

small group communication Communication involving a small number of people who can see and speak directly with one another, as in a business meeting.

social news sites Web sites dedicated to specific kinds of news or entertainment (e.g., Digg, Daytripper, Campus Reader).

socioeconomic status (SES) A demographic variable that includes income, occupation, and education.

source The person who creates a message, also called a *sender*. The speaker transforms ideas and thoughts into messages and sends them to a receiver, or an audience.

source qualifier A brief description of the source's qualifications.

source reliability The qualities that determine the value of a source, such as the author's background and reputation, the reputation of a publication, the source of data, and how recent the reference is.

spatial pattern of arrangement A pattern of organizing main points in order of their physical proximity or direction relative to each other; used when the purpose of a speech is to describe or explain the physical arrangement of a place, a scene, or an object.

speaker credibility The quality that reveals that a speaker has a good grasp of the subject, displays sound reasoning skills, is honest and nonmanipulative, and is genuinely interested in the welfare of audience members; a modern version of *ethos*.

speaking extemporaneously A type of delivery that falls somewhere between impromptu and written or memorized deliveries. Speakers delivering an extemporaneous speech prepare well and practice in advance, giving full attention to all facets of the speech—content, arrangement, and delivery alike. Instead of memorizing or writing the speech word for word, they speak from an outline of key words and phrases.

speaking from manuscript A type of delivery in which the speaker reads the speech verbatim—that is, from prepared written text that contains the entire speech, word for word.

speaking from memory A type of delivery in which the speaker puts the entire speech, word for word, into writing and then commits it to memory.

speaking impromptu A type of delivery that is unpracticed, spontaneous, or improvised.

speaking outline A delivery outline to be used when practicing and actually presenting a speech.

speaking rate The pace at which a speech is delivered. The typical public speech occurs at a rate slightly less than 120 words per minute.

special occasion speech A speech whose general purpose is to entertain, celebrate, commemorate, inspire, or set a social agenda.

specific speech purpose A refined statement of purpose that zeroes in more closely than the general purpose on the goal of the speech. See also *general speech purpose.*

speech of acceptance A speech made in response to receiving an award. Its purpose is to express gratitude for the honor bestowed on the speaker.

speech of inspiration A speech whose purpose is to inspire or motivate the audience to consider positively, reflect on, and sometimes even to act on the speaker's words.

speech of introduction A short speech whose purpose is defined by two goals: to prepare or "warm up" audience members for the speaker and to motivate them to listen to what the speaker has to say.

speech of presentation A speech whose purpose is twofold: to communicate the meaning of the award and to explain why the recipient is receiving it.

staff report A report that informs managers and other employees of new developments relating to personnel that affect them and their work.

statistics Quantified evidence; data that measure the size or magnitude of something, demonstrate trends, or show relationships with the purpose of summarizing information, demonstrating proof, and making points memorable.

story An account of events. See also *narrative.*

style The specific word choice, sentence structure, and rhetorical devices (techniques of language) that speakers use to express their ideas.

subject heading A word or phrase chosen by information specialists to describe and group related materials in a library catalog, database, or subject directory.

subject (Web) directory A searchable database of Web sites organized by categories (e.g., Yahoo! Directory).

subordinate points Ideas subordinate to others that are thus given relatively less weight. In an outline, they are indicated by their indentation below the more important points.

summary Part of a conclusion to a speech; a restatement of points covered. Also, a brief overview of someone else's thoughts, words, or ideas.

supporting material Examples, narratives, testimony, facts, and statistics that support the speech thesis and form the speech.

supporting points Information (examples, narratives, testimony, and facts and statistics) that clarifies, elaborates, and verifies the speaker's assertions.

symposium A formal meeting at which several speakers deliver short speeches on the same topic.

synchronous communication Communication in which people exchange messages simultaneously, in real time. See also *real-time presentations.*

table A systematic grouping of data or numerical information in column form.

talking head A speaker who remains static, standing stiffly behind a podium, and so resembles a televised shot of a speaker's head and shoulders.

target audience Those individuals within the broader audience who are most likely to be influenced in the direction the speaker seeks.

task roles Types of roles that directly relate to the accomplishment of the objectives and missions of a group. Examples include "recording secretary" and "moderator."

team debate format A debate in which a team of two or more people opposes a second team, with each person having a speaking role.

team presentation A type of oral presentation prepared and delivered by a group of three or more people.

testimony Firsthand findings, eyewitness accounts, and opinions by people, both lay (nonexpert) and expert.

theoretical research presentation An oral presentation focusing on studies that attempt to analyze and explain a phenomenon; frequently delivered in social scientific fields.

thesis statement The theme, or central idea, of a speech that serves to connect all the parts of the speech in a single line. The main points, supporting material, and conclusion all relate to the thesis.

toast A brief tribute to a person or an event being celebrated.

topical pattern of arrangement A pattern of organizing main points as subtopics or categories of the speech topic.

topic mapping A brainstorming technique in which words are laid out in diagram form to show categorical relationships among them; useful for selecting and narrowing a speech topic. Also called *mind mapping.*

town hall meeting A type of forum in which citizens deliberate on issues of importance to the community.

transitions Words, phrases, or sentences that tie speech ideas together and enable a speaker to move smoothly from one point to the next.

trustworthiness The quality of displaying both honesty and dependability.

two-sided message In persuasive speaking, a message that mentions opposing points of view and refutes them. See *one-sided message.*

typeface A specific style of lettering, such as Arial, Times Roman, or Courier. Typefaces come in a variety of fonts, or sets of sizes (called the "point size"), and upper and lower cases.

values Our most enduring judgments about what is good and bad in life, as shaped by our culture and our unique experiences within it.

visualization An exercise for building confidence in which the speaker, while preparing for the speech, closes his or her eyes and envisions a series of positive feelings and reactions that will occur on the day of the speech.

vocal fillers Unnecessary and undesirable sounds or words used by a speaker to cover pauses in a speech or conversation. Examples include "uh," "hmm," "you know," "I mean," and "it's like."

vocal variety The variation of volume, pitch, rate, and pauses to create an effective delivery.

vodcast A podcast with video clips. See *podcast*.

voice A feature of verbs in written and spoken text that indicates the subject's relationship to the action; verbs can be either active or passive.

volume The relative loudness of a speaker's voice while giving a speech.

voluntary audience As opposed to a captive audience, an audience whose members have chosen to attend.

warrant The link between a claim and evidence. See also *reasoning*.

Webinar Real-time presentations, including training sessions, seminars, and other presentations that connect presenters and listeners through their computers or mobile devices, regardless of where they are in the world.

word association A brainstorming technique in which one writes down ideas as they come to mind, beginning with a single word.

working outline A preparation or rough outline using full sentences in which the speaker firms up and organizes main points and develops supporting points to substantiate them.

Notes

CHAPTER 1

1. Vickie K. Sullivan, "Public Speaking: The Secret Weapon in Career Development," *USA Today*, 133 (May 2005): 24.

2. Graduate Management Admission Council, *2011 Corporate Recruiters' Survey*, http://www.gmac.com/community/media/p/987.aspx.

3. U.S. Census Bureau, Table 398: "Resident Population of Voting Age and Percent Casting Votes—States: 2000 to 2010," *Statistical Abstract of the United States: 2012*, http://www.census.gov/compendia/statab/2012/tables/12s0398.pdf; CIRCLE (The Center for Information & Research on Civic Learning and Engagement), "Youth Voting," October 2, 2011, http://www.civicyouth.org/quick-facts/youth-voting/; Pew Research Center for the People & the Press, "Who Votes, Who Doesn't, and Why," October 18, 2006, http://people-press.org/reports/display.php3?ReportID=292.

4. For a discussion of Daniel Yankelovich's three-step process by which public judgments occur, see Yankelovich, *Coming to Public Judgment* (Syracuse, NY: Syracuse University Press, 1991).

5. W. Barnett Pearce, "Toward a National Conversation about Public Issues," in *The Changing Conversation in America: Lectures from the Smithsonian*, ed. William F. Eadie and Paul E. Nelson (Thousand Oaks, CA: Sage, 2002), 16.

6. Robert Perrin, "The Speaking-Writing Connection: Enhancing the Symbiotic Relationship," *Contemporary Education* 65 (1994): 2.

7. David C. Thomas and Kerr Inkson, *Cultural Intelligence: People Skills for a Global Business* (San Francisco: Berrett-Koehler Publishers, 2004), 14.

8. Ibid.

9. William Avram, "Public Speaking," *Compton's Online Encyclopedia*, accessed June 10, 2000, www.comptons.com/encyclopedia/.

10. Lloyd F. Bitzer, "The Rhetorical Situation," *Philosophy and Rhetoric* (Winter 1968): 1–14.

CHAPTER 3

1. James C. McCroskey, "Classroom Consequences of Communication Anxiety," *Communication Education* 26 (1977): 27–33; James C. McCroskey, "Oral Communication Apprehension: A Reconceptualization," in *Communication Yearbook* 6, ed. M. Burgoon (Beverly Hills: Sage, 1982), 136–70; Virginia P. Richmond and James C. McCroskey, *Communication Apprehension, Avoidance, and Effectiveness*, 5th ed. (Boston: Allyn & Bacon, 1998).

2. Adapted from James C. McCroskey, "Oral Communication Apprehension: A Summary of Recent Theory and Research," *Human Communication Research* 4 (1977): 79–96.

3. C. Kane, "Overcoming Stage Fright—Here's What To Do," *Christine Kane* (blog), April 24, 2007, http://christinekane.com/blog/overcoming-stage-fright-heres-what-to-do/.

4. R. Behnke, C. R. Sawyer, and R. Chris, "Milestones of Anticipatory Public Speaking Anxiety," *Communication Education* 48 (April 1999): 165–72.

5. David-Paul Pertaub, Mel Slater, and Chris Barker, "An Experiment on Public Speaking Anxiety in Response to Three Different Types of Virtual Audience," *Presence: Teleoperators and Virtual Environments* 11 (2002): 678–80.

6. Joe Ayres, "Coping with Speech Anxiety: The Power of Positive Thinking," *Communication Education* 37 (1988): 289–96; Joe Ayres, "An Examination of the Impact of Anticipated Communication and Communication Apprehension on Negative Thinking, Task-Relevant Thinking, and Recall," *Communication Research Reports* 9 (1992): 3–11.

7. S. Hu and Joung-Min Romans-Kroll, "Effects of Positive Attitude toward Giving a Speech on the Cardiovascular and Subjective Fear Responses during Speech in Speech Anxious Subjects," *Perceptual and Motor Skills* 81, no. 2 (1995): 609–10; S. Hu, T. R. Bostow, D. A. Lipman, S. K. Bell, and S. Klein, "Positive Thinking Reduces Heart Rate and Fear Responses to Speech-Phobic Imagery," *Perceptual and Motor Skills* 75, no. 3, pt. 2 (1992): 1067–76.

8. M. T. Motley, "Public Speaking Anxiety Qua Performance Anxiety: A Revised Model and Alternative Therapy," *Journal of Social Behavior and Personality* 5 (1990): 85–104.

9. Joe Ayres, C. S. Hsu, and Tim Hopf, "Does Exposure to Performance Visualization Alter Speech Preparation Processes?" *Communication Research Reports* 17 (2000): 366–74.

10. Joe Ayres and Tim S. Hopf, "Visualization: Is It More Than Extra-Attention?" *Communication Education* 38 (1989): 1–5.

11. Herbert Benson and Miriam Z. Klipper, *The Relaxation Response* (New York: HarperCollins, 2000).

12. Laurie Schloff and Marcia Yudkin, *Smart Speaking* (New York: Plume, 1991), 91–92.

13. Lars-Gunnar Lundh, Britta Berg, Helena Johansson, Linda Kjellén Nilsson, Jenny Sandberg, and Anna Segerstedt, "Social Anxiety Is Associated with a Negatively Distorted Perception of One's Own Voice," *Cognitive Behavior Therapy* 31 (2002): 25–30.

CHAPTER 4

1. *The Compact Edition of the Oxford English Dictionary*, 1971 ed., 2514.

2. Cited in Edward P. J. Corbett, *Classical Rhetoric for the Modern Student* (New York: Oxford University Press, 1990).

3. Rebecca Rimel, "Policy and the Partisan Divide: The Price of Gridlock," speech given at the Commonwealth Club in San Francisco, November 2004, Pew Charitable Trusts Web site, www.pewtrusts.org.

4. Susan Grogan Faller, Steven E. Gillen, and Maureen P. Haney, "Rights Clearance and Permissions Guidelines," paper prepared by law firm of Greenebaum Doll & McDonald, Cincinnati, Ohio, 2002.

5. W. Barnett Pearce, "Toward a National Conversation about Public Issues," in *The Changing Conversation in America: Lectures from the Smithsonian*, ed. William F. Eadie and Paul E. Nelson (Thousand Oaks, CA: Sage, 2002), 16.

6. W. Gudykunst, S. Ting-Toomey, S. Suweeks, and L. Stewart, *Building Bridges: Interpersonal Skills for a Changing World* (Boston: Houghton Mifflin, 1995), 92.

7. Ibid.

8. Michael Josephson, personal interview, May 10, 1996.

9. Ibid.

10. Rebecca Moore Howard, "A Plagiarism Pentimento," *Journal of Teaching Writing* 11 (1993): 233.

11. Francie Diep, "Fast Facts about the Japan Earthquake and Tsunami," *Scientific American*, March 14, 2011, http://www.scientificamerican.com/article.cfm?id=fast-facts-japan.

12. "How to Recognize Plagiarism," Indiana University, Bloomington, School of Education Web site, accessed June 16, 2002, www.indiana.edu/.

13. "Copyright Basics," United States Copyright Office Web site, www.copyright.gov, includes works classified as literary, musical, dramatic, choreographic, pictorial, graphic, sculptural, audiovisual, sound recording, and architectural.

14. Steven E. Gillen, "Rights Clearance and Permissions Guidelines," paper prepared by the law firm Greenebaum Doll & McDonald, Cincinnati, Ohio, 2002.

15. "Fair Use," United States Copyright Office Web site, accessed July 21, 2011, http://www.copyright.gov/.

CHAPTER 5

1. Kathy Thompson, Pamela Leintz, Barbara Nevers, and Susan Witkowski, "The Integrative Listening Model: An Approach to Teaching and Learning Listening," *Journal of General Education* 53 (2004): 225–46.

2. Andrew Wolvin and C. Coakley, *Listening*, 4th ed. (Dubuque, IA: Wm. C. Brown, 1992), 28.

3. Laura Janusik, "Time Spent Listening and Communicating," International Listening Association, section on "Listening Facts," http://www.listen.org/.

4. J. Flynn, T. Valikoski, and J. Grau, "Listening in the Business Context: Reviewing the State of Research," *International Journal of Listening*, 22, no. 2 (2008): 141–51.

5. H. E. Chambers, *Effective Communication Skills for Scientific and Technical Professionals* (Cambridge, MA: Perseus Publishing, 2001).

6. Graduate Management Admissions Council, "2011 Corporate Recruiters' Survey," http://www.gmac.com/community/media/p/987.aspx.

7. Philip Vassallo, "Dialogue: Speaking to Listen: Listening to Speak," *ETC* (Fall 2000): 306–13.

8. Dirk Heylen, "Understanding Speaker-Listener Interactions," paper presented at the Interspeech 2009 International Speech Communication Association Conference, http://www.interspeech2009.org/conference/.

9. S. Golen, "A Factor Analysis of Barriers to Effective Listening," *Journal of Business Communication* 27 (1990): 25–36.

10. Thanks to Barry Antokoletz of New York City College of Technology for suggesting the inclusion of these strategies.

11. Thomas E. Anastasi Jr., *Listen! Techniques for Improving Communication Skills*, CBI series in Management Communication (Boston: CBI Publishing, 1982), 35.

12. Ibid.

CHAPTER 6

1. James C. McCroskey, Virginia P. Richmond, and Robert A. Stewart, *One on One: The Foundations of Interpersonal Communication* (Englewood Cliffs, NJ: Prentice Hall, 1986).

2. Daniel O'Keefe notes that although attitudes and behavior are "generally consistent," there are "a large number of possible moderating variables," including the relative demands of the behavior, whether there is a vested position, and others: Daniel J. O'Keefe, *Persuasion: Theory & Research*, 2nd ed. (Thousand Oaks, CA: Sage, 2002), 17.

3. Ibid.

4. "Tip Sheet: Communicating about Biodiversity," Biodiversity Project Web site, accessed May 20, 2010, http://www.biodiversityproject.org/docs/publicationsandtipsheets/communicatingaboutbiodiversity_tipsheet.pdf.

5. Ibid.

6. McCroskey, *One on One*, 76.

7. Herbert Simon, *Persuasion in Society* (Thousand Oaks, CA: Sage, 2001), 385–87.

8. Kenneth Burke, *A Rhetoric of Motives* (Berkeley, CA: University of California Press, 1969).

9. Nick Morgan, *Working the Room: How to Move People to Action through Audience-Centered Speaking* (Cambridge, MA: Harvard Business School Press, 2003).

10. E. R. Behrman and Nevzer Stacey, eds., *The Social Benefits of Going to College* (Ann Arbor, MI: University of Michigan Press, 2000).

11. Pew Forum on Religion & Public Life, *U.S. Religious Landscape Survey*, February 2008, http://religions.pewforum.org/pdf/report-religious-landscape-study-full.pdf.

12. Daniel Canary and K. Dindia, eds., *Sex Differences and Similarities in Communication* (Mahwah, NJ: Lawrence Erlbaum, 1998).

13. Center for Disease Control and Prevention, "People with Disabilities: Living Healthy," updated July 25, 2011, http://www.cdc.gov/Features/disabilities/.

14. U.S. Census Quick Facts, July 11, 2011, http://quickfacts.census.gov/qfd/states/00000.html; American Community Survey Brief, "Place of Birth of the Foreign-born Population, 2009," October 2010, http://www.census.gov/prod/2010pubs/acsbr09-15.pdf.

15. U.S. Department of State, "Independent States of the World Fact Sheet," April 13, 2011, http://www.state.gov/s/inr/rls/4250.htm.

16. E. D. Steele and W. C. Redding, "The American Value System: Premises for Persuasion," *Western Speech* 26 (1962): 83–91; Robin M. Williams Jr., *American Society: A Sociological Interpretation*, 3rd ed. (New York: Alfred A. Knopf, 1970).

17. Richard D. Lewis, *When Cultures Collide: Leading across Cultures,* 3rd ed. (Boston: Intercultural Press-Nicholas Brealey International, 2005), 27.

18. Rushworth M. Kidder, *Shared Values for a Troubled World: Conversations with Men and Women of Conscience* (San Francisco: Jossey-Bass, 1994).

CHAPTER 8

1. Richard F. Corlin, "The Coming Golden Age of Medicine," *Vital Speeches of the Day* 68, no. 18 (2002).

2. Jonathan Drori, "Every Pollen Grain Has a Story," speech posted on TED Web site, April 2010, http://www.ted.com/talks/lang/eng/jonathan_drori_every_pollen_grain_has_a_story.html.

3. Quoted in K. Q. Seelye, "Congressman Offers Bill to Ban Cloning of Humans," *New York Times*, March 6, 1997, sec. A:3.

4. Mark Turner, *The Literary Mind* (New York: Oxford University Press, 1996).

5. Barack Obama, "The Great Need of the Hour," speech given in Atlanta, GA, January 20, 2008, www.barackobama.com/2008/01/20/remarks_of_senator_barack_obam_40.php.

6. Earle Gray, "Want to Be a Leader? Start Telling Stories," *Canadian Speeches* 16, no. 6 (2003): 75(2).

7. Testimony of Derek P. Ellerman to Subcommittee on Human Rights and Wellness, Committee on Government Reform, United States House of Representatives, July 8, 2004 (Polaris Project), www.polarisproject.org/polarisproject/news_p3/ DPETestimony_p3.htm.

8. Rodney Reynolds and Michael Burgoon, "Evidence," in *The Persuasion Handbook: Developments in Theory and Practice*, ed. J. P. Dillard and M. Pfau (Thousand Oaks, CA: Sage, 2002), 427–44.

9. J. C. Reinard, "The Empirical Study of the Persuasive Effects of Evidence: The Status after Fifty Years of Research," *Human Communication Research* 15 (1988): 3–59.

10. 2010 Census Briefs, "Age and Sex Composition, 2010," http://www.census.gov/prod/cen2010/briefs/c2010br-03.pdf.

11. "A380-800: New Generation, New Experience," Airbus Web site, http://www.airbus.com/aircraftfamilies/passengeraircraft/a380family/a380-800/.

12. American Lung Association, "Trends in Tobacco Use," July 2011, http://www.lungusa.org/finding-cures/our-research/trend-reports/Tobacco-Trend-Report.pdf.

13. National Conference of State Legislatures, "State Unemployment Rates for May, 2011," June 17, 2011, http://www.ncsl.org/?tabid=13308.

14. Jose Antonio Vargas, "The Face of Facebook," *New Yorker*, September 20, 2010: 54–63.

15. Center on Budget and Policy Priorities, "Behind the Numbers: An Examination of the Tax Foundation's Tax Day Report," April 14, 1997, www.cbpp.org/taxday.htm.

16. Roger Pielke Jr., "The Cherry Pick," *Ogmius: Newsletter for the Center for Science and Technology Research* 8 (May 2004), http://sciencepolicy.colorado.edu/ogmius/archives/issue_8/index.html.

CHAPTER 9

1. "Identifying Primary and Secondary Sources," Indiana University, Bloomington, Libraries page, accessed July 25, 2011, www.libraries.iub.edu/index.php?pageId=1483.

2. Gregory Ferenstein, "Jimmy Wales, Wikipedia Go to College," FastCompany, July 6, 2011, http://www.fastcompany.com/1765182/jimmy-wales-on-wikipedia-becoming-official.

CHAPTER 10

1. Susan Gilroy, "The Web in Context: Virtual Library or Virtual Chaos?" Lamont Library of the Harvard College Library Web site, accessed May 5, 2005, hcl.harvard.edu/lamont/resources/guides/.

2. Elizabeth Kirk, "Evaluating Information Found on the Internet," The Sheridan Libraries of the Johns Hopkins University, last modified February 12, 2002, www.library.jhu.edu/researchhelp/general/evaluating/ index.html.

3. Jorgen J. Wouters, "Searching for Disclosure: How Search Engines Alert Consumers to the Presence of Advertising in Search Results," *Consumer Reports WebWatch*, November 8, 2004, www.consumerwebwatch.org/dynamic/search-report-disclosureabstract.cfm.

4. "Database Search Tips," Massachusetts Institute of Technology Libraries, accessed August 30, 2011, http://libguides.mit.edu/content.php?pid=36863&sid=271371.

CHAPTER 11

1. Ralph Underwager and Hollida Wakefield, "The Taint Hearing," *IPT* 10 (1998). Originally presented at the 13th Annual Symposium in Forensic Psychology, Vancouver, BC, April 17, 1997, accessed September 1, 2007, www.ipt-forensics.com/journal/volume10/j10_7.htm#en0.

2. Institute for Writing and Rhetoric, "Sources and Citation at Dartmouth College," produced by the Committee on Sources, May 2008, www.dartmouth.edu/~writing/sources/sources-citation.html.

CHAPTER 12

1. Gordon H. Bower, "Organizational Factors in Memory," *Cognitive Psychology* 1 (1970): 18–46.

2. Murray Glanzer and Anita R. Cunitz, "Two Storage Mechanisms in Free Recall," *Journal of Verbal Learning and Verbal Behavior* 5 (1966): 351–60.

3. E. Thompson, "An Experimental Investigation of the Relative Effectiveness of Organization Structure in Oral Communication," *Southern Speech Journal* 26 (1960): 59–69.

4. R. G. Smith, "Effects of Speech Organization upon Attitudes of College Students," *Speech Monographs* 18 (1951): 292–301.

5. H. Sharp Jr. and T. McClung, "Effects of Organization on the Speaker's Ethos," *Speech Monographs* 33 (1966): 182ff.

CHAPTER 13

1. R. G. Smith, "Effects of Speech Organization upon Attitudes of College Students," *Speech Monographs* 18 (1951): 547–49; E. Thompson, "An Experimental Investigation of the Relative Effectiveness of Organizational Structure in Oral Communication," *Southern Speech Journal* 26 (1960): 59–69.

2. Robert X. Cringely, "Timeline," *Nerds 2.0.1: A Brief History of the Internet*, PBS.org, www.pbs.org/opb/nerds2.0.1/timeline/.

CHAPTER 14

1. Mark B. McClellan, speech presented at the fifth annual David A. Winston lecture, Washington, DC, October 20, 2003, www.fda.gov/oc/speeches/2003/winston1020.html.

CHAPTER 15

1. Ron Hoff, *I Can See You Naked,* rev. ed. (Kansas City: Andrews McMeel, 1992), 41.

2. William Safire, *Lend Me Your Ears: Great Speeches in History* (New York: W.W. Norton, 1992), 676.

3. Bas Andeweg and Jap de Jong, "May I Have Your Attention? Exordial Techniques in Informative Oral Presentations," *Technical Communication Quarterly* 7, no. 3 (Summer 1998): 271–84.

4. Kenneth Burke, *A Rhetoric of Motives* (Berkeley: University of California Press, 1950).

5. Marvin Runyon, "No One Moves the Mail Like the U.S. Postal Service," *Vital Speeches of the Day* 61, no. 2 (November 1, 1994): 52–55.

6. C. A. Kiesler and S. B. Kiesler, "Role of Forewarning in Persuasive Communication," *Journal of Abnormal and Social Psychology* 68 (1964): 547–69, cited in James C. McCroskey, *An Introduction to Rhetorical Communication,* 8th ed. (Boston: Allyn & Bacon, 2001), 253.

7. Robert L. Darbelnet, "U.S. Roads and Bridges," *Vital Speeches of the Day* 63, no. 12 (April 1, 1997): 379.

8. Andeweg and de Jong, "May I Have Your Attention?" 271.

9. Elpidio Villarreal, "Choosing the Right Path," speech delivered to the Puerto Rican Legal Defense and Education Fund Gala in New York City, October 26, 2006, *Vital Speeches of the Day* 72, no. 26 (2007): 784–86.

10. Hillary Rodham Clinton, "Women's Rights Are Human Rights," speech delivered to the United Nations Fourth World Conference on Women, Beijing, China, September 5, 1995.

CHAPTER 16

1. Robert Harris, "A Handbook of Rhetorical Devices," July 26, 2002, VirtualSalt Web site, www.virtualsalt.com/rhetoric.htm.

2. Peggy Noonan, *Simply Speaking: How to Communicate Your Ideas with Style, Substance, and Clarity* (New York: Regan Books, 1998), 51.

3. Dan Hooley, "The Lessons of the Ring," *Vital Speeches of the Day* 70, no. 20 (2004): 660–63.

4. James E. Lukaszewski, "You Can Become a Verbal Visionary," speech delivered to the Public Relations Society of America, Cleveland, Ohio, April 8, 1997. Executive Speaker Library, www.executive-speaker.com/lib_moti.html.

5. Loren J. Naidoo and Robert G. Lord, "Speech Imagery and Perceptions of Charisma: The Mediating Role of Positive Affect," *Leadership Quarterly* 19, no. 3 (2008): 283–96.

6. Ibid, phrase taken from President Franklin Delano Roosevelt's 1933 inaugural address; he used the phrase again in a 1942 speech.

7. L. Clemetson and J. Gordon-Thomas, "Our House Is on Fire," *Newsweek,* June 11, 2001, 50.

8. Andrew C. Billings, "Beyond the Ebonics Debate: Attitudes about Black and Standard American English," *Journal of Black Studies* 36 (2005): 68–81.

9. Sylvie Dubois, "Sounding Cajun: The Rhetorical Use of Dialect in Speech and Writing," *American Speech* 77, no. 3 (2002): 264–87.

10. Gloria Anzaldúa, "Entering into the Serpent," in *The St. Martin's Handbook,* eds. Andrea Lunsford and Robert Connors, 3rd ed. (New York: St. Martin's Press, 1995), 25.

11. *The Concise Oxford Dictionary of Linguistics* (New York: Oxford University Press, 1997).

12. Cited in William Safire, *Lend Me Your Ears: Great Speeches in History* (New York: W.W. Norton, 1992), 22.

13. "Barack Obama's New Hampshire Primary Speech," Nashua, NH, January 8, 2008, *New York Times*, www.nytimes.com/2008/01/08/us/politics/08text-obama.html?pagewanted=a11.

14. Lunsford and Connors, *The St. Martin's Handbook,* 345.

CHAPTER 17

1. James C. McCroskey, *An Introduction to Rhetorical Communication,* 8th ed. (Englewood Cliffs, NJ: Prentice Hall, 2001), 273.

2. Robbin Crabtree and Robert Weissberg, *ESL Students in the Public Speaking Classroom: A Guide for Teachers* (Boston: Bedford/St.Martin's, 2000), 24.

CHAPTER 18

1. Stephen M. Smith and David R. Shaffer, "Celerity and Cajolery: Rapid Speech May Promote or Inhibit Persuasion through Its Impact on Message Elaboration," *Personality and Social Psychology Bulletin* 17, no. 6 (December 1991): 663–69.

2. Kyle James Tusing and James Price Dillard, "The Sounds of Dominance: Vocal Precursors of Perceived Dominance during Interpersonal Influence," *Human Communication Research* 26 (2000): 148–71.

3. Susan Berkley, "Microphone Tips," *Great Speaking* ezine 4, no. 7 (2002), Great Speaking Web site, www.antion.com.

4. Walt Wolfram, "Everyone Has an Accent," *Teaching Tolerance Magazine* (Fall 2000): 18, www.tolerance.org/teach/magazine/features.jsp?p=0&is=17&ar=186.

CHAPTER 19

1. Reid Buckley, *Strictly Speaking: Reid Buckley's Indispensable Handbook on Public Speaking* (New York: McGraw-Hill, 1999), 204.

2. Robert Rivlin and Karen Gravelle, *Deciphering the Senses: The Expanding World of Human Perception* (New York: Simon & Schuster, 1998), 98; see also A. Warfield, "Do You Speak Body Language?" *Training & Development* 55, no. 4 (2001): 60.

3. Buckley, *Strictly Speaking,* 209.

4. Albert Mehrabian, *Silent Messages* (Belmont, CA: Wadsworth, 1981); Mike Allen, Paul L. Witt, and Lawrence R. Wheeless, "The Role of Teacher Immediacy as a Motivational Factor in Student Learning: Using Meta-Analysis to Test a Causal Model," *Communication Education* 55, no. 6 (2006): 21–31.

5. J. P. Davidson, "Shaping an Image That Boosts Your Career," *Marketing Communications* 13 (1988): 55–56.

6. Carmine Gallo, *The Presentation Secrets of Steve Jobs* (New York: McGraw-Hill, 2009), 181.

CHAPTER 20

1. Richard E. Mayer, *Multimedia Learning* (Cambridge: Cambridge University Press, 2005); Edward R. Tufte, *Visual Explanations: Images and Quantities, Evidence and Narrative* (Cheshire, CT: Graphics Press, 1997).

2. J. Doumont, "The Cognitive Style of PowerPoint: Slides Are Not All Evil," *Technical Communication* 52, no. 1 (2005): 64–70.

3. G. Jones, "Message First: Using Films to Power the Point," *Business Communication Quarterly* 67, no. 1 (2004): 88–91.

CHAPTER 21

1. Nancy Duarte, "Avoiding the Road to Powerpoint Hell," *Wall Street Journal*, January 22, 2011.

2. Nancy Duarte, *Slide:ology: The Art and Science of Creating Great Presentations*. (Cambridge, MA: O'Reilly, 2008), 92.

3. Edward Tufte, "PowerPoint Is Evil," *Wired* 11 (2003), www.wired .com/wired/archive/11.09/ppt2_pr.html.

CHAPTER 23

1. Katherine E. Rowan subdivides informative communication into *informatory discourse,* in which the primary aim is to represent reality by increasing an audience's awareness of some phenomenon, and *explanatory discourse,* with the aim to represent reality by deepening understanding. See Katherine E. Rowan, "Informing and Explaining Skills: Theory and Research on Informative Communication," in *Handbook of Communication and Social Interaction Skills,* ed. J. O. Greene and B. R. Burleson (Mahwah, NJ: Erlbaum, 2003), 403–38.

2. Nick Morgan, "Two Rules for a Successful Presentation," *Harvard Business Review Blog* ("The Conversation"), May 14, 2010, http://blogs .hbr.org/cs/2010/05/two_rules_for_a_successful_pre.html; H. E. Chambers, *Effective Communication Skills for Scientific and Technical Professionals* (Cambridge, MA: Perseus Publishing, 2001).

3. Vickie K. Sullivan, "Public Speaking: The Secret Weapon in Career Development," *USA Today*, May 2005, 24.

4. E. Thompson, "An Experimental Investigation of the Relative Effectiveness of Organization Structure in Oral Communication," *Southern Speech Journal* 26 (1966): 59–69.

5. Howard K. Battles and Charles Packard, *Words and Sentences*, bk. 6 (Lexington, MA: Ginn & Company, 1984), 459.

6. Katherine E. Rowan, "A New Pedagogy for Explanatory Public Speaking: Why Arrangement Should Not Substitute for Invention," *Communication Education* 44 (1995): 236–50.

7. S. Kujawa and L. Huske, *The Strategic Teaching and Reading Project Guidebook*, rev. ed. (Oak Brook, IL: North Central Regional Educational Laboratory, 1995).

8. Shawn M. Glynn et al., "Teaching Science with Analogies: A Resource for Teachers and Textbook Authors," National Reading Research Center, Instructional Resource no. 7, Fall 1994, 19.

9. Ibid., 19.

10. Altoona List of Medical Analogies, "How to Use Analogies," Altoona Family Physicians Residency Web site, accessed August 5, 2010, www.altoonafp.org/analogies.htm.

11. Tina A. Grotzer, "How Conceptual Leaps in Understanding the Nature of Causality Can Limit Learning: An Example from Electrical Circuits" (paper presented at the annual conference of the American Educational Research Association, New Orleans, April 2000), http:// pzweb.harvard.edu/Research/UnderCon.htm.

12. Neil D. Fleming and C. Mills, "Helping Students Understand How They Learn," *Teaching Professor* 7, no. 4 (1992).

13. Thompson, "An Experimental Investigation," 59–69.

CHAPTER 24

1. Richard E. Petty and John T. Cacioppo, *Communication and Persuasion: Central and Peripheral Routes to Attitude Change* (New York: Springer-Verlag, 1986).

2. Kathleen Reardon, *Persuasion in Practice* (Newbury Park, CA: Sage Publications, 1991), 210.

3. Elpidio Villarreal, "Choosing the Right Path" (speech delivered to the Puerto Rican Legal Defense and Education Fund Gala in New York City, October 26, 2006), *Vital Speeches of the Day* 72, no. 26 (2007): 784–86.

4. Kim Witte and Mike Allen, "A Meta-Analysis of Fear Appeals: Implications for Effective Public Health Campaigns," *Health Education and Behavior* 27 (2000): 591–615.

5. Joseph R. Priester and Richard E. Petty, "Source Attributions and Persuasion: Perceived Honesty as a Determinant of Message Scrutiny," *Personality and Social Psychology Bulletin* 21 (1995): 637–54.

See also Kenneth G. DeBono and Richard J. Harnish, "Source Expertise, Source Attractiveness, and the Processing of Persuasive Information: A Functional Approach," *Journal of Personality and Social Psychology* 55 (1987): 541.

6. B. Soper, G. E. Milford, and G. T. Rosenthal, "Belief When Evidence Does Not Support the Theory," *Psychology and Marketing* 12 (1995): 415–22, cited in Stephen M. Kosslyn and Robin S. Rosenberg, *Psychology: The Brain, the Person, the World* (Boston, MA: Allyn & Bacon, 2004), 330.

7. Richard Petty and John T. Cacioppo, "The Elaboration Likelihood Model of Persuasion," in *Advances in Experimental Social Psychology*, vol. 19, ed. L. Berkowitz (San Diego: Academic Press, 1986), 123–205; Richard Petty and Duane T. Wegener, "Matching versus Mismatching Attitude Functions: Implications for Scrutiny of Persuasive Messages," *Personality and Social Psychology Bulletin* 24 (1998): 227–40.

8. The model of argument presented here follows Stephen Toulmin, *The Uses of Argument* (New York: Cambridge University Press, 1958), as described in James C. McCroskey, *An Introduction to Rhetorical Communication*, 6th ed. (Englewood Cliffs, NJ: Prentice Hall, 1993).

9. Dennis S. Gouran, "Attitude Change and Listeners' Understanding of a Persuasive Communication," *Speech Teacher* 15 (1966): 289–94; J. P. Dillard, "Persuasion Past and Present: Attitudes Aren't What They Used to Be," *Communication Monographs* 60 (1966): 94.

10. M. Allen, "Comparing the Persuasive Effectiveness of One- and Two-Sided Messages," In *Persuasion: Advances through Meta-Analysis*, ed. M. Allen and R. W. Preiss (Cresskill, NJ: Hampton Press, 1998), 87–98.

11. James C. McCroskey, *An Introduction to Rhetorical Communication*, 9th ed. (Englewood Cliffs, NJ: Prentice Hall, 2005).

12. Edward P. J. Corbett, *Classical Rhetoric for the Modern Student*, 4th ed. (New York: Oxford University Press, 1999).

13. S. Morris Engel, *With Good Reason: An Introduction to Informal Fallacies*, 6th ed. (Boston: Bedford/St. Martin's, 2000), 191.

14. Jennifer Aaker and Durairaj Maheswaran, "The Impact of Cultural Orientation on Persuasion," *Journal of Consumer Research* 24 (December 1997): 315–28.

15. Jennifer L. Aaker, "Accessibilty or Diagnosticity? Disentangling the Influence of Culture on Persuasion Processes and Attitudes," *Journal of Consumer Research* 26 (March 2000): 340–57.

16. Kristine L. Fitch, "Cultural Persuadables," *Communication Theory* 13 (February 2003): 100–123.

17. Ibid.

18. Jennifer L. Aaker and Patti Williams, "Empathy versus Pride: The Influence of Emotional Appeals across Cultures," *Journal of Consumer Research* 25 (1998): 241–61.

19. Ibid.

20. Ibid.

21. Alan Monroe, *Principles and Types of Speeches* (Chicago: Scott, Foresman, 1935).

22. Herbert Simon, *Persuasion in Society* (Thousand Oaks, CA: Sage Publications, 2001), 385–87.

CHAPTER 25

1. Roger E. Axtell, *Do's and Taboos of Public Speaking: How to Get Those Butterflies Flying in Formation* (New York: Wiley, 1992), 150

2. Colin Firth Oscar Acceptance Speech, *Huffington Post* (Entertainment section), February 28, 2011, http://www.huffingtonpost.com/2011/02/28/colin-firth-oscar-acceptance-speech n 829054.html.

3. The Reliable Source, "White House Correspondents' Dinner: President Obama Cracks Wise," *Washington Post*, May 2, 2010, http://voices.washingtonpost.com/reliable-source/2010/05/white_house_correspondents_din_3.html.

CHAPTER 26

1. Sheri Jeavons, "Webinars that Wow: How to Deliver a Dynamic Webinar," sponsored by Citrix GoToMeeting, http://news.citrixonline.com/download_a_webinar/?attend_a_webinar=Y&paged=2.

2. Kami Griffiths and Chris Peters, "10 Steps for Planning a Successful Webinar," TechSoup, January 27, 2009, http://www.techsoup.org/learningcenter/training/page/1252.cfm.

3. Ken Molay, "Best Practices for Webinars," Adobe Connect Web site, http://www.adobe.com/products/acrobatconnectpro/webconferencing/pdfs/Best_Practices_for_Webinars_v4_FINAL.pdf.

4. Patricia Fripp, "15 Tips for Webinars: How to Add Impact When You Present Online," *eLearn Magazine*, July 7, 2009, http://elearnmag.org/featured.cfm?aid=1595445.

5. Ibid.

CHAPTER 27

1. C. M. Anderson, B. L. Riddle, and M. M. Martin, "Socialization in Groups," in *Handbook of Group Communication Theory and Research*, ed. Lawrence R. Frey, Dennis S. Gouran, and Marshall Scott Poole. (Thousand Oaks, CA, Sage, 1999): 139–63; A. J. Salazar, "An Analysis of the Development and Evolution of Roles in the Small Group," *Small*

Group Research 27 (1996): 475–503; K. D. Benne and P. Sheats, "Functional Roles of Group Members," *Journal of Social Issues* 4 (1948): 41–49.

2. Dan O'Hair and Mary Wiemann, *Real Communication*, 2nd ed. (New York: Bedford/St. Martin's, 2012), 266.

3. Ibid., 268.

4. W. Park, "A Comprehensive Empirical Investigation of the Relationships among Variables of the Groupthink Model," *Journal of Organizational Behavior* 21 (2000): 874–87; D. T. Miller, and K. R. Morrison, "Expressing Deviant Opinions: Believing You Are in the Majority Helps," *Journal of Experimental Social Psychology* 45, no. 4 (2009): 740–47.

5. O'Hair and Wiemann, *Real Communication*, 266.

6. Geoffrey A. Cross, "Collective Form: An Exploration of Large-Group Writing," *Journal of Business Communication* 37 (2000): 77–101.

7. Irving Lester Janis, *Groupthink: Psychological Studies of Policy Decisions and Fiascoes* (Berkeley: University of California Press, 1982).

8. Ibid.

9. Victor H. Vroom and Philip Yetton, *Leadership and Decision Making* (Pittsburgh: University of Pittsburgh Press, 1973); C. Pavitt, "Theorizing about the Group Communication-Leadership Relationship: Input-Process-Output and Functional Models," in *Handbook of Group Communication Theory and Research,* ed. Frey, Gouran, and Poole, 313–34.

10. L. Richard Hoffman and Norman R. F. Maier, "Valence in the Adoption of Solutions by Problem-Solving Groups: Concept, Method, and Results," *Journal of Abnormal and Social Psychology* 69 (1964): 264–71.

11. John Dewey, *How We Think* (Boston: D.C. Heath Co, 1950).

CHAPTER 28

1. Maureen Farrell, "In Picture: Ten Presentation Killers," Forbes.com, August 1, 2007, http://www.forbes.com/2007/08/01/microsoft-powerpoint -presentation-ent-sales-cx_mf_0801byb07_torpedo_slide_9.html.

2. Lin Kroeger, *The Complete Idiot's Guide to Successful Business Presentations* (New York: Alpha Books, 1997), 113.

CHAPTER 29

1. For a review, see Priscilla S. Rogers, "Distinguishing Public and Presentational Speaking," *Management Communication Quarterly* 2 (1988): 102–15; Frank E. X. Dance, "What Do You Mean 'Presentational' Speaking?" *Management Communication Quarterly* 1 (1987): 270–81.

2. "Business Ethics," Business for Social Responsibility Web site, 2001–2002, accessed October 2, 2002, www.bsr.org/BSRResources/ WhitePaperDetail.conf.

3. William L. Benoit, *Accounts, Excuses, and Apologies: A Theory of Image Restoration Strategies* (Albany: State University of New York Press, 1995).

4. Ibid.

CHAPTER 30

1. With continuing thanks to Michal Dale of Southwest Missouri State University's Department of Communication.

CHAPTER 31

1. Robert Anholt, *Dazzle 'Em with Style: The Art of Oral Scientific Presentation* (New York: W. H. Freeman and Company, 1994).

CHAPTER 32

1. Deanna P. Daniels, "Communicating across the Curriculum and in the Disciplines: Speaking in Engineering," *Communication Education* 51 (July 2002): 3.

2. Ibid.

3. H. J. Scheiber, "The Nature of Oral Presentations: A Survey of Scientific, Technical, and Managerial Presentations," *IPCC 92 Santa Fe. Crossing Frontiers. Conference Record* (September 29–October 3, 1992): 95–98, doi: 10.1109/IPCC.1992.672998.

CHAPTER 33

1. James M. Henslin, *Sociology: A Down-to-Earth Approach,* 11th ed. (Boston: Allyn & Bacon, 2011), 136.

2. William E. Thompson and James V. Hickey, *Society in Focus: An Introduction to Sociology,* 2nd ed. (New York: HarperCollins, 1996), 39.

CHAPTER 35

1. Rick Sullivan and Noel McIntosh, "Delivering Effective Lectures," JHPIEGO Strategy Paper, December 1996, The Reading Room, http://www.reproline.jhu.edu/english/6read/6training/lecture/delivering _lecture.htm#Characteristics.

CHAPTER 36

1. J. M. Brown and N. A. Schmidt, "Strategies for Making Oral Presentations about Clinical Issues: Part I. At the Workplace," *Journal of Continuing Education in Nursing* 40, no. 4 (2009): 152–53, accessed January 19, 2012, CINAHL with Full Text, EBSCOhost.

2. With thanks to Patricia Gowland, R.N., M.S.N., O.C.N., C.C.R.C., Executive Director of Cancer Research and Patient Navigation, Vanguard Health, Chicago and Associate Director of Clinical Research, University of Illinois at Chicago Cancer Center, for her review of presentation types.

APPENDIX B

1. Patricia Nelson, "Handling Questions and Answers," Toastmasters International, Edmonton and Area, revised November 3, 1999, http://www.ecn.ab.ca/toast/qa.html.

2. Diane DiResta, *Knockout Presentations: How to Deliver Your Message with Power, punch, and Pizzazz* (Worcester, MA: Chandler House Press, 1998), 236.

3. Ibid., 237.

4. Lillian Wilder, *Talk Your Way to Success* (New York: Eastside Publishing, 1986), 279.

APPENDIX C

1. Patricia Nelson, "Handling Questions and Answers," Toastmasters International, Edmonton and Area, revised November 3, 1999, http://www.ecn.ab.ca/toast/qa.html.

2. Daria Price Bowman, *Presentations: Proven Techniques for Creating Presentations that Get Results* (Holbrook, MA: Adams Media, 1998), 177.

3. Oklahoma Society of CPAs (OSCPA), "Tips for Successful Media Interviewing," accessed June 10, 2006, http://www.oscpa.com/?757.

APPENDIX D

1. E. Flege, J. M. Munro, and I. R. A. McKay, "Factors Affecting Strength of Perceived Foreign Accent in a Second Language," *Journal of the Acoustical Society of America* 97 (1995): 312.

2. The content in this section is based on Robbin Crabtree and Robert Weissberg, *ESL Students in the Public Speaking Classroom*, 2nd ed. (Boston: Bedford/St. Martins, 2003), 23.

3. M. C. Florez, "Improving Adult ESL Learners' Pronunciation Skills," *National Clearinghouse for ESL Literacy Education*, 1998, www.cal.org/NCLE/DIGESTS/Pronun.htm.

4. Ibid.

5. Robert Anholt, *Dazzle 'Em with Style: The Art of Oral Scientific Presentation* (New York: W. H. Freeman & Co, 1994), 156.

Acknowledgments

TEXT CREDITS

Page 19: Joe Ayres and Tim S. Hopf. "Visualization: Is It More than Extra-Attention?" From *Communication Education*, Volume 38 (1989), pp. 1-5. Reprinted by permission of Taylor & Francis Ltd. www.informaworld.com.

Pages 225-230: J.K. Rowling, Commencement Speech, Harvard University (2008). Reprinted by permission of Harvard University Public Affairs and Communications Department.

PHOTO CREDITS

53: (top-bot) Royalty Free/Getty Images, Manfred Ruiz/Getty Images; **66:** (L and R) Title page and p. 229 from *Predictably Irrational: The Hidden Forces That Shape Our Decisions* by Dan Ariely. Copyright © 2008 by Dan Ariely. Reprinted by permission of Harper Collins Publishers; **68:** Reproduced with permission. Copyright ©2010 Scientific American, a division of Nature America, Inc. All rights reserved; **80:** (L and R) Courtesy of Nobel Media AB, **89:** (top-bot) Courtesy of Pew Internet, Courtesy of Peter Urban; **172:** (top-bot and L-R) Royalty Free/Getty Images, Royalty Free/Getty Images, iStock photo, Royalty Free/Getty Images; **173:** Royalty Free/Getty Images; **235:** Courtesy of David England.

Index

abstract language, 135
academic articles, review of, 255
acceptance, speeches of, 221
action step, in motivated
    sequence, 205–6
active listening, 31
active voice, 137, 161
activity presentation, for
    group, 273
ad hominem argument, 24, 199
advanced search function, of
    search engines, 84, 85
affirmative side, in debate, 256
after-dinner speeches, 223–24
age, of audience, 40
agenda, for group
    communication, 239
Agnew, Spiro, 139
agora (public square), 3–4
alliteration, 139
almanacs, 64
American Psychological
    Association. See APA
    documentation system
analogies, 135–36
    in informative speech, 180
    reasoning by, 198
    in scientific and mathematical
    presentations, 264
anaphora, 139
anecdotes, 57
Anholt, Robert, 299
animation effects
    (PowerPoint), 169
anti-group roles, 239
antithesis, 140
anxiety
    boosting one's confidence
        and, 18–19, 22
    identifying causes of, 15–16
    management of, 14–22
    performance, 17
    preparation, 17
    pre-performance, 17
    pre-preparation, 16
APA documentation system,
    281–84
apathetic audience, 209
appeal to tradition fallacy, 201
appearance, on television,
    294–95
architecture design review, 266

argument(s)
    addressing other side of, 197
    claims in, 195
    in debates, 256–57
    devil's advocacy, 240, 241
    dialectical inquiry, 240, 241
    in persuasive speeches, 190,
        195–201
Aristotle, 4, 190, 192
Armstrong, Neil, 140
arrangement. See also
    organization of speech
articles. See also citations;
    documentation systems
    recording and citing, 68–69
articulation, 148
    by non-native English
    speakers, 298
arts courses, presentation
    speeches in, 270–72
asynchronous
    communication, 234
atlases, 65
attention step, in motivated
    sequence, 204
attire, during speeches, 153
attitudes, of audience, 36, 37
attribution, 26
audience. See also audience
    analysis; delivery of speech
    attitudes toward topic and,
        37–38
    call to action for, 132
    central processing by, 194
    common ground with,
        127–28
    for crisis-response
        presentations, 252
    cultural differences in, 43–44,
        201–2
    engaging, 142
    ethical speech and, 248
    facial expressions and,
        150–51
    feelings toward occasion, 25
    identify disposition of, 208–9
    inclusion in speech, 6
    interviewing and surveying,
        44–46
    introduction and, 126–28
    listening by, 30–34
    motivation of, 263

audience (*continued*)
   for online presentations, 238
   on-the-job, 260–61
   peripheral processing by, 194
   persuasive speech
      organization and, 202–9
   for presentational speaking,
      247–48
   for progress report, 251
   for proposal, 250
   psychology of listeners, 36–39
   public speaking anxiety and,
      15–22
   respecting values of, 23
   for sales presentations,
      248–49
   source perception by, 87
   for special-occasion speeches,
      219–25
   speech topic and, 128
   for staff reports, 250
   for team presentations, 243
   types of, 209
audience analysis, 9–10, 36–46
   demographics and, 40–42
   for gauging existing
      knowledge, 176
audience-centered approach,
   8, 36
audio, 159
autocratic leaders, 241
averages, statistical, 60

balance, of organization, 100
bandwagoning fallacy, 199
bar graph, 157, 158
barriers to listening, 33
begging the question fallacy, 199
beliefs, of audience, 36, 37, 41
biased language, rooting out, 140
biases
   of speaker, 33
   on Web sites, 77
bibliography, working, 269
Bing, 72
biographical resources, 64
blogs, 70
   as information sources, 78–79
   locating, 62, 70
   oral citations of, 91–92
body language
   and delivery of speech,
      143, 150
   on television, 194
body of speech, 12, 96
boldface, in presentation aids, 163

books. *See also* citations;
      documentation systems
   access, 73
   oral citation of, 90–91
   of quotations, 73
   recording and citing, 90–91
   as sources, 62
Boolean operators, in keyword
      searches, 83
brainstorming, 48, 50–51
breathing
   techniques for anxiety
      management, 20
   voice projection and, 146
brief examples, 56
business and professional
      ethics, 248
business situations,
      presentations in, 247–53

Calapinto, John, 27–28
call to action, 132
canned speeches, 223
canons of rhetoric, 4
captive audience, 38, 39, 247–48
careers
   business presentations skills
      and, 253
   public speaking in, 2–3
career success, from public
      speaking, 2, 253
case conference, in nursing and
      allied health courses, 275–76
case study
   in classroom, 252–53
   clinical, 275
categorical pattern, 110
causal (cause-effect) pattern of
      arrangement, 107–8
causal reasoning, in persuasive
      speeches, 198–99
causes, underlying, 111, 181
celebration, speeches of, 219
central idea. *See* thesis statement
central processing, 194
channel, 8
charts, 157, 158
   flip charts, 160
cherry-picking, in statistical
      presentation, 61
Chicago Manual of Style
      documentation system,
      278–80
chronological organization,
      106, 182
Cicero, 4

citations. *See also*
    documentation systems;
    specific systems
  of articles and periodicals,
    68–69
  for fact and statistics
    sources, 26
  of Internet sources, 80–81
  oral, 86, 90–92, 93
  in PowerPoint
    presentations, 171
  in presentation aids, 93
  for quotations, paraphrases,
    and summaries, 26, 27–28,
    81, 94
  for sources in speeches,
    26–28, 66–67, 80–81,
    85–94
  style of, 67, 69
claims, in argument,
    195–96, 256
classroom, case study
    presentation in, 252–53
classroom discussion
    presentation, 273
clichés, 136
clinical case study, 275
Clinton, Hillary Rodham, 132
clip art, in PowerPoint
    presentation, 166, 170
closed end questions, 45
closure, in conclusion, 130–31
co-culture (social community),
    of audience, 41
code-switching, 136–37
coherence, of organization, 100
collaboration, with
    interviewee, 71
colleagues, as audience, 260
collectivist cultures, 202
colloquial expressions, 138
color
  in presentation aids, 163
  subjective interpretations
    of, 163–64
commemoration, speeches
    of, 219
commencement address, sample
    of, 225–30
commercial factors, in
    research, 82
common ground, with audience,
    127–28
common knowledge citations,
    26–27
communication

asynchronous, 234
  dialogic, 31
  in groups, 238–47
  in informative speech,
    178–80
  mediated, 294–95
  nonverbal, 150
  process of, 7
  public speaking as, 6–8
community service learning
    project, 215–19
comparative advantage pattern,
    206, 249
compare and contrast
    speeches, 271
computer-generated
    presentation aids, 159
concise language, 11
conclusion, 12, 96, 225
  in arts and humanities
    speeches, 271
  preparing, 130–33
  transition to, 103
concrete language, 135
confidence
  boosting, 18–19, 22
  in speaking, 142
conflict, in group
    communication, 240
connotative meaning, 138
consultative leaders, 241
context, of speech, 8, 46
controversial topics, debates
    over, 256, 268
conversation, speeches as, 18
conversation stoppers, 24
coordinate points, 99, 100
coordination, in outlines, 13
copyright, 29
  PowerPoint presentations
    and, 171
core values, appeals to, 201, 202
Corlin, Richard F., 56
Coulter, John, sample outline
    by, 115–19, 121–23
Council of Science Editors.
    See CSE documentation
    system
Creative Commons
    (organization), 29
credibility. *See also* reliability
  in persuasive speech, 191–92
  of sources, 88–89
  of speaker, 22, 128–29, 130
  words for, 136–40
crisis-response presentations, 252

critical audience, 209
cross-cultural values, 43
CSE documentation system,
    288–91
cultural background, of
    audience, 41
cultural barriers, to listening, 33
cultural intelligence, 6
cultural norms, appeals to,
    201, 202
cultural premises, 201, 202
cultural sensitivity, 137–38
culture
    adapting to audience culture,
        43–44
    addressing in persuasive
        speeches, 201–2

Darbelnet, Robert I., 129
data
    in social science
        presentations, 270
    in technical
        presentations, 266
database
    on general search engines, 78
    subject-specific, 74
debates, 256
    in arts and humanities
        courses, 271
    about controversial social
        science issues, 268
    formal, 257
    strong arguments in, 256–57
    taking sides in, 256
    tips for winning, 258
decision making, in groups, 240
declarative sentence, main point
    as, 97
decoding, 7
deductive reasoning, in
    persuasive speeches, 198
deep Web, 73
defamatory speech, 23–24
defensive listening, 32
definition, in informative
    speech, 179
delegative leaders, 241
    delivery of source
        information, 90
delivery cues, 120
delivery of speech, 14
    body language and, 143, 150
    methods of, 142–45
    nonverbal, 14
    online, 234

planning and practicing for,
    153–54
speaking outline for,
    120–23, 124
voice control in, 146–50
delivery outline, 112
demographics, audience, 10,
    40–42, 44
demonstration, in informative
    speech, 178, 179, 181
denotative meaning, 138
derivative works, copyright
    and, 29
description, in informative
    speech, 179, 270–71
design, of presentation aids,
    161–64
Design Template
    (PowerPoint), 167
devil's advocacy argument,
    240, 241
Dewey, John, six-step reflective
    thinking process of, 242
diagram, 156
dialect, 149–50
dialectical inquiry, 240, 241
dialogic communication, 31
digital collections, as
    sources, 63
digital projectors, 159
dignity, 24
directness, 142
directories, on Web, 79
direct quotation, 27, 28, 67, 94
disability, of audience
    members, 42
discussion, in arts and
    humanities courses, 271
disinformation, 78
    distinguishing, 75–78
displays, methods of 159–61
distractions
    listening and, 31–32
    during speech delivery, 8, 237
DLP projectors, 159
documentation systems
    APA, 281–84
    Chicago Manual of Style,
        278–80
    CSE, 288–91
    IEEE, 291–92
    MLA, 284–88
DOI (digital object
    identifier), 281
domain, Web source evaluation
    and, 76

dress (attire)
  during speeches, 153
  on television, 294–95
Drori, Jonathan, 56
dyadic communication, 6

education courses, presentation
    speeches in, 272–74
education level, of audience, 41
ego-focused emotions, 201–2
Ehlers, Vernon, 56
either-or fallacy, 199
elaboration likelihood model of
    persuasion, 194
electronic resources, 72–85. *See
    also* Internet
  legal uses of, 171
emotions
  cultural responses to, 201–2
  in persuasive speech,
    190–91
encoding, 7
encyclopedias, 64
engagement with audience, 142
engineering design review, 265
English language. *See also*
    language
  non-native speakers of,
    296–99
entertainment, speeches of, 219
enthusiasm
  in online presentations, 233
  in speech, 142
epiphora (epistrophe), 139
equipment, for virtual delivery,
    232–33
ESL. *See* non-native speakers of
    English
ethics
  business and
    professional, 248
  in public speaking, 22–29
ethnic background, of audience,
    41, 43–44
ethos, 22, 191, 192
eulogies, 222–23
evidence
  in arguments, 195, 256–57
  evaluation of, 33
  in persuasive speech, 195, 197
evidence-based practice (EBP)
    presentation, 274–75
examples, 56
  transitions between, 103
expert audience, 260
expertise, of speaker, 248

expert testimony, 57, 92
explanation, in informative
    speech, 178, 179–80
extemporaneous speaking,
    144–45
extended examples, 56
eye contact
  key-word outlines for,
    113–14
  during speeches, 143, 151
  on television, 194

face-to-face (FtF) speaking,
    232. *See also* online
    presentations
facial expressions, during
    speeches, 150–51
fact(s), 58. *See also* citations;
    documentation systems
  claims of, 196
fact books, 64
fairness, of speaker, 25
fair use, 29
  Creative Commons licensing
    for, 29
  materials for PowerPoint
    presentation, 171
fallacies, in reasoning, 24,
    199–201
faulty analogy, 136
feedback, 7
  constructive and
    compassionate, 34
  to improve speeches, 21,
    298–99
feedback loop, 31
field study presentation, 263
figures of speech, 135
First Amendment, 23
Firth, Colin, 221
fixed-alternative questions,
    45, 295
flip charts, 159, 160
flowcharts, 157, 158
flowing the debate, 257
fonts, for presentation aids,
    162–63
footnotes, 85
  in PowerPoint
    presentations, 171
formal debates, 257
formality, of presentational
    speaking, 247
forum, 4, 246–47
fragments. *See* sentence
    fragments

free speech, rights of, 23–24
frequency, statistical, 59
full-sentence transitions, 101–4

Garza, Richard, 182–83
gender
    of audience, 42
    stereotyping by, 42
gender-neutral language,
    137–38
general-interest magazines, 63
general speech purpose, 49
gestures, during speeches,
    21, 152
global opinion polls, cross-
    cultural surveys and, 43
goals
    of group communication, 239
    of leadership, 241
    of team presentations, 243
Google, 72, 78
Google Docs, 164
government information
    for online presentations, 235
    publications, 63
graphics
    in presentation aids, 264
    in scientific and mathematical
        presentations, 264
graphs, 157, 158
groups
    active participation in, 241
    activity presentation to, 273
    communication in, 238–47
    decision making in, 240
    Dewey's six-step reflective
        thinking process for, 242
groupthink, 240

Handout Master (PowerPoint),
    166, 169
handouts, 159, 160
hasty generalization fallacy, 200
hate speech, 25
health courses, presentation
    speeches in, 274–76
hierarchy of needs (Maslow),
    192, 193
hostile audience, 209
humanities courses,
        presentation speeches in,
    270–72
humor
    in after-dinner speeches, 224
    in introduction, 127
hypothetical example, 56

identification, with speaker, 39,
    127–28
idioms, 33, 138
IEEE documentation system,
    291–92
"I have a dream" speech
    (King), 139
imagery, 135, 267
immediacy, nonverbal, 152
impromptu speaking, 143–44
inclusive speakers, 6
income, of audience, 41
indentation, of supporting
    points, 98
individual debate format, 257
individualist cultures, 202
inductive reasoning, in
    persuasive speeches, 198
information. *See also* sources;
        specific types
    critically analyzing, 74–75
    defined, 75
    facts and statistics as, 98, 126,
        127, 197
    locating supporting
        material, 12
    new and interesting, 177
    unusual, in introduction, 127
informative speeches, 10, 50, 54,
    176–89
    arranging points in pattern,
        182–83
    in arts and humanities
        courses, 270–71
    communicating in, 178–80
    reducing confusion in,
        180–82
    sample of, 183–89
    strategies for explaining
        complex information, 181
    subject matter of, 177, 178
Inkson, Kerr, 6
insider audience, 260
inspiration, speeches of, 219,
    224–25
Institute of Electrical and
        Electronics Engineers.
    See IEEE documentation
        system
integrity, 24
interactive communication,
        public speaking as, 7–8
internal previews, as transitions,
    103, 105, 177
internal summaries, 103,
    105, 177

Internet. *See* online entries;
sources; Web entries
connection for online
presentations, 232
recording source information
from, 85
search tools on, 78–85
sources on, 72–85
interview. *See also* citations;
documentation systems
audience attitudes and, 45
conducting, 70–71
media, 295
oral citation for, 92
intonation, in speaking, 146
introduction, 12, 96
motivating audience
with, 129
preparing, 126–30
speeches of, 220, 221
invective, 24
invention, as canon of
rhetoric, 4
issues-based conflict, in group
communication, 240
italics, in presentation
aids, 163

Jackson, Jesse, 139
jargon, 133–34, 296
Jesus, 139
Jobs, Steve, 153
journal articles. *See also*
magazines
on Internet, 73

key-word outline, 113–14
keyword searches, 82, 83
Kim, Krista, 183
King, Martin Luther, Jr., 139
Kruckenberg, David, 183–89

language
abstract, 135
active and passive voice in,
137–38
alliterative, 139
biased, 140
concise, 11
concrete, 135
culturally sensitive, 137–38
denotative vs. connotative
meaning and, 138
figures of speech in, 135–36
gender-neutral, 137–38
imagery in, 135

lasting impression from,
138–40
repetition and, 134, 138–39
rhetorical devices and, 133
simple, 133–34
using, 133–40
words to build credibility,
136–40
language patterns, in dialects,
149–50
lavaliere microphone, 149
lay audience, 260
lay testimony, 57–58, 92
lazy speech, 148
LCD displays, 159
leadership
style of, 241
of team, 243
leading questions, 70
learning styles, appeal of
informative speeches to,
181, 182
lectures, 272
library portal, finding print and
online sources with, 72–75
licenses, for copyrighted
works, 29
Lincoln, Abraham, 140
line graph, 157, 158
listeners. *See* audience; listening
listening, 30–34
active, 31
attitudes toward speaker and,
38–39
attitudes toward topic and,
37–38
cultural barriers to, 33
defensive, 32
distractions to, 31–32
feedback loop and, 31
help with, 177
learning by, 297
nonverbal cues and, 33
obstacles to, 31–33
responsible, 31
retention and, 30
literature review, in social
sciences, 268, 269
loaded questions, 70
logical fallacies, 199–201
logos, 190, 192

magazines. *See also* journal
articles
on Internet, 74
as sources, 63

main points, 11, 96–98, 101
  in arts and humanities
    speeches, 271
  as declarative sentences,
    97–98
  organizing, 182–83, 202–8
  in parallel form, 98
  preview of, 129, 220
  restricting number of, 97–98
  for single idea, 97–98
  transitions between, 101–4
maintenance roles, in groups, 239
malapropisms, 137
manuscript, speaking from,
    142–43
Maslow, Abraham, 192, 193
mass communication, 6
masters (PowerPoint), 169
mathematics courses,
    presentation speeches in,
    263–64
Matthew (Bible), 140
McClellan, Mark B., 113
mean, statistical, 60
meaning, denotative and
    connotative, 138
Mease, Paige, 17
media interview, 295
median, statistical, 60
mediated communication,
    294–95
meditation, for anxiety
    management, 18, 20
medium, 8
memory,
  speaking from, 143
message, 8
  customizing for audience, 38
  demographics of audience
    and, 40–42
  focusing on, 154
metaphors, 135
  mixed, 136
methods/procedure
    presentation, 262
microphone, using, 149
Microsoft PowerPoint, 164–74.
    See also PowerPoint
    presentations
mini-lecture presentation, 272
misinformation, 75
  distinguishing, 75–78
mixed audience, 260
mixed metaphors, 136
MLA documentation system,
    284–88

mode, statistical, 60
model, 156
moderators
  of group communications, 239
  of panel discussions, 245, 246
Modern Language Association.
    See MLA documentation
    system
monologue, 31
Monroe, Alan, motivated
    sequence pattern by,
    203–6, 207
Morris, Lee, 16
motivated sequence
  pattern (Monroe), 203–6, 207
  in sales presentation, 249
  sample of speech, 214–19
motivation
  of audience, 263
  in introduction, 129, 263
  in persuasive speech, 189–90
movement. *See also* body
    language
  for anxiety management, 21
multimedia, 159
mumbling, 148

narrative
  as organizational pattern, 111
  sharing of, 57
naturalness, in speech, 142
needs, Maslow's hierarchy of,
    192, 193
need step, in motivated
    sequence, 204–5
negative side, in debate, 256
nesting, in keyword searches, 83
newspapers, as sources, 63
noise, 8
non-native speakers of English,
    tips for, 296–99
non sequitur fallacy, 200
nonverbal behavior, in team
    presentations, 244
nonverbal communication, 150
nonverbal cues, in listeners, 33
nonverbal delivery, 14
nonverbal immediacy, 152
Noonan, Peggy, 134
normal view (PowerPoint), 168
norms, cultural, 201, 202
notecards, for delivery
    cues, 121
note-taking, 66–67, 68–69
  for Internet sources, 81, 85
  recording references and, 72

nursing and allied health courses, presentations in, 274–76

Obama, Barack, 57, 139, 222
objectivity, of Web sites, 77
Obracay, Kristen, 15
occupations, of audience, 41
offensive speech, avoiding, 25
one-sided message, 197
online-only magazine. *See also* citations; documentation systems
citations for, 91
online presentations
delivery mode for, 234
planning checklist for, 237–38
platforms for, 234–37
preparation of, 232–37
unique demands of, 232
online sources. *See also* Internet; Web sites
from library portal, 72–75
online video. *See also* citations; documentation systems
citation for, 92
on-the-job audiences, preparing for, 260–61
open-ended questions, 45–46
opinion(s), of audience, 197
opinion polls, about audience attitudes, 43, 46
oral citations, 86, 90–92, 93
oral paraphrase, 28
oral scientific presentation, 261–62
oral style, 5–6
oral summary, 28
oratory, 143
history of, 3–4
organization of speech, 13, 96–105, 96–111, 144
blending patterns for, 106
causal (cause-effect), 107–8
chronological, 106
of crisis-response presentations, 252
of informative speeches, 177, 182–83
main points in, 97–98
in narrative pattern, 111
pattern for, 105–11
of persuasive speeches, 202–8
problem-solution, 108–10

of progress reports, 251–52
of proposals, 250
of sales presentations, 249
spatial, 107
of staff reports, 250–51
supporting points in, 98–99
topical, 110–11
transitions and, 101–5
unified, coherent, and balanced, 100
other-focused emotions, 202
outlines, 12–13, 112–24
key-word, 113–14
for main and supporting points, 97, 98–99
phrase, 113
sentence, 113
speaking, 112, 120–23
working, 13, 112, 114–19
overhead transparency, 159–60

paid listings (sponsored links), 82
pandering, 40
panel discussions, 245–46
parable, 57
parallel form, 98
parallelism, 98, 139–40
paraphrase. *See also* citations; documentation systems
citations for, 27–28, 94
notes for, 67
oral, 28
Parrish, Mary, 16
participation, in groups, 241
participative leaders, 241
passive voice, 137
pathos, 190, 192
pattern
of speech, 144
for speech organization, 13, 182–83
pauses, in speaking, 147
percentages, statistical, 59
performance anxiety, 17. *See also* anxiety
periodicals, as sources, 63
peripheral processing, by audience, 194
personal experiences, in speeches, 12
personal interview, oral citation style of, 92
personal pronouns, 134
person-based conflict, in group communications, 240

persuasive speech, 10, 50, 54, 189–219
  arguments in, 195–201
  credibility in, 191–92
  culture and, 201–2
  evidence in, 197
  listener needs in, 192, 193
  mental engagement in, 194–95
  motivation in, 189–90, 194
  organization of, 202–8
  problem-cause-solution sample of, 203, 209–14
  reason and emotion in, 190–91
  refutation pattern in, 207–8
  sound arguments in, 195–201
  in technical presentations, 265–67
phrase outline, 113
phrases, 134
  transitional, 104
pictograms, 157, 158
pictures, 156–57, 169
pie graph, 157, 158
pitch, vocal, 146
plagiarism, 26
  avoiding, 85
planning, of speech, 153–54
podcast, 235
poetry, collections of, 65
policy, claims of, 196, 202
policy recommendation report, 269
political affiliation, of audience, 42
Poplin, Stephanie, 214–19
positive attitude, anxiety and, 18
poster presentation, 160, 258–60
posters, 156, 159, 160
posture, during speeches, 152
PowerPoint presentations, 164–74
  avoiding technical glitches in, 172–73
  commands for running, 174
  copyright infringement and, 171
  entering and editing text, 169
  Help menu, 171
  inserting objects into slides, 169–70
  masters, 169
  presentation options, 159–60
  "Record Narration" feature and, 236

slide layouts, 168
  transition and animation effects, 169
  venue for, 172–73
  view options, 168
practice, 13–14, 121, 153–54. *See also* rehearsal
preexisting knowledge, of audience, 197
premises, cultural, 201
preparation, for online presentations, 232–33
preparation anxiety, 17
preparation outline, 110
pre-performance anxiety, 17
pre-preparation anxiety, 16
presentation aids, 13, 156–74
  crediting sources in, 93
  designing, 161–64
  PowerPoint and, 164–74
  in scientific and mathematical presentations, 264
  for team presentations, 244
  in technical presentations, 266
  types of, 156–61
presentational speaking, 247, 255–61
presentations. *See* online presentations; presentation aids; presentation speeches
presentation speeches, 221–22. *See also* presentation aids
  in arts and humanities courses, 270–72
  in business and professional situations, 247–53
  compare and contrast, 271
  debates as, 256–58
  in education courses, 272–74
  in group settings, 238–42
  in nursing and allied health courses, 274–76
  poster sessions as, 258–59
  program evaluation presentation, 269
  review of academic articles as, 255
  in science and mathematics courses, 261–64
  in social science courses, 267–70
  team presentations as, 243–47
  in technical courses, 265–67

previews
of main points, 129
of topic and purpose, 128
as transitions, 103, 105
preview statement, 105
Prezi, 164
primacy effect, 97
primary sources, 62, 70–71
print articles. *See also* citations;
documentation systems
oral citation of, 91
print sources, from library
portal, 72–75
problem-cause-solution pattern,
203, 249
sample speech, 209–14
problem-solution pattern,
108–10, 202–3, 249
professional situations,
presentations in, 247–53
program evaluation program, 269
progress reports, in businesses,
251–52
projectors, 159–60
pronouns
gender and, 138
personal, 134
pronunciation, 148, 298
propaganda, 75
distinguishing, 75–78
proposals
in businesses, 249–50
quality improvement, 275
props, 156
prototype, 265
Publication Manual of the
American Psychological
Association. *See* APA
documentation system
public discourse, positive, 24
public domain, 29
public forum, 4
public speaking. *See also* anxiety;
speech(es)
defined, 7
ethical, 22–29
steps in process of, 9
published sources, about
audience attitudes, 46
purpose of speech, 49–50
general, 49
main points and, 96–97
preview in introduction, 128
reiterating in conclusion, 130
specific, 10, 51

quality improvement
proposal, 275
question-and-answer sessions,
292–93
questionnaire, for audience
members, 45
questions
in interviews, 70–71
in introduction, 127
quotation marks, in keyword
searches, 83
quotations. *See also* citations;
documentation systems
books of, 65
citations for, 27–28,
81–82, 94
direct, 27, 28, 67
in introduction, 127

radio
oral citations of programs, 92
speaking on, 295
rate of speaking, 147
real-time presentations, 234
reason
in argument, 190–91
in persuasive speech,
190–91
reasoning
by analogy, 198
in arguments, 257
causal, 198–99
deductive and inductive,
198–99
evaluation of, 34
fallacies in, 24, 199–201
in persuasive speeches,
198–99
receiver, 7
reckless disregard for truth, 24
recorded presentations, 234
red herring fallacy, 200
refereed journals, as sources, 63
reference works, 64–65
oral citation of, 91
recording, 72
reflective thinking, Dewey's six-
step method of, 242
refutation
in debate, 257
as organizational pattern,
207–8
rehearsal, of team presentations,
244–45
relaxation response, 19–20

reliability
   of sources, 87, 88–89
   of statistics, 60
religion, of audience, 42
repetition, 134
   for rhythm, 138–39
reports. *See* specific types
request for funding
   presentation, 266
research. *See also* Internet;
    sources
   evaluating needs for, 61
   Internet, 62
   presentation on theoretical,
    268, 269
   primary, 62, 70–71
   qualitative, 267
   quantitative, 267
   secondary, 62–70
research overview presentation,
   262–63
research presentation, 261–62
resolution, in debate, 256
respect, for audience, 25
responsibility
   of listener, 31
   of speaker, 25
restate-forecast transition,
   101–3
review
   of academic articles, 255
   of social sciences
    literature, 268
rhetoric (oratory)
   canons of, 4
   history of, 3–4
rhetorical devices, 133
rhetorical questions
   in introduction, 127
   transitions as, 103, 104
rhetorical situation, 8
rhythm, repetition for, 138–39
rights, of free speech, 23–24
roast, as speech, 222
roles
   in group communications, 239
   in team presentations, 243
Roosevelt, Franklin D., 135
Roth, Lisa, 209, 210–14
rough outline, 110
Rowling, J. K., sample
   commencement address
   by, 225–30
rules of engagement, for public
   discourse, 3, 24
Runyon, Marvin, 128

Safire, William, 127
sales presentation (sales pitch),
   248–50
Sanford, Jenna, 20
sans serif typefaces, 162, 163
satisfaction step, in motivated
   sequence, 205
scale questions, 45, 295
scanning, 151
science courses, presentation
   speeches in, 261–64
scientific talk, 261
screencast, 235
scriptwriting, 32
search engines, 72–73, 78,
   79–82
searches, smart, 82–85
search tools, 78–85
secondary sources, 62–70
selective perception, 30
sentence fragments, 134
sentence outline, 113
serif typefaces, 162, 163
service learning presentation,
   259–60
SES. *See* socioeconomic status
setting, of speech, 46
shared meaning, 8
shift report, in nursing and
   allied health courses, 276
"Shock Jock" syndrome, 137
signposts, 104
simile, 135
Simon, Herbert, 208–9
simple language, 133–34
six-by-six rule, of visual
   design, 161
skills, public speaking as, 2,
   4–6
Slide Master (PowerPoint), 169
SlideRocket, 164
slides (PowerPoint), 168
slippery slope fallacy, 200
small group communication,
   6, 238
smart searches, 82–85
social agenda, speeches that
   set, 219
social news sites, 70
social phenomena, explanations
   of, 269
social science courses,
   presentation speeches in,
   267–70
socioeconomic status (SES), of
   audience, 41

software
  digital audio recording, 235–36
  multimedia, 159
  PowerPoint, 164–74
sound, in PowerPoint
    presentation, 170–71
sound arguments, constructing,
    195–201
source (sender), 7
sources. *See also* citations;
      documentation systems;
      information; research
  audience perception of, 87
  citing, 61, 67, 69, 81, 85–94
  crediting, 26–28
  delivery in speech, 90
  establishing trustworthiness
      of, 86–87
  evaluating, 71–72
  on Internet, 72–85
  locating supporting material,
      55–61
  overview with sample oral
      citations, 90–92, 93
  primary, 62, 70–71
  print and online, 90–92
  qualifiers of, 87
  recording and citing, 66–69,
      80–81
  reliability of, 87, 88–89
  secondary, 62–70
spatial pattern of arrangement,
    107, 266
speaker
  audience's feelings toward,
      38–39
  credibility of, 22, 128–29,
      130, 191–92
  expertise of, 197, 248
speaking outline, 13, 112,
    120–21
  sample, 121–23
  steps in creating, 120, 124
speaking rate, 147
special occasion speeches, 10,
    50, 219–31
  of acceptance, 221
  after-dinner, 223–24
  to celebrate, 219
  to commemorate, 219
  to entertain, 219
  eulogies and other tributes,
      222–23
  to inspire, 219, 224–25
  of introduction, 220, 221
  of presentation, 221–22

  roast as, 222
  sample commencement
      address, 225–30
  to set social agendas, 219
  toast as, 222
specific speech purpose, 51
speech(es). *See also* citations;
      documentation systems
  canons of rhetoric as parts
      of, 4
  delivery practice for, 153–54
  informative, 176–89
  major parts of, 12
  online, 65
  organizing, 96–111
  outlining of, 12–13, 112–24
  overview of, 9–14
  persuasive, 189–219
  practice of, 13–14, 121,
      153–54
  presentational, 247
  purpose of, 10, 49–50
  signaling end of, 130–31
  source citation in, 61, 69, 81
  special occasion, 219–31
  topic of, 47–48
speech anxiety. *See* anxiety
speech points
  in narrative organizational
      pattern, 111
  organization of, 99
  in problem-solution pattern,
      108–10
  in spatial pattern, 107
  in topical pattern of
      arrangement, 110–11
sponsored links, 82
staff reports, 250–51
statistics, 58–61. *See also*
      citations; documentation
      systems
  cherry-picking of, 61
  ethical presentation of,
      60–61
  selective use of, 59
stereotypes, 42, 138
stop-time technique, for anxiety
      control, 17
story (narrative)
  in introduction, 127
  sharing of, 57
  structuring, 57
stress, controlling in speech-
      making, 20
stretching, for anxiety
      management, 21

style, 133
    citation, 67, 69, 81
    oral, 5–6
subject (Web) directories,
    purposes of, 79–82
subject heading searches, on
    Internet, 83–84
subject matter, of informative
    speeches, 177, 178
subject-specific databases, 74
subordinate points, 13, 99, 100
subordination, in outlines, 13
summary
    citations for, 27–28, 94
    of key points, 130
    notes for, 67, 69
    oral, 28
    as transitions, 103, 105
supporting material, 12, 58
    developing, 55–61
    locating, 62–72
    oral citations of, 93
supporting points, 98–99, 101
    transitions between, 104
surveys
    of audience members,
        45–46
    in primary research, 71
sympathetic audience, 209
symposium, 245
synchronous
    communication, 234

tables, 157, 158, 170
talking head, 152
task roles, in groups, 239
team leader, 243
team presentations, 243–47,
    255–56
technical presentations, 265–67
television
    oral citations of programs, 92
    speaking on, 294–95
temporal pattern, 106
testimony, 57–58
    oral citations of, 92
theoretical research
    presentation, 268, 269
thesis statement, 11, 51–55
    in arts and humanities
        speeches, 271
    focus through, 55
    main points and, 96–97
Thomas, David C., 6
timing, of speech, 154
toast, as speech, 222

topical pattern of arrangement,
    110–11, 182, 183
topic (mind) mapping, 48–49
topic of speech, 10
    listeners' feelings toward,
        37–38
    narrowing of, 50–51, 52–53
    preview in introduction, 128
    reiterating in conclusion,
        131–32
    selecting, 47–49
town hall meeting, 246–47
transition(s), 101–5
    as listener guides, 102–3, 177
    previews and summaries
        as, 105
    to signal end of speech,
        130–31
    between team speakers, 244
    techniques for, 101–5
    words and phrases for, 104
transition effects
    (PowerPoint), 169
treatment plan reports, in
        nursing and allied health
        courses, 275–76
tributes, speeches as, 222–23
truncation, in keyword
        searches, 83
trustworthiness
    of sources, 71–72
    of speaker, 25
truth, reckless disregard
        for, 24
Tufte, Edward, 162
two-sided message, 197
typefaces, for presentation aids,
    162–63

underlining, in presentation
    aids, 163
uninformed audience, 209
unity, of organization, 100

value(s)
    of audience, 23, 36–37, 41
    claims of, 196
    core, 201, 202
    cross-cultural, 43
    universal, 44
Verdery, Morgan, 18
video(s), 159. *See also* citations;
        documentation systems
    online, 234–35
    in PowerPoint presentation,
        170–71

video recording
of speech practice, 154
Villarreal, Elpidio, 131–32,
190–91
virtual delivery, in online
presentations, 232–33
visual aids. *See also*
presentation aids
for online presentations,
233
visualization, for anxiety
management, 18–19
visualization step, in motivated
sequence, 205
vocal delivery, 14
vocal fillers, 147
vocal variety, 148
for non-native English
speakers, 298–99
in online presentations, 233
vodcast, 140, 235
voice control
in speaking, 146–50
on television, 194
voice of verbs
active, 137
passive, 137
voice projection, 146
volume, of speaking, 146
voluntary audience, 39

warrants (reasons), in
argument, 195
watchdog sites, 75
Web directories, 79
Webinars, 236–37
Weblog. *See* blogs

Web sites. *See also* citations;
documentation systems;
Internet
citation for, 81–82
evaluating, 76–77
oral citation of
organization, 91
source credits on, 81–82
Web sources. *See also* Internet
recording and citing, 81
Wikipedia, 64
Wilson, Phil, 135
word(s)
accurate uses of, 136
pronunciation and
articulation of, 146
"Shock Jock" syndrome
and, 137
transitional, 104, 105
word association, for
brainstorming, 48
working outline, 13, 112, 114–19
sample of, 114, 115–19
working world, audience types
in, 260
Works Cited
in informative speech,
188–89
in motivated sequence
speech, 218–19
in problem-cause-solution
persuasive speech, 214
worksheets, in PowerPoint
presentation, 170

Yahoo!, 78
YouTube, 72

SAMPLE SPEECHES

Informative Speeches

*John Kanzius and the Quest to Cure
Cancer, David Kruckenberg*   **184**

Student David Kruckenberg describes a promising new way to treat cancer.

Persuasive Speeches

Emergency in the Emergency Room, Lisa Roth   **210**

Student Lisa Roth investigates the crisis in emergency room care and advocates a claim of policy—the overhauling of the emergency room system.

*The Importance of Community Engagement
and Volunteerism, Stephanie Poplin*   **215**

Organizing her speech using Monroe's motivated sequence pattern, student Stephanie Poplin argues that volunteering can enrich our lives.

Special Occasion Speeches

*2008 Harvard University Commencement
Address, J. K. Rowling*   **225**

J. K. Rowling, author of the Harry Potter books, speaks to inspire and share life lessons with the 2008 graduating class of Harvard University.

VISUAL GUIDES

Selecting a Topic

*From Source to Speech: Narrowing Your Topic
to Fit Your Audience*   52

Locating Supporting Materials

From Source to Speech: Recording and Citing Books   66

*From Source to Speech: Recording and Citing
Articles from Periodicals*   68

Finding Credible Sources on the Internet

From Source to Speech: Evaluating Web Sources   76

*From Source to Speech: Recording and Citing
Web Sources*   80

Citing Sources in Your Speech

*From Source to Speech: Demonstrating Your
Sources' Reliability and Credibility*   88

Organizing the Speech

*From Point to Point: Using Transitions to Guide
Your Listeners*   102

A Brief Guide to Microsoft PowerPoint

*From Slide Show to Presentation: Getting Ready
to Deliver a PowerPoint Presentation*   172

QUICK TIPS

Voice Your Ideas in a Public Forum 4

Speak with Purpose 10

Envision Your Speech as a Conversation 18

Stretch Away Stress 21

Seek Pleasure in the Occasion 21

Follow the Rules of Engagement 24

Beat the Odds by Listening 30

Custom-Fit Your Message 38

Be Authentic 40

Be Sensitive to Disability When Analyzing an Audience 42

Consult Global Opinion Polls 43

Explore Topics on CQ Researcher 48

Use the Thesis Statement to Stay Focused 55

Give the Story Structure 57

Use a Variety of Supporting Materials 58

Use Statistics Selectively—and Memorably 59

Avoid Cherry-Picking 61

Mix It Up with Both Primary and Secondary Sources 62

Use Watchdog Sites to Check the Facts 75

Find the Right Subject Headings 84

Consider Audience Perception of Sources 87

Credit Sources in Presentation Aids 93

Save the Best for Last—or First 97

Spend Time Organizing Speech Points 99

Blend Organizational Patterns 106

Find Freedom with the Topical Pattern 110

Sometimes Only Exact Wording Will Do 120

When Not to Preview Your Topic 128

When Establishing Credibility Is Especially Key 130

Bring Your Speech Full Circle 132

Experiment with Phrases and Sentence Fragments 134

Avoid Clichés and Mixed Metaphors 136

Avoid the "Shock Jock" Syndrome 137

Denotative versus Connotative Meaning 138

Breathe from Your Diaphragm 146

Control Your Rate of Speaking 147

Avoid Meaningless Vocal Fillers 147

Stand Straight 152

Learn from the Legends 153

Practice Five Times 154

Hold the Handouts 160

Beware of "Chartjunk" 162

Using Serif and Sans Serif Type 162

Enlighten Rather than Advocate 176

Reveal the Backstory 178

Use Analogies Accurately 180

Expect Modest Results 190

Base Your Emotional Appeals on Sound Reasoning 191

Show Them the Reward 194

Respond to the Introduction 221

Commemorate Life—Not Death 223

Be Yourself When Using Humor 224

Tailor Your Message to the Audience and Occasion 225

Sounding Enthusiastic Online 233

Put a Face to the Speaker(s) 237

Handling Trolls Online 239

Optimize Decision Making in Groups 240

Team Cohesion Pays Off 243

Be Mindful of Your Nonverbal Behavior 244

Speak Ethically at Work 248

Adapt the Motivated Sequence to the Selling Situation 248

Build Career Skills 253

Flowing the Debate 257

What Do Science-Related Courses Include? 261

Make the Introduction Motivating 263

What Are the Technical Disciplines? 265

Prepare Technical Presentations Carefully 267

Narrow Your Topic 269

Be Prepared to Lead a Discussion 271

Be an Active Lecturer 273

Check for Correct Articulation 298

CHECKLISTS

Getting Started

Steps in Gaining Confidence 22
An Ethical Inventory 25
Correctly Quote, Paraphrase, and Summarize Information 28
Dealing with Distractions While Delivering a Speech 32

Development

Respond to the Audience as You Speak 39
Reviewing Your Speech in the Light of Audience Demographics 44
Identifying the Speech Topic, Purpose, and Thesis 55
Evaluating Your Research Needs 61
Finding Speeches Online 65
Identifying Paid Listings in Search Results 82

Organization

Reviewing Main and Supporting Points 101
Choosing an Organizational Pattern 111
Steps in Creating a Working Outline 114
Tips on Using Notecards or Sheets of Paper 121
Steps in Creating a Speaking Outline 124

Starting, Finishing, and Styling

Guidelines for Preparing the Introduction 126
How Effective Is Your Introduction? 130
Guidelines for Preparing the Conclusion 131
How Effective Is Your Conclusion? 133
Use Language Effectively 140

Delivery

Practice Check for Vocal Effectiveness 148
Tips on Using a Microphone 149
Tips for Using Effective Facial Expressions 151
Broad Dress Code Guidelines 153

Presentation Aids

Incorporating Presentation Aids into Your Speech 161
Apply the Principles of Simplicity and Continuity 164
Using PowerPoint Presentations Effectively 165
Ensuring Legal Use of Media Acquired Electronically 171

Types of Speeches

Strategies for Explaining Complex Information 181
Possible Matches of Organizational Patterns with Speech Types 183
Structure the Claims in Your Persuasive Speech 196
Be a Culturally Sensitive Persuader 202
Steps in the Motivated Sequence 207
Preparing a Speech of Introduction 220

Online, Group, and Business Contexts

Creating a Podcast 236
Team Presentation Tips 246

Speaking across the Curriculum

Tips for Winning a Debate 258
Evaluating Your Original Research Presentation 262
Tips for Preparing Successful Scientific Presentations 264

CONTENTS

PART 1 · GETTING STARTED 1

1. BECOMING A PUBLIC SPEAKER 2
   A Vital Life Skill
   Classical Roots
   Learning to Speak
   Speech as Communication
   An Interactive Process

2. SPEECH OVERVIEW 9
   Audience Analysis
   Topic Selection
   Speech Purpose
   Thesis Statement
   Main Points
   Supporting Materials
   Separate Speech Parts
   Outline
   Presentation Aids
   Delivery

3. SPEECH ANXIETY 14
   Causes of Anxiety
   Onset of Anxiety
   Boosting Confidence
   Relaxation Techniques
   Using Movement
   Learning from Feedback

4. ETHICS 22
   Audience Trust
   Audience Values
   Free Speech and Responsibility
   Positive Public Discourse
   Ethical Ground Rules
   Avoiding Offensive Speech
   Avoiding Plagiarism
   Fair Use, Copyright,
   and Ethics

5. LISTENING 30
   Selective Listening
   Responsible Listening
   Exchanging Ideas
   Listening Obstacles
   Active Listening
   Evaluating Evidence
   Feedback

PART 2 · DEVELOPMENT 35

6. AUDIENCE ANALYSIS 36
   Psychology
   Demographics
   Culture
   Seeking Information
   Setting and Context

7. TOPIC AND PURPOSE 47
   Where to Begin
   General Speech Purpose
   Narrowed Topic
   • From Source to Speech:
     Narrowing Your Topic to Fit Your
     Audience
   Specific Speech Purpose
   Thesis Statement

8. DEVELOPING SUPPORT 55
   Examples
   Stories
   Testimony
   Facts and Statistics
   Oral References

9. LOCATING SUPPORT 62
   Secondary Sources
   • From Source to Speech: Citing
     Books
   • From Source to Speech: Citing
     Periodicals
   Generating Primary Sources:
   Interviews and Surveys
   Evaluate Sources
   Recording References

10. INTERNET RESEARCH 72
    Using a Library Portal
    Information, Propaganda,
    Misinformation, and Disinformation
    • From Source to Speech:
      Evaluating Web Sites
    Internet Search Tools
    • From Source to Speech: Citing
      Web Sites
    Smart Searches
    Recording Sources

11. CITING SOURCES 85
    Source Information
    • From Source to Speech:
      Demonstrating Source Credibility
    Sample Oral Citations
    Citing Summaries and Paraphrases

PART 3 · ORGANIZATION 95

12. ORGANIZING THE SPEECH 96
    Main Points
    Supporting Points
    Coordination and Subordination
    Organization
    Transitions
    • From Point to Point: Using
      Transitions

13. ORGANIZATIONAL PATTERNS 105
    Chronological
    Spatial
    Causal (Cause-Effect)
    Problem–Solution
    Topical
    Narrative

14. OUTLINING THE SPEECH 112
    Create Two Outlines
    Outline Formats
    Working Outlines
    Speaking Outlines

PART 4 · STARTING,
FINISHING, AND STYLING 125

15. INTRODUCTIONS AND
    CONCLUSIONS 126